SERVICE QUALITY MANAGEMENT IN HOSPITALITY AND TOURISM

M. C. METTI

ANMOL PUBLICATIONS PVT. LTD.
NEW DELHI - 110 002 (INDIA)

ANMOL PUBLICATIONS PVT. LTD.

H.O.: 4374/4B, Ansari Road, Darya Ganj,
New Delhi-110 002 (India)
Ph.: 23278000, 23261597

B.O.: No. 1015, Ist Main Road, BSK IIIrd Stage
IIIrd Phase, IIIrd Block
Bangalore - 560 085 (India)
Visit us at: www.anmolpublications.com

Service Quality Management in Hospitality and Tourism

ISBN 978-81-261-3231-7

PRINTED IN INDIA

Printed at Mehra Offset Press, Delhi.

SERVICE QUALITY MANAGEMENT IN HOSPITALITY AND TOURISM

Contents

Preface

It is probable that service industries will dominate the new millennium, with service quality management at the forefront of many of the key issues. Whilst recognizing that the focus is on the hospitality and tourism industries, a solid chapter covering the services sector, followed by relating to the specifics of the hospitality and tourism industries would broaden the readership's base, and provide a greater conceptual framework for the book.

This would differentiate the text and provide a solid benchmark for future writing and research in this area. One of the issues with many current texts written for tourism and hospitality studies is that they cover similar information.

This can be a challenge to provide a strong conceptual framework by including a holistic nexus inclusive of strategic management, operational management and marketing foci to the topic. Again, the inclusion of case studies and review and discussion questions to emphasise learning experiences would add to the quality.

The range of topics examining nascent service management issues is, without a doubt, a challenge that has successfully been undertaken with a team of international scholars who clearly know and care about service quality management. Due to the theoretical and practical experience highlighted, it makes for reading for both academic and industry purposes; thus being useful to both practitioner managers and educators. This book would be suitable for both undergraduate and graduate students. Therefore it fills a difficult dual-purpose niche excellently.

Author

Chapter 1

Service Quality in Hospitality

SATISFACTION AND BEHAVIOURAL INTENTIONS

A primary goal of park and recreation agencies is to provide opportunities from which users may derive satisfaction. This goal stems from a belief that users who are highly satisfied with their experience are likely to be repeat visitors, to be loyal users, to disseminate positive word-of-mouth communications to others, and to be supporters of the providing agency. The centrality of satisfied users to an agency accomplishing its mission and securing its future well-being, accounts for the substantial literature on satisfaction research in the leisure field which dates back at least to the 1960s.

Delivering quality service will be one of the major challenges facing hospitality managers in the opening years of the next millennium. It will be an essential condition for success in the emerging, keenly competitive, global hospitality markets. While the future importance of delivering quality hospitality service is easy to discern and to agree on, doing so presents some difficult and intriguing management issues. Since the delivery of hospitality service always involves people, these issues centre on the management of people, and in particular on the interactions between guests and staff, interactions that are called service encounters.

In the eyes of our guests, our hospitality businesses will succeed or fail depending on the cumulative impact of the service encounters in which they have participated. It is easy to check the importance of managing these service encounters. Think back to the last time you visited a hotel or restaurant. How did you feel about the quality of the experience? Was it one that you would recommend to others? What were the specific interactions that made a difference? If you can't remember, is this something that should matter to the hospitality business concerned?

Surely something should have gone especially well? Service encounters are the building blocks of quality hospitality service. How can hospitality businesses manage them more effectively? We suggest a two step process in the evaluation of a service chain. First, hospitality managers should identify each encounter in the chain that they wish to take apart, and then single out those that are of operational or strategic significance - in effect, focusing in on the few encounters that really make a difference to guest experience and thus to the bottom line.

Second, apply what we have called the 6 S's to improving these critical encounters through effective redesign. While the first step may seem obvious, it is important to identify a service chain and then to break it down into the component encounters. Just how much detail is needed? Too much detail takes time and resources, and may confuse rather than clarify. Too little and we may miss important problems.

The process is iterative, with more detail needed in some areas and less in others, and with an overriding consideration that the chain is assessed not just from the point of view of a manager but also from that of a guest. Which are the encounters that really matter? Those that add significant value to the guest, those that cost in time or money, those that help to differentiate the business from its competitors, and those where significant innovation is possible or occurring. Hospitality service encounters run the gamut from those that are very trivial to those that are highly critical.

They vary greatly in their nature and may be simple or complex, standard or custom, low tech or high tech, remote or friendly, low or high skill, frequent or occasional, and so on. They can be instrumental dealing with the performance of necessary utilitarian activities or can involve emotion-laden hospitality events. An initial management task is to understand a service encounter by discerning and dealing with those attributes that are most important to guests.

In doing so, pertinent questions must be raised about the specific service encounter(s) under consideration. With respect to a particular service encounter, hospitality managers might raise many questions like the following:

a. Exactly what happened?

b. What were the guest reactions?

c. Should it be done differently?

d. What resources would assure optimal performance?

e. What changes should be made?

f. How can such changes best be put into effect?

The specific encounter(s) under consideration will, of course, indicate the kinds of questions that should be pursued. It is important to obtain adequate information to understand the situation thoroughly.

Determining the context of a situation relating to a hospitality encounter that has gone wrong establishes parameters for improvement. All this is part of the second step. With the information at hand hospitality managers can organize, and analyze the data and it is here that the 6S approach can help. These are:

1. Specification
2. Staff
3. Space
4. System
5. Support
6. Style

Specification means clearly detailing information about the what, when, where, and how, of service encounters. It requires giving careful thought to the linkages between particular service encounters and others in the service chain.

The starting point for hospitality service encounter analysis is specifying clearly the overall service strategy and what it is designed to achieve. Is the purpose cost or service quality leadership? Is it to provide unique service values, customized or standardized, complex or simple, frequent or occasional? Is it to provide service at any reasonable cost?

Is service limited to a luxury package, or does it include budget travellers? Which staff members are involved in providing the service? What skills do they need? What training has been provided? How committed are they to service goals? Is team cooperation or individual empowerment required? What attitudes are appropriate-- friendly, open, helpful, warm service, or efficient, unobtrusive, uninvolving, unthreatening service? What staff members deal with guests? How close are the 'backroom' staff to guests? Are staff presentations and appearances appropriate?

To what extent are guests involved in the provision of service? What skill, knowledge, information, or experience do guests need to fulfill their roles? What are likely guest expectations? What communication occurred between guest and service provider? Did the dynamics of the exchange proceed smoothly? Do any language and cultural barriers exist? Where will the service encounter occur? Is the space appropriately designed to facilitate the service encounter? Is there adequate space to handle each of the activities such as waiting, completing forms, storing or handling luggage, assembling tours? Is signage appropriate? Is the decor attractive to guests and supportive of activities that have to be carried out?

Are the necessary systems to support the encounter in place? Is the information necessary to respond effectively to guests' needs readily available? Is the appropriate technology being fully used? Are the interfaces between different functions such as housekeeping and front office, sales and front office, fully operational? What measurements of quality, or performance, are in use? Are they the most helpful for both service providers and managers? Are the criteria for success clearly defined? Is everyone involved aware of guest needs and concerns? Are the service providers given the facilities and financial and human support needed to do the job?

Is the technology appropriate? Have employees been given the training needed? Are incentive and reward systems geared to the tasks to be performed? Is supervision supportive? Does organization structure help or hinder performance?Are the suggested procedures appropriate? How should the service encounter be conducted, given the enterprise culture? Is the management style, and marketing orientation, appropriate for the tasks? Do service providers have the appropriate attitudes? Is the right emphasis being placed on service quality?

When hospitality managers have carried out this two step process they will be in an excellent position to make decisions that will both improve the quality of hospitality services provided and guest perceptions of them. Zeroing in on hospitality service quality in this manner will help hospitality businesses meet the service challenges of the millennium, enhance their market positions, and reap the associated profit rewards.

More recently a related stream of research in the leisure field has emerged in the area of service quality. This research stream stems from the pioneering work of Parasuraman, Berry and Zeithaml in the marketing field. They were the first to conceptualize and operationalize the concept of service quality in 1985 and have remained prominent contributors to the service quality literature as it has grown exponentially in the last decade.

The dominant theory used in the conceptualization of both service quality and satisfaction has been the expectancy-disconfirmation paradigm. This paradigm is derived from two processes: the development of expectations of outcomes, and the disconfirmation judgment that results from comparison of the perceived outcomes against these expectations. Confirmation results when the actual performance matches initial expectations. When performance exceeds or falls short of expectations, positive or negative disconfirmation results. Positive disconfirmation leads to satisfaction or perceptions of high service quality, while negative disconfirmation leads to dissatisfaction or perceptions of low service quality.

This common theoretical basis has resulted in considerable confusion in differentiating the satisfaction and service quality constructs. The literature is replete with reports that use the two terms interchangeably as synonyms and do not recognize them as distinctively different constructs.

For example, Howat el al. evaluated visitor satisfaction by using indicators based on Parasuraman et al.'s five dimensions of service quality. Despite this confusion there is a consensus that satisfaction and service quality are different constructs. The purpose of this study was to empirically explore the relationship between the two constructs and their impact on behavioural intentions.

Conceptual Framework and Hypotheses

The conceptual framework which guided development of the study's hypotheses. The framework examines service quality and satisfaction at two levels: the transaction level and the global level. At the global level, the model depicts overall service quality and overall visitor satisfaction as two different constructs which influence behavioural intentions.

At the transaction level, the concepts of quality of performance and quality of experience are conceptualized as direct antecedents of overall service quality and overall satisfaction. Quality of performance refers to visitors' perceptions of the attributes of a facility that are controlled by management. Quality of experience is defined as the psychological outcomes which visitors derive from visiting a facility. It reflects visitors' perceived benefits they obtain from the experience.

Oliver notes that visitors are likely to use more dimensions to form quality of experience judgments than quality of performance judgments. He maintains that the dimensions underlying quality judgments are rather specific, whether they are cues or attributes. Satisfaction judgments, however, can result from any dimension, quality-related or not. Quality of performance is only one dimension that influences quality of experience, which is influenced by a broader array of inputs.

The two constructs are likely to be positively correlated, but the relationship is unlikely to be linear. It has been pointed out that a high quality experience may result even when quality of performance is perceived to be low because, for example, social group interactions are sufficiently positive to offset the low quality service. The opposite can also occur when a low quality of experience results, even though perceived quality of performance is high.

For example, visitors ma y recently have had a bad experience while traveling to the site, such as receiving a speeding ticket, so they are not in a receptive mood to enjoy the experience. Thus, there are likely to be occasions when the quality of experience has relatively little to do with the quality of an agency's performance in delivering the service.

The production of a recreational experience involves both visitors and resources. Management can only provide opportunities such as services and facilities. How visitors avail themselves of those opportunities determines the quality of experience they receive. Since visitors' participation is involved in delivering the service it means that a recreation experience can be influenced, both by the services provided by suppliers and the emotional states brought to the site by visitors. The quality of performance provided by recreation suppliers can be controlled by management, while factors brought to the site by visitors are outside a supplier's control.

Quality of performance positively influences visitors' quality of experience.

Visitors' perceptions of performance quality on each attribute strongly influence their overall perceptions of service quality while quality of experience which is comprised of a set of specific psychological benefits leads to overall visitor satisfaction.

Like quality of experience and overall satisfaction, quality of performance and overall service quality are two distinct constructs. Quality of experience refers to the specific benefits people obtain, while overall satisfaction is visitors' levels of satisfaction towards their total experience with the recreation service, i.e., it is the summation of the specific benefits.

Quality of performance relates to evaluation of specific service attributes, while overall service quality is the evaluation of the quality of the service in general, rather than that of particular attributes. Perceptions of individual attributes and specific benefits are conceptualized as being compensatory. The compensatory nature of attributes was tested by Lue, Crompton and Stewart in the context of multi-destination travel behaviour.

Lue et al. reported that destinations could offset negative attributes, if they were perceived to provide other attributes that visitors preferred. Thus, the authors concluded that service attributes were compensatory and cumulative. Visitors can have perceptions of high overall quality or high levels of overall satisfaction, even though they perceive specific service attributes to have low quality or they are not satisfied with particular benefit dimensions of the experience.

Over time, the summation of visitors' evaluative beliefs about individual service attributes will contribute to their overall evaluation of service quality of the recreation service. Likewise, visitors' overall satisfaction is a summation state of the psychological outcomes they have experienced over time. As Bitner and Hubbert pointed out, multiple positive/negative experiences, which occur within a visit, are likely to lead to a high/low level of overall satisfaction.

Perceptions of the quality of performance of individual attributes influence perceptions of overall service quality. Perceptions of the quality of experience relating to individual benefits influence overall satisfaction. The model postulates that quality of performance has impact not only on overall service quality, but also on overall visitor satisfaction. Likewise, visitors' quality of experience influences their perceptions of overall service quality.

When visitors perceive a leisure service's attributes to be high quality, they are likely to experience higher levels of overall satisfaction with the service. At the same time, the stronger the psychological benefits that visitors obtain from their visits, the more positive attitude they are likely to have towards overall service quality.

Quality of experience positively impacts visitors' perceptions of overall service quality. Quality of performance positively impacts visitors' levels of overall satisfaction.

Visitors' levels of overall satisfaction contribute to their attitudes towards overall service quality. This follows the conceptualization of the relationship between service quality and satisfaction suggested by Parasuraman, Berry and Zeithami and Teas. It suggests that high levels of overall satisfaction lead to perceptions of high overall service quality, while low levels of overall satisfaction result in perceptions of low overall service quality.

The direction of this flow derives from the recognition that overall satisfaction is experience specific while overall service quality is not. Since overall service quality is visitors' perceptions of overall performance, visitors can have a general impression towards the quality of a recreation site even if they have never been there. This can occur when visitors have acquired knowledge of the site from external sources such as word-of-mouth communication, television programmes, or newspaper or magazine articles.

For example, based on their knowledge of Yellowstone National Park, potential visitors may have a general impression of the quality of the park, even though they have never visited it. However, they cannot express their levels of overall satisfaction with it because this impression can only be formed after visiting and experiencing the benefits the park offered at least once. Levels of overall satisfaction can only be derived from firsthand experience.

Overall satisfaction positively influences overall service quality. Once visitors form an overall evaluation toward service quality and toward overall satisfaction, the model indicates that these judgments are likely to influence visitors' future behavioural intentions. Thus, when a visitor perceives an attraction to have high overall service quality, the individual is likely to say positive things about the attraction and to come back and visit it again in the future.

Likewise, if a visitor's level of overall satisfaction is high with the attraction, the individual is likely to disseminate positive word-of-mouth about the attraction and to visit it again in the future. Overall service quality is positively associated with visitors' behavioural intentions. Overall satisfaction is positively associated with visitors' behavioural intentions. To test the hypotheses in the study, data were collected from visitors to Aransas National Wildlife Refuge in Texas.

During a two-weekend period, one adult member from each of the 355 visitor groups entering the interpretive centre in this time period was given a questionnaire, a pre-paid envelope and a cover letter explaining the purpose and the importance of the study. Participants were requested to complete and return the questionnaire in the enclosed pre-paid envelope. A drawing for a $500 US savings bond was used as an incentive to encourage response.

A modified Dillman approach was used to collect the data. It involved one postcard reminder and two other follow-ups, which included replacement questionnaires, to those who did not respond. These procedures resulted in the return of 282 completed instruments (81% response rate). There was almost an equal proportion of male (50.3%) and female (49.7%)

respondents, and 62.5% of the sample were aged between 40 and 69. Over 83% had at least one college degree and 34% were retired. Almost half of the respondents (47%) had an income in the $30,000 to $60,000 range, while 18.4% reported incomes over $90,000. First time visitors to the refuge constituted 51.6% of the sample while 53.1% resided within the state of Texas.

Five constructs were included in the hypotheses that were tested. They were: quality of performance, quality of experience, overall service quality, overall visitor satisfaction, and visitors' future behavioural intentions. Quality of performance was operationalized by a list of attributes of the wildlife refuge selected from a pool developed from previous literature and from extended discussions with refuge managers.

They were categorized into six domains and an expert panel, which included the researchers and refuge managers, was used to select five items from those assigned to each domain to represent the dimensions of that domain. The six domains were Education and Conservation, Staff/Volunteers, Comfort Amenities, Cleanliness, Information, and Wildlife.

A pretest using a sample of university students was conducted to examine the validity and reliability of these scales. Responses to the items were measured on 7-point Likert-type scales anchored by "very poor" and "excellent". A factor analysis on the pretest sample resulted in the number of items being reduced from a total of 30 to 25, and in some reassignment of items and re-tiding of the domains.

To evaluate the factor structure in the scales for the construct of quality of performance, data from the study's respondents were subjected to a principal components factor analysis of the six scales (not the individual items) to see if the six scales were unifactorial (i.e. if the six scales were measuring the same construct). The analysis confirmed that they were, but a low communality estimate and low reliability resulted in one factor, Wildlife, being dropped. The scales used to measure the quality of performance construct, with their factor loadings and reliabilities. The identification code is the label given to each scale in the measurement model which is discussed in the next section.

The benefit items used to operationalize quality of experience were adapted from the Recreation Experience Preference scales (REP) that have been used in past benefits research. Manfredo et al. demonstrated the reliability and validity of 19 REP scales using a meta-analysis of 36 studies. The expert panel used in the current study judged that 15 of the 19 REP scales potentially could be relevant to a refuge visitation experience. Items were measured on 7-point Likert-type scales anchored by "strongly disagree" and "strongly agree".

After a pretest with the university student sample, the 51 items drawn from the 15 domains were reduced to 39 items, which were assigned to 8 domains. The eight domains were: Nature Appreciation/Learning, Achievement, Introspection/Nostalgia, Escape, Similar People, Physical Fitness, Family Togetherness and New People. A factor analysis using principal component factor analysis was also conducted on the sample data to examine th e factor structure of the scales measuring the construct.

The factor analysis resulted in 2 factors. As shows, six of the eight scales loaded on Factor 1 while Similar people and Family Togetherness loaded on Factor 2. As a result, a decision had to be made regarding whether to treat the second factor as a separate variable distinctively different from the latent quality of experience variable, or just to delete the second factor. Since the objective of the present study was to test the proposed theoretical model rather than to explore an additional latent construct, and there was no theoretical rationale for adding a second dimension into the structural model, it was decided to delete the two scales Similar People and Family Togetherness from the study.

Overall service quality was measured on a 10-point scale with a single item that asked respondents their perceptions of overall quality of the refuge's attributes. The anchors on the scale were, extremely low quality and extremely high quality. Responses ranged from 4 to 10, but 89% were in the 7 to 10 range and the mean was 8.2. This manifest variable is labeled V19 in the measurement model.

Overall satisfaction was measured with a 4-item, 7-point modified semantic differential scale. This scale was originally adapted by Childress and Crompton from Crosby and Stephens. Since there were no pre-determined domains among the items measuring overall satisfaction, a factor analysis was conducted on the four individual items. As expected, the principal component method extracted only one factor, meaning that the scale was unifactorial. The Cronbach's alpha reliability score for the scale was .97.

The final construct, behavioural intentions, was measured with a seven-item, 7-point scale derived from Zeithaml, Berry and Parasuraman. Respondents were requested to indicate how likely they were to take each of the seven actions (1 = not at all likely and 7 = extremely likely). The seven items were not unifactorial because two factors were extracted from the principal component factor analysis on the 7 items.

The loadings of the items are listed. One item was deleted because it did not have a salient loading above. 40 on either factor. The two items loaded on Factor 2 were also deleted for the same reason as the two items in quality of experience were deleted. One of the items from Factor 1 was also deleted to improve the reliability measure of behavioural intentions (reliability score increased from .78 to .84 after deleting the item).

The Measurement Model

The naming of its components follows Bender's (1989) convention. Since overall service quality was measured by a single item scale, it was a manifest variable (V19), labeled with the letter "V" for variable. Quality of performance (Fl), quality of experience (F2), overall satisfaction (F3) and behavioural intentions (F4) are latent variables prefaced by the letter "F" for factor.

The quality of performance construct (Fl) was measured by the five manifest variables Vi through V5. The quality of experience construct (F2) was measured by manifest variables V6 through Vii. The overall satisfaction construct (F3) was measured by manifest variables V12 to V15. The behavioural intention construct (F4) was measured by manifest variables V16 through V18 which are keyed.

V1 through V5 represent the five scales that measured the quality of performance construct. Each of these variables was calculated as the grand mean score of respondents' ratings of each item in the individual scale. For example, in the first scale "Education and Conservation" (Vi) there were five items. V1 is the average score of respondents' ratings on these five items. The same method was applied to V6 through Vii. However, V12 through V19 were the respondents' actual responses to each individual item.

The measurement model posits no unidirectional paths between latent variables. Instead, a covariance is estimated to connect each latent variable with every other latent variable. This is indicated by the curved, two-headed arrow connecting each F variable and V19 to every other F variable. Letter "L" represents the coefficients of the "V" variables to "F" factors. Letter "E" represents measurement errors for each manifest variable. Letter "C" represents covariance between latent factors and the manifest variable V19.

The measurement model was estimated using the maximum likelihood method, and the goodness of fit indices. It has been recommended that the model chi-square test be used as a goodness of fit index, with a smaller chi-square value (usually non-significant chi-square test) indicating a better model fit. The chi-square value for the initial measurement model was statistically significant. However, the chi-square test usually is not considered as the absolute standard by which the goodness of fit of the model is judged because it is sensitive to sample size.

Other tests, such as goodness of fit index (GFI), adjusted goodness of fit index (AGFI), Bender's comparative fit index (GFI) and Bender and Bonett's non-normed fit index (NNFI), should also be used to judge the goodness of fit of the model. Values over .9 on these indices indicate an acceptable fit. The indices in Table 5 pro vided mixed support for the initial measurement model because only the CFI was larger than .90. It was thus concluded that there was a problem with the model's fit.

To identify the problem, the patterns of normalized residuals, parameter significance tests, and LaGrange multiplier tests were examined. All coefficients were significant, indicating the indicators were good measures of the underlying latent factors. However, of the ten largest standardized residuals, nine of them were related to V6, which is the variable "Nature Appreciation/Learning" measuring quality of experience (F2). Nine of the ten largest LaGrange multipliers tests were also related to V6.

The researchers' interpretation of this problem was that nature appreciation and learning about nature is so pervasive in a visit to a wildlife refuge that it permeates into all aspects of the experience. Given the premise that to experience nature was such a dominant pervasive theme in the process of visiting the refuge, it would be represented in the model even if it was excluded as an explicit variable. Thus, V6 was eliminated from the measurement model, and the model was re-calibrated.

Goodness of fit indices for the re-specified measurement model are also presented. The t values for the coefficients of the standard factor loadings were still all significant. Moreover, NNFI now exceeded .9, and the GFI improved to .86. The results indicated that the revised measurement model had a reasonable fit to the data. Therefore, this measurement model was tentatively accepted as the study's "final" measurement model.

Reliability and validity of the constructs and their indicators were assessed. The reliability of an indicator variable is the square of the correlation between a latent factor and that indicator. In this case, the R-square values are indicator reliabilities which indicate the percent of variance in the indicator that is explained by the common factor that it is supposed to measure. Overall satisfaction indicators had very high reliabilities, while reliabilities for quality of performance indicators, quality of experience indicators (from .24 to .81) and behavioural intention indicators were relatively low.

A composite reliability index for each latent factor was calculated to measure the internal consistency of the indicators measuring a given factor. This procedure is similar to the use of Cronbach's alpha for measuring the scale reliability of multiple items in a scale. The composite reliability for latent factor overall satisfaction was .96. Although indicator reliabilities for quality of performance, quality of experience and behavioural intentions were relatively low, the composite reliabilities for these factors were .79, .83 and .81, respectively, which all exceeded the minimally acceptable level of .70 reliability for scale instruments? The relatively high composite reliabilities suggested that the individual scales, when taking as a group, performed fairly well in the model.

Convergent validity and discriminant validity of the constructs were assessed to see if the indicators were measuring what they were intended to measure. Convergent validity is demonstrated when different scales are used to measure the same construct, and scores from these different scales are strongly correlated. In the confirmatory analysis, convergent validity was examined by reviewing the t tests for the factor loadings.

Hatcher states: "if all factor loadings for the indicators measuring the same construct are statistically significant (greater than twice their standard errors) this is viewed as evidence supporting the convergent validity of those indicators". In the present model testing, all t tests were significant providing evidence to support the convergent validity of the indicators.

Discriminant validity is demonstrated when different scales are used to measure different constructs and the correlations between the measures are relatively weak. Discriminant validity for the latent factors was assessed by performing confidence interval tests. The confidence interval was calculated by adding or subtracting two standard errors around the correlation between two factors.

If this confidence interval includes the value of 1.0, then it is very likely that, for the actual population, the two factors are perfectly correlated. In the present model testing, none of the confidence intervals approached 1.0, demonstrating the discriminant validity of all measures used in the study.

It differs from the model that depicts the causal relationship among exogenous and endogenous variables. An exogenous variable is an independent variable whose causes lie outside the model. In this case, quality of performance is the only exogenous variable in the structural model. In contrast to exogenous variables, the postulated causes of endogenous variables are included in the model. In the current model, quality of experience, overall service quality, overall satisfaction and behavioural intentions are all endogenous variables.

The standard errors for the factor loadings and path coefficients in the initial structural model were not near zero, and none of them appeared to be unacceptably small. All factor loadings that were tested had t values greater than 1.96. All of the path coefficients were significant (.05 level) except for the path from F2 to V19. The goodness of fit indices for the structural model indicated the model has a relatively good fit to the data. However, these indices represent the overall fit of the measurement model and the structural model combined.

The current theoretical model consists of a relatively small number of latent variables and a relatively large number of indicator variables. This suggests that indices of overall model fit may be more influenced by the fit of the measurement model than by the fit of the structural model.

However, the present study is more concerned with the fit of the structural model than the fit of the measurement model. Therefore, the relative normed-fit index (RNFI) was calculated to evaluate the fit of only the structural model when free from the influence of the fit of the measurement model. The RNFI for the structural model was .94, indicating a reasonably good fit of the theoretical model without considering how well the latent variables were measured by their indicators.

Since both the measurement model and the structural model had relatively good fit to the data, it was necessary to perform a chi-square difference test to determine whether there was a significant difference between the fit provided by the structural model and that provided by the measurement model. This test provides evidence for the nomological validity of the structural model. The difference chi-square value between the structural and the measurement model was 20.07, which was greater than the critical value of 13.82 with df = 2.

Thus, there was a significant difference (.001) between the fit provided by the measurement model and the fit provided by the structural model. In other words, the fit of the structural model was significantly poorer than the fit of the measurement model. This result suggested that the structural model contained some misspecifications that needed to be modified.

To identify sources of the misspecifications in the model, the modification indices were reviewed. The multivariate Wald tests suggested the path from F2 to V19 should be deleted. This was consistent with the factor loadings' significance tests because the t-test for the coefficient of the path from F2 to V19 was found to be non-significant (.05 level). It indicated that the relationship between quality of experience and overall service quality was not significant. Thus, this path was eliminated from the model.

They were relatively similar to the initial structural model, but it was marginally more parsimonious. The chi-square difference test was conducted on the measurement model and the revised structural model to see if the structural model had a reasonable fit with the data, like the measurement model did. The test was highly significant, revealing that there were still mis-specifications in the revised model 1.

Wald tests conducted on the initial structural model did not reveal any additional causal paths between latent constructs that could be deleted without affecting the model's fit. Thus, results of LaGrange multiplier tests were reviewed to identify new causal paths that should be added to the model. The results showed that paths should be added from two variables to F4, together with a path from F2 to F4.

Since V8 and V9 are indicators of F2, a path from F2 to F4 should be added to the model. There was previous empirical evidence to support the direct influence of quality of experience on visitors' future behavioural intentions. This evidence is discussed later in the paper. A path from quality of experience (F2) to behavioural intentions (F4) was then added and the new model, revised model 2, was then estimated.

The fit indices for revised model 2 were all higher than those of revised model 1 and the parsimonious NF1 did not decrease, meaning that revised model 2 was as parsimonious as revised model 1. The RNFI for revised model 2 was 0.99 indicating that revised model 2 was a much better fit than revised model 1, independent of the measurement model. All of the coefficient estimates of the standard loadings were significant and in the predicted direction. The distribution of normalized residuals for revised model 2 was symmetrical and centreed on zero. Only three of the normalized residuals were greater than the absolute value of 2.0, and the largest of the three was 2.7.

The chi-square difference test between the measurement model and the revised structural model 2 resulted in a value of 1.23, which was much smaller than the critical value of 13.82.

Thus, the chi-square test was not significant, indicating that the fit of revised model 2 was not significantly different from the fit of the measurement model in which the F variables were free to covary. In other words, the causal relationships described in the revised model 2 successfully explained the observed relationships between the latent constructs.

The addition of the causal path from quality of experience to behavioural intentions resulted in revised model 2 being superior to revised model 1, and this addition did not decrease the model's parsimony. Thus, this model was the final model for the study. All parameter estimates in the final model were significant at [alpha] = .05. Standardized instead of unstandardized coefficients were then used to evaluate the strength of path coefficients estimated, because the variables involved were not measured on the same scale.

Effects of Exogenous and Endogenous Variables

The standardized coefficients for each path in the model. They represented the strength of the direct effect of an exogenous variable on an endogenous variable, and that of one endogenous variable on another. The direct effect refers to the influence of one variable on another that is not mediated by any other variables in the model. Bollen noted that the direct and indirect effects can help to answer important questions regarding the influence of one variable on another, but "it is the total effect that is more relevant". He explained that the direct effect could be misleading when the indirect effect has an opposite sign, for in such cases the total effect may not be as strong as the direct effect shows.

The direct, indirect and total effects of all endogenous and exogenous variables in the final model. Direct effects, according to Bollen, "are the influences of one variable on another that are not mediated by any other variable... Indirect effects are ones that are mediated by at least one other variable, and the total effects are the sum of direct and indirect effects". While direct effects as the values of direct path coefficients, indirect effects are calculated by multiplying all the path coefficients for each route of indirect influence.

If an independent variable has more than one route of indirect influence on a dependent variable, then the indirect effects for each route are summed to calculate the overall indirect effects of the independent variable on the dependent variable. Quality of performance (F1) had a positive direct effect on quality of experience (F2) (.48).

Quality of performance had a stronger direct effect (.31) on overall satisfaction, than did quality of experience (.23). In addition, quality of performance also indirectly influenced overall satisfaction through quality of experience (indirect effects of .11 = .48 X .23). Thus, the total effects of quality of performance on overall satisfaction (.42) were stronger than those of quality of experience (.23).

Overall service quality is directly and/or indirectly influenced by quality of performance, quality of experience and overall satisfaction. Quality of performance not only directly contributed to overall service quality, but it also indirectly influenced overall service quality through two routes. One route was through quality of experience [right arrow] overall satisfaction right arrow overall service quality, while the second route was through overall satisfaction right arrow overall service quality.

Thus, quality of experience had total effects of .73 on overall service quality, with a direct influence of .60 and an indirect influence of .13 (.13 .48 X .23 X .30 + .31 X .30). The direct influence of overall satisfaction on overall service quality was .30. Since the direct path from quality of experience to overall service quality was not supported by the data, quality of experience only had an indirect influence of .07 (.07 = .23 X .30) on overall service quality through overall satisfaction. Thus, of the three independent variables that impact overall service quality, quality of performance had the highest degree of influence on overall service quality.

Visitors' future behavioural intentions were either directly or indirectly influenced by quality of performance, quality of experience, overall service quality and overall satisfaction. Quality of performance had the strongest total effect (.62) on behavioural intentions even though it did not have any direct effect on this variable. While overall satisfaction had the second strongest total effects (.59) on behavioural intentions, its direct effect was the highest (.41). Quality of experience both directly (.29) influenced behavioural intentions, and indirectly (.11) influenced it through overall satisfaction and overall service quality. Overall service quality had the lowest total effect (.26) on behavioural intentions among all variables.

Hypothesis 1 stated that quality of performance has a positive direct influence on quality of experience because perception of service attributes can contribute to the benefits visitors receive from their visiting experience. This hypothesis is shown as the path from F1 to F2. The standardized coefficient of this path was .48. The t value was 7.29, which was significant at [alpha] = .001. The significant coefficient provided evidence of support for hypothesis 1.

Hypothesis 2 explored the relationship between visitors' perceptions of individual attributes' performance and their perceptions of overall service quality and is shown as the path from F1 to V19. Hypothesis 2 was supported since the t-test for the path coefficient was significant (t value of 12.49), indicating that visitors' perceptions of quality of performance positively influenced their perceptions of the overall service quality of the refuge.

The specific benefits visitors received that constituted their quality of experience were expected to relate positively to their overall satisfaction level. The greater the perceived psychological benefits visitors obtained from the visit, the higher it was anticipated would be their levels of overall satisfaction with the refuge in general. This relationship, indicated by the path from F2 to F3, was found to be significant at an alpha level of .05 with a t value of 2.82, so Hypothesis 3 was supported.

It was hypothesized that quality of experience would influence overall service quality. In the initial structural model, the path coefficient from F2 to V19 was found to be non-significant, and thus was eliminated from the model, so Hypothesis 4 was not supported.

Hypothesis 5 stated that perceptions of quality of performance of the refuge's individual attributes positively influenced overall satisfaction. The higher the perceived quality of individual service attributes, the higher it was anticipated would be the levels of overall satisfaction. The significant coefficient (t value of 3.85) from path F1 to F3 enabled Hypothesis 5 to be supported.

It was postulated that the higher visitors' overall satisfaction was with the refuge, the higher would be their perceptions of overall service quality. The path from F3 to V19 was significant (t value of 5.46) so Hypothesis 6 was supported.

Visitors' future behavioural intentions were expected to be influenced positively by both overall service quality and overall satisfaction. When visitors have high perceptions of overall service quality and high levels of overall satisfaction with the refuge, they are more likely to visit the refuge again in the future or to encourage their friends to do so. The path coefficients from V19 to F4 and from F3 to F4 were both found to be significant, so hypotheses 7 and 8 were both supported.

The results provided empirical support for the conceptualization of service quality and satisfaction. However, it was found that the particular psychological benefits visitors obtained from the visit did not contribute to their perceptions of service quality in a major way. They only contributed to overall service quality indirectly through overall visitor satisfaction (indirect effect of .07).

This finding of the study contradicts those who insist transaction-specific satisfaction influences overall service quality. One explanation for this contradiction lies in the different conceptualizations of satisfaction at the transaction level. The present study views satisfaction at the transaction level as the specific benefits received from a visit, while others have considered it to be evaluation of individual service attributes, or as overall satisfaction with the service.

While the study found that both visitors' evaluations of individual service attributes and their levels of overall satisfaction directly influenced their perceptions of overall service quality, when satisfaction was conceptualized as psychological benefits visitors receive at the transaction level, it did not contribute to overall service quality directly. This provides evidence supporting the distinction between quality of performance and quality of experience, and it also reinforces the notion that satisfaction should be specified at both the transaction level and the global level. Thus, when studying the relationship between satisfaction and service quality in general, the inter-relationship among transaction-level concepts and global-level concepts should be considered.

Hypothesis 6 supported the proposition that visitors who were satisfied with their overall experience at the refuge tended to have high evaluations of its overall quality. Although there is evidence that overall service quality and visitor satisfaction are independent of each other, "the main issue to be resolved is whether customers distinguish between customer satisfaction and service quality in their own minds". The present study did find discriminant validity between overall service quality and overall satisfaction.

In addition, the results showed that the total effects of overall satisfaction on overall service quality were relatively low. This implies that although they are correlated, overall service quality and overall satisfaction are not the same construct. Support for hypotheses 7 and 8 suggests that high levels of visitor satisfaction, and/or perceptions of high service quality are likely to reinforce visitors' intentions of using the service again in the future and to engage in positive word-of-mouth communication with their family and friends.

However, the influence of overall service quality on behavioural intentions was found to be much weaker than that of overall satisfaction. Indeed, the results showed that overall service quality contributed least to behavioural intentions among all four constructs examined (i.e. quality of performance, quality of experience, overall satisfaction and overall service quality).

In addition to the direct influences of overall service quality and overall satisfaction on behavioural intentions, this study also found that quality of experience directly contributed to behavioural intentions. This relationship was not hypothesized in the proposed model. The decision to add the path in the revised structural model was made because previous studies have provided empirical evidence for the influence of transaction-specific satisfaction on behavioural intentions.

For example, Westbrook studied the relationship of consumption-based psychological responses and post-purchase processes. He reported that both negative and positive dimensions of psychological responses were directly related to satisfaction judgments, complaint behaviour and word-of-mouth communication.

These results suggest that when visitors' psychological responses to particular benefits are strong enough, they can impact their future behavioural intentions. If visitors are not satisfied with specific benefits derived from the current visit, they may not return even if overall quality of the service is considered to be good.

The issue of understanding the relationship between service quality and visitor satisfaction from a manager's perspective starts with a fundamental question: should management focus on visitor satisfaction or on perceived service quality? Thus, Dabholkar has noted that practitioners "are not interested in the difference between these concepts per se, but are interested in both concepts mainly as predictors of customer behaviour".

Thus, two aspects of the study are likely to be of especial interest to managers. First, it confirmed that improved service quality and visitor satisfaction can result in repeat visitation and positive word-of-mouth. Second, it clarified the relationship between service quality and satisfaction, and found that both constructs had an independent effect on visitors' future behavioural intentions.

Service quality and satisfaction at the global level are overall evaluations. However, the study suggests that change in overall evaluations starts with changes in perceptions of quality of performance and quality of experience. Hence, the priority of managers is at the transaction level of service quality and satisfaction.

From management's perspective, quality of performance should be viewed as the most important aspect of a service, for as Berry and Parasuraman noted: "Service quality is the foundation of services marketing". While the refuge's attributes are under the control of the managers, benefits visitors obtain during the trip are not. Although quality of visitors' experience is partially a response to management's performance, in part it is also a reaction to factors that are brought to the refuge by visitors themselves.

Further, the subjectivity of the psychological outcome of a refuge visit experience determines that tourism managers cannot control the psychological benefits visitors obtain from each visit. Thus, at the transaction level, service quality is most important for managers. To influence visitors' future decisions, managers can improve the attributes of a refuge.

Crompton and Lamb pointed out "Citizens don't buy programmes or service; they buy the expectation of benefits. Programmes themselves are not marketable. Only their benefits have a value to client groups. A service programme is simply a vehicle for the user benefits that it conveys". Results of the study confirmed that quality of performance is only one factor that influences visitors' benefits obtained.

However, it is the most accessible means available to management to achieve the ultimate goal — realization of benefits sought by visitors. Although structural equation modeling procedures deal with causal models, they do not establish causal relationships. Bollen asserts that "At best they show whether the causal assumptions embedded in a model match a sample of data" .

Thus, results of the study only verify that the proposed relationships among constructs in the conceptual model for the most part were supported by the sample data collected for this study. An important next step is to fit the proposed model to other samples of data so that its validity can be examined.

Findings of the study supported the influence of overall satisfaction on overall service quality which suggests that overall service quality is a higher level construct. However, this is not conclusive because structural equation modeling shows only whether the relationship conceptualized in the model has support from the sample data.

Although the impact of overall satisfaction on overall service quality was conceptualized based on previous studies, there is also evidence in the literature that there may be a reciprocal effect between overall service quality and satisfaction. Future research could usefully examine this possible effect in order to determine which construct is superordinate at the global level.

A related topic that awaits further research is examination of the interrelationships among dimensions of latent constructs in the model. The purpose of the present study was to test the structural model and, thus, it did not focus on examining the dimensions of the constructs. Future studies could investigate what service attributes contribute most to visitors' quality of experience, and what benefits should be promoted to current and potential visitors. In addition, the Nature Appreciation/ Learning dimension was eliminated in this study because of its overwhelming influence on the model.

This may be an important issue for future studies to address, because it seems likely that one or two powerful variables may consistently overwhelm similar models in leisure contexts where respondents are highly involved users.

Chapter 2

The Organization of Global Service

THE PERCEIVED VALUE OF A SERVICE

Most Hospitality Operators use the term "Quality" somewhere in their advertising and promotion. What exactly does that mean? One would compile multiple responses, as Management tried to define "Quality". The same would be said for their Staff, and, just as importantly, the Guest. We all have different perspectives. Hospitality invites a Quality Experience, but, if expectations are not met, you have a disappointed Guest, reduced Revenue, unhappy employees and a deteriorating reputation.

So, what is the Value of Quality: the Concept, the Experience and Reward, and how does this relate to your Hospitality Business?Recent research has revealed that few leisure providers integrate marketing techniques into programming efforts and that "leisure service agencies have long attempted to serve diverse and, at times, non-responsive populations". A marketing perspective would suggest leisure and tourism providers analyze the needs and desires of their participants, in order to develop the most appropriate delivery methods. In doing so, leisure/tourism programmers may benefit by attracting more responsive and possibly more loyal participants.

Quality is a Process. There are Performance Standards created, communicated and implemented. The Standards are reviewed constantly to stress Continual Improvement. Success

Stories are heralded. Problem Areas are immediately addressed. Steady "feed back" is required. This is not a one day exercise. Quality must become integral to your Business Performance.

Does your definition of Quality translate to the Guest's expectations? Hospitality Operations are boldly diverse. We present to the Consumer various locations, architecture, ambiance, price, amenity, and activity. When they make a reservation - book a room, a table, or a ticket - the Guest has an Expectation. Now, we must deliver and not create a disconnect, because we may be at cross purposes with our Guest and their concept of Quality.

How do we create a "common ground" to meet these expectations and avoid the false steps in fully serving our Guest? The Quality Process begins with recognized, reasonable Hospitality Performance Standards. All parties understand cleanliness. The environment you represent must be clean and not assault the five senses. We need to feel safe and secure. We require certain "creature comforts".

We look for our needs to be attended with some courtesy, accuracy, speed and pleasant attitude. Finally, we expect the facility to present an acceptable appearance / condition. These elements are how you will be judged by your Guest. They represent the Benchmarks for a memorable Quality experience or not. These Performance Standards are the foundation, and the Guest needs to know you are serious and sincere. Particularly for those Destinations which are Family oriented, recognize that the greatest influence on where the Family will stay, dine and recreate is the Mother, and she holds Quality Standards dearly.

The success of a Process needs to be measured - a Performance Evaluation. Where do you rate with these Hospitality Standards? Do you deliver, and, just as importantly, does your Staff? Your Quality message must be communicated daily. Your Staff must abide by your Message. Clear guidelines, need to be in place, practiced and assessed.

Attention to detail and meeting the Guest's needs are the Mantra. There are many means to evaluate your Performance: the personal relationship you have with your Guests; in-house mechanisms, like Comment Cards; Mystery Shop Services; Assessment Companies; and formal Guest Satisfaction Systems. They are all meaningful. Further, many leisure and tourism providers would benefit by obtaining a more consistent participant base as it has been shown that it is six times less expensive to plan marketing strategies for retaining consumers, than it is to attract new consumers.

In the field of marketing, the construct of perceived value has been identified as one of the most important measures for gaining competitive edge, and has been argued to be the most important indicator of repurchase intentions.

Yet, in regards to leisure and tourism services, repurchase intentions and consumer loyalty are often predicted solely by measures of consumer satisfaction, and/or service quality. Woodruff (1997) states, "if consumer satisfaction measurement is not backed up with in-depth learning about customer value and related problems that underlie their evaluations, it may not provide enough of the customer's voice to guide managers where to respond".

Further, just because a consumer is "satisfied" with a product/service, does not necessarily mean the product/service is a good value. It is quite possible a consumer who is very satisfied with a product or service, may consider it a poor value if the costs for obtaining it a re perceived to be too high. On the contrary, a moderately satisfied consumer may find a service to have good value, if they believe they receive good utility for the price paid.

Since perceived value has been found to be an important indicator of repurchase intentions it is believed leisure/tourism providers could benefit from refined measures of the construct. Valid and reliable measures of perceived value would allow for comparison of value between leisure/tourism programmes, and would allow individual leisure/tourism providers the ability to identify the dimensions of perceived value in which they perform well or poor.

While recent multidimensional scales have been created for measuring the perceived value of tangible products, a multi-dimensional scale for the measurement of perceived value of intangible products (services) does not exist. Thus, the purpose of the current study is to develop a multidimensional scale for the measurement of perceived value of a service.

Perceived value has been defined as "the consumer's overall assessment of the utility of a product based on perceptions of what is received and what is given". Within this definition, Zeithaml (1988) identified four diverse meanings of value:

(1) Value is low price,

(2) Value is whatever one wants in a product,

(3) Value is the quality that the consumer receives for the price paid, and

(4) Value is what the consumer gets for what they give. The majority of past research on perceived value has focused on the fourth definition.

A fundamental base for the conceptualization of perceived value of a service was developed by Zeithaml. Her research utilized focus groups and in-depth consumer interviews to explore the relationships between consumers' perceptions of price, quality and value. The focus groups were utilized to determine the salient attributes and variables related to perceived value, while the interviews were utilized to reveal the causal links among product attributes, quality and value. Open ended questions were then used to examine the information needed to make judgments about quality and value (i.e., advertising and packaging).

Results of her study showed that perceived quality leads to perceived value, which leads to purchase intentions. Both intrinsic (i.e., how the purchase makes you feel) and extrinsic attributes (i.e., reputation of the product/service), as well as price, were found to be positively related to perceived quality. Moderating variables of perceived value included perceived sacrifice (non-monetary price), extrinsic attributes and intrinsic attributes. Overall, Zeithaml reported quality, price (monetary and non-monetary), reputation of the product/service and how the product/service makes one feel (emotional response) were dimensions related to perceived value.

Similarly, the Profit of Impact Marketing Strategies (PIMS) study conceptualized value as the relationship between quality and price. They ascertained competitive success is obtained through "perceived relative value" of the total package of products and services that influence customer behaviour. Relative value, is the value received from one product/service, in comparison to similar offerings.

According to Bojanic: "the notion of relative perceived value results in three possible value positions: (1) offering comparable quality at a comparable price, (2) offering superior quality at a premium price, or (3) offering inferior quality at a discounted price." Perceived value may thus be altered if management changes what they are doing, a competitor changes what they are doing, or if consumer's desires or needs change.

More recently, Parasuraman and Grewal (2000) conceptualized perceived value as a dynamic construct consisting of four value types: acquisition value, transaction value, in-use value and redemption value. They define acquisition value as the benefits received for the monetary price given, and transaction value as the pleasure the consumer receives for getting a good deal. In-use value is the utility derived from utilization of the product/service, while redemption value is the residual benefit received at the time of trade-in or end of life (products) or termination (for services). Utilizing these definitions, the relevance of each of the four dimensions are different during varying times of the product/services life (i.e., acquisition and transaction value are most salient during purchase, while in-use value and redemption value are more pertinent after purchase).

While all of these theorized frameworks aid in the understanding of perceived value, they do not offer measures for collecting perceived value data. Perceived value is most commonly measured by using a self-reported, unidimensional measure asking respondents to rate the value they received for their purchase. The problem with a one-dimensional measures is that it assumes that consumers have a shared meaning of value. Zeithaml states, "quality and value are not well differentiated from each other and from similar constructs such as perceived worth and utility."

Thus, it has been argued that one-dimensional measures of perceived value lack validity. Another inherent problem is unidimensional measures result in the knowledge of how well one is rated for value, but give no specific direction on how to improve value.

It is believed that a formal measurement tool for the perceived value of a service, would allow comparisons similar to comparisons of service quality that are now available due to Parasuraman, Zeithaml and Berry's (1988) SERVQUAL scale and Cronin and Taylor's SERVPERF scale. With the use of reliable and valid multi-dimensional measures, leisure and tourism providers should be able to identify the dimensions in which they are succeeding and/or failing in regards to both their own past measures and those of their competition.

Current efforts to measure perceived value have shown it is difficult to quantify perceived value. Kantamneni and Coulson focused on the development of a multi-dimensional measure of perceived value of a product. They utilized undergraduate business students to identify potential measurable dimensions of a product's perceived value. Results identified the distinct factors of societal value, experiential value, functional value and market value.

Societal value was termed to be the product's benefit/ value to society. Experiential value was related to the senses:

if the product feels, smells and looks good, while functional value was related to whether or not the product is reliable and safe. The final factor, market value, was the product's worth regarding price for value. Another multi-dimensional scale for the measurement of perceived value of a product was presented by Sweeney, Soutar and Johnson.

Utilizing exploratory factor analysis of 29 items generated from a literature review, the factors of quality, emotional response, price and social emerged as dimensions of perceived value of a product. Quality referred to how well the product was made, and emotional response to how a product made the consumer feel. Price was operationalized as whether or not the money paid for the product was reasonable, and social as the impression that the purchase of the product had on others.

While the aforementioned studies show promise for the measurement of perceived value of tangible products, there is need for a different scale to be developed for measuring the perceived value of a service. Past research has shown that scales developed for measuring a product's perceived value are difficult to use when measuring perceived value of a service. Further, the dimensions inherent in a service differ from those of a product. Lovelock argued that services differ from products in that they are intangible, perishable, variable and inseparable. Thus, multi-dimensional measures of a service must consider these properties.

Following the theoretical model conceptualized by Zeithaml, current conceptual frameworks, and the properties of a service, multiple dimensions of perceived value of a service can be identified. Most researchers agree that perceived value is a comparison of what a consumer "receives," with what the consumer "gives" for the attainment of a product or service. Perceived price is what a consumer gives up or sacrifices in order to obtain a product.

While some consumers may know the exact price of the service purchased, others may only remember (encode) that their purchase was expensive or inexpensive in relation to past purchases. Still others may not encode a price at all. Consumers also evaluate non-monetary costs in their determination of quality received for price paid. Non-monetary costs include such things as time, search costs, brand image and convenience. It is therefore a combination of both perceived monetary and non-monetary costs that equate to consumers' overall perceived sacrifice which, in turn, affects their perception of product or service value.

In regards to what a consumer "receives" past research has identified emotional response, or the joy received from purchase, and quality as dimensions of perceived value of a product/service. Further, the product/services reputation has been identified as an influence on consumer's perceived quality, and perceived value. Thus it could be argued that dimensions of what a consumer receives from the purchase of a service include: the emotional response to the service, quality received from the service, and the reputation of the service rendered. While the dimensions related to what is given, consist of monetary and non-monetary (behavioural) price.

Utilizing these dimensions, a hypothetical model of one of the roles that perceived value plays in the assessment of a service. It is suggested that the perceptions of service quality leads to the purchase and experience rendered by the service. This experience results in the perception of the value received from the service. It is further postulated that perceived value influences intention to reinvest in the service experience, and how positively or negatively individuals talk to others about their service experience.

This process then effects future assessments of the quality of a service. While it has been postulated that perceived value changes during different stages of a purchase, the proposed scale will only measure perceived value after completing a purchase. Thus the role that perceived value plays in the decision-making processes of the current conceptualization can only occur after service has been rendered.

Instrument Development

The operational definition of the construct of perceived value that was used to guide development of the scale was "the consumer's overall assessment of utility of a product based on perceptions of what is received and what is given. Further, perceived value was a priori conceptualized as a multi-dimensional construct, including the dimensions of quality, emotional response, monetary price, behavioural price, and reputation. Since reliability has consistently been found to be the most important dimension of quality for recreation and tourism managers, quality was defined as a consumer's judgment about a product or service's overall excellence or superiority.

Emotional response was defined as a descriptive judgment regarding the pleasure that a product or service gives the purchaser. The definition utilized for monetary price was the price of a service as encoded by the consumer. Behavioural price was defined as the price (non-monetary) of obtaining a service, which included the time and effort, used to search for the service. Finally, reputation was defined as the prestige or status of a product or service, as perceived by the purchaser, based on the image of the supplier.

The initial pool of items was accumulated from various scales developed by others relating to the construct of perceived value. Fifty-two items were acquired from a review of both scientific and popular literature.

In order to examine the scale's external validity and generalizeability it was administered to samples on two different seven-day Caribbean cruises, on board the same vessel. To ensure that cruise passengers taking back-to-back cruises were not sampled twice, the two samples were taken three weeks apart. One questionnaire was distributed to each cabin on board the vessel that was accommodated by a paying cruiser on the second to the last evening of the cruise. A letter was included with the questionnaire explaining that only one member in the room was to complete it, and that it was to be returned to their cabin steward.

The scale was operationalized by asking participants to rate each item on a scale from 1, definitely false, to 5 definitely true for their cruise on board the vessel. The survey also included single-item measures of overall perceived value and overall satisfaction. Overall perceived value was measured by asking respondents to rate the value received for their money when purchasing their cruise. The single item, 10-point scale, was anchored by extremely poor value and extremely good value.

A total of 591 questionnaires were distributed during the first cruise, and 592 during the second. Of these 394 (66.7%) and 398 (67.2%) completed questionnaires were returned from the first and second sample respectively. Among passengers who participated, the average age was 51.6, the median household income was $75,000 to $99,999, 58.7% were female and, on average, respondents had taken 8.1 cruises in their lifetime.

Eight expert judges, from four different universities (all faculty members with Ph.D.'s and expertise in service marketing), were selected to refine and edit the initial 52 items for content validity. The judges were given the following operational definition of perceived value: the consumer's overall assessment of a product, or service's utility based on the perceptions of what is received and what is given. They were also given operational definitions for the proposed dimensions of quality, emotional response, perceived monetary price, behavioural price and reputation.

Consistent with Zaichowsky and Lee and Crompton (1992), each of the judges were first asked to rate each of the 52 items as either clearly representative, somewhat representative or not representative of the perceived value construct. The judges were also asked to assign each of the items as either "clearly representative" or "somewhat representative" to one of the five proposed dimensions of perceived value. They were further asked to identify if any items were representative of more than one dimension.

Following the same criteria utilized by Lee and Crompton, a series of rules were established in order to determine whether or not each item was to be discarded. An item was also discarded if less than five of the eight-member panel assigned it to the same dimension. This process resulted in 25 of the 52 items being eliminated.

The judges were further asked to: a) edit and improve the items to improve their clarity, readability and content, b) identify any items which they believed may be objectionable to respondents and c) offer any suggestions they felt might improve the study. This process resulted in the slight rewording of one item, and the removal of two others. The items removed were due to the judges' belief that the items were too similar to others in the scale. In both cases, the item with the weakest rating by the panel of judges was removed.

The resultant scale consisted of 25 items. Of these items, four were assigned to the dimension of "quality", six to "perceived monetary price", and five each to "emotional response", "behavioural price" and "reputation".

To examine dimensionality and internal reliability of the scale items, a convenience sample of 344 undergraduate students was used. Students were selected from two undergraduate tourism classes, and three undergraduate marketing classes. All students who attended the class periods on the date the questionnaire was administered were asked to complete a questionnaire. To enable a majority of the students to be familiar with the service context, respondents were asked to rate each of the 25 items as they related to lunch at a well-known fast food restaurant.

Respondents were further asked the last time that they had experienced a lunch at the restaurant. Only respondents who had been to the restaurant within the last month were included in the study. Of the respondents included in the study (n 278), approximately one half (51%) were female. Respondents had visited the restaurant 3.6 times on average in the last month.

In order to validate the a-priori assignment of the 25 items to their respective dimensions (as assigned by the expert panel), confirmatory factor analysis (CFA) was employed. The analyses were conducted with the use of the SAS System's proc calis procedures and followed guidelines suggested by Hatcher. Fit indices were chosen following recommendations by Hu and Bender. Fit indices included in the current investigation are the Bender comparative fit index, or CFI, Bender and Bonett, normed fit index, or NFI, and Joreskog and Sorbum root-meansquare residual, or RMSR.

Both the CFI and NFI may range in value from 1.0 to 0.0. According to Bender (1989), a fit index of 0.0 is associated with a "null" model (one specifying that all items are uncorrelated), while a fit index of 1.0 represents a "saturated" model (a model with zero degrees of freedom that perfectly reproduces the original covariance matrix). Values greater than 0.9 indicate a good fit of the data, while values higher than 0.95 indicate an excellent fit of the data. Conversely, An RMSR of less than .10 suggests a good fit of the data.

Since both the CFI and NFI are greater than 0.90, and the RMSR is less than .10, results suggest that the model is a good fit of the data. This finding further suggests, that each item is uniquely related to the factor to which it was assigned. A review of the resultant Wald and Lagrange tests did not suggest any conceptually sound changes to the model. Therefore, the proposed model was tentatively accepted, pending further tests to examine its reliability and validity.

The resultant standardized path coefficients are displayed. The t-tests investigating the null hypothesis that each of the coefficients are equal to zero were all significant, suggesting that all paths were assisting in the prediction of their assigned factors. These results provided evidence supporting the convergent validity of the indicators.

Composite reliability is analogous to coefficient alpha, and reflects the internal consistency of the indicators measuring each CFA factor. Results show that all five factors have composite reliability scores greater than 0.70. Utilizing the criteria set for the current analysis, this suggests that each of the factors are reliably measuring their respective constructs.

Combined, these findings support the reliability and internal validity of the hypothesized model. Since the model was found to be a good fit of the data and all paths were found to be significant, it is suggested that the proposed scale effectively measured the pretest subjects' perceived value. Thus, the scale was tentatively accepted, pending further examination and given the name SERV-PERVAL scale.

In order to further test the reliability of the 25 item SERV-PERVAL scale, separate confirmatory factor analyses (CFA) were conducted on the two samples of cruisers. The analyses were conducted utilizing the procedures described previously. Since the CFI and NFI fit indices for both samples are greater than 0.90 and the RMSR scores are less than .10, results suggest that both models are good fits of the data.

This finding also suggests, that each item is uniquely related to the factor to which it was assigned. Further, review of the resultant Wald and Lagrange tests did not suggest any conceptually sound changes. Therefore, the models were tentatively accepted, pending further tests to examine their reliability and validity.

The resultant standardized path coefficients are displayed. The t-tests investigating the null hypothesis that each of the coefficients were equal to zero were all significant, suggesting that all paths are assisting in the prediction of their assigned factors. These results provide evidence supporting the convergent validity of the indicators.

Results show that all five factors from both samples have reliability scores greater than 0.90. Utilizing the criteria set for the current analysis, this suggests that all of the factors are reliably measuring their respective constructs for both data sets. Combined, these findings support the reliability and validity of the hypothesized models.

Since the model was found to be a good fit of the data and all paths were found to be significant, it is suggested that the proposed scale effectively measured the proposed factors of perceived value for both samples. To further validate the scale, the perceived value factors were tested for criterion validity (sometimes called predictive validity).

According to Babbie, criterion validity is demonstrated if scores from the developed scale show expected relationships with one or more external variables that provide direct measure of the construct measured. It would be expected that each of the five factors would be positively related to an overall measure of perceived value. Thus, Pearson's correlations were employed to examine the relationships between each of the factors of perceived value, and overall perceived value. All five factors correlated positively and significantly to overall perceived value for both samples.

To further examine criterion validity, multiple regression with overall perceived value as the dependent variable, and the factors of perceived value as independent variables was employed. It would be expected that the five factors would explain a majority of the variance in perceived value. The regression analysis predicting perceived value was significant and explained 63.5% of the variance in the model.

Therefore results suggest that the proposed five factors of perceived value are related to the construct of perceived value (have criterion validity). Further validation of the scale was completed by testing the factors of perceived value for discriminant validity. Discriminant validity can be examined by comparing the inter-correlations of the constructs to the square root of the average variance extracted. The square root of the average variance for each of the factors is greater than any of the inter-correlations of the constructs. This finding suggests that the factors of perceived value have discriminant validity.

Results demonstrated a valid and reliable five dimensional scale for measuring perceived value. With the use of a panel of experts, the scale was judged to have content validity. The scale consisted of five interrelated, but unique dimensions: quality, emotional response, monetary price, behavioural price and reputation.

Utilizing CFA on the data from a pretest, and two separate samples, the generated items were found to saliently load uniquely on their predicted factors. Further, all of the resultant standardized path coefficients were found to significantly assist in the prediction of their assigned factors. This finding provided evidence of the convergent validity of the proposed indicators.

In order to confirm the reliability of the five factors, composite reliability scores for each of the factors were computed. All reliability scores for the three samples were deemed acceptable, suggesting that each of the factors were reliably measuring their respective constructs. Criterion validity was investigated by examining the correlations between perceived value and each of the factors. It was found that perceived value was positively and significantly related to each of the five factors. Finally, discriminant validity was investigated by comparing the inter-correlations of the constructs to the square root of the average variance for each of the factors. It was revealed that discriminant validity was found for each of the factors of perceived value.

While the current methods were thorough, the study was limited to a specific context. More research is necessary to determine how generalizeable the scale is across service sectors. Also, the future research should examine interrelationships between each of the factors. While the identified dimensions are unique, the causal paths between each dimension would assist in theoretical development of the construct of perceived value. It is believed that this knowledge would assist leisure and/or tourism management in better understanding the role each of the dimensions play in consumers' decision making processes. It is also recommended that future research examine the redundancy of items in the scale.

Redundant items could thus be removed to make the scale more succinct, and less taxing on respondents. Further, it is possible that potential dimensions of perceived value were not identified in the final instrument and the items included were not exhaustive of the five dimensions identified. Thus, it is suggested that future research examine the potential addition of both different factors and different items.

As suggested by Havitz, marketing literature, while seldom utilized in leisure research, is consistent with many of the important "perspectives within the leisure literature". It is thus postulated that the adaptation of tools in the field of marketing, for the fields of recreation and tourism may have far reaching benefits for leisure and tourism providers.

Since there are currently no multidimensional measures of perceived value of a service, and evaluations of perceived value of a service have been found to differ from evaluations of products, it is believed that the current conceptualization is important to leisure and tourism providers. Further, it has been suggested that current perceived value measures are difficult to quantify, though perceived value has been recognized as one of the most salient determinants of purchase intentions and repeat visitation. Thus it is hoped that, similar to the Parasuraman et al., the scale offered here will facilitate comparison of value within, and across services.

Since the seminal work of Chandler, the notion of a linkage between strategy and structure has become widely accepted-that is, if an organization is to implement its strategy most effectively, it needs the appropriate structure and support systems. At the same time, it needs the flexibility to exploit strategic options that arise from environmental changes. However, at least in the short run, a firm cannot easily change its organizational structure, and this may be a major impediment to its ability to change its strategy.

In an increasingly globally integrated world, firms attempting to become major players in their industry need to cope with and exploit environmental changes and adjust their organizational structure to create what Bartlett and Ghoshal (1989) termed "transnational" organizations. In other words, firms need to be able simultaneously to achieve local responsiveness, global efficiency. and the creation of knowledge (learning).

Chandler based his conclusions on a study of four of the largest corporations in the United States – General Motors, Dupont, Standard Oil, and Sears Roebuck – of which only Sears Roebuck was a service organization. Indeed, much of the literature on both the strategy of multinational firms and organizational structure has emanated from studies of large and powerful manufacturing firms, notwithstanding the ever-increasing importance of large multinational firms in service industries.

While some of these service industries have more in common with MNEs producing goods, others are quite different. The purpose of this paper is to explore the effects of globalization on the organizational structures and systems of service firms in general, and professional service firms in particular. The paper postulates certain relationships between key success factors in multinational professional service firms and the structure and systems of these firms. The resulting propositions help provide the basis for a contingency theory of organizational structure and systems.

In the first section, some of the contributions to organization design theory and to organizational taxonomies are briefly surveyed. In the second section, some of the relevant theories on the organizational structure of multinational enterprises are reviewed. The third section discusses the globalization of services, while the fourth proposes a taxonomy of multinational service firms by the key factors contributing to their success, and it hypothesizes on the implications for organizational design.

This analysis is offered as preliminary to devising a contingency theory of organizations for service multinationals' particularly professional service multinationals. Organization theory is a positive theory focused on understanding organizations. On the basis of its findings, the organization focuses its design on normative solutions, that is, on the optimal means of creating an organization to achieve given goals and missions. Organization theory has moved a long way from the belief prevailing at the beginning of the century in immutable general laws of organization design or in the classical depiction of a "machine" organization.

March and Simon summarized the state of the art as follows: "Much of what we know or believe about organizations is distilled from common sense and from the practical experience of executives. The great bulk of this wisdom and lore has never been subjected to the rigorous scrutiny of scientific methods". Many assertions have since been tested to check whether or not they are supported by the facts. In addition, the importance of such factors as information, motivation, power, conflict. and innovation have been subjected to much scrutiny.

Moreover, different theses have also been tested in a variety of national and cultural contents. The organizational structure of the firm has been shown to be a reflection of its operating environment. Lawrence and Lorsch examined the firm's differentiation and integration characteristics in three industries. By differentiation, they meant orientations toward goals, time, and interpersonal relationships, as well as toward the degree of formality of the structure; by integration, they meant the degree of collaboration among departments working on common projects.

They demonstrated that these characteristics depend on the degree of turbulence in the environment: in a highly stable environment, organizations tend to be much more integrated, whereas in a turbulent environment, differentiation becomes more necessary. In Lawrence and Lorsch's model, complex tasks are performed through increased task specialization and subsequent coordination.

The different needs in different stages tn an organizational evolution have also been recognized. Child called attention to the importance of growth as a means of meeting the aspirations of the participating members of the organization. Kimberly argued for a dynamic perspective – researching the different stages in the life cycle of organizations – from creation to transformation to maturity and then decline. Pfeffer and Salancik distinguished between internally generated growth, to achieve individual or organizational goals, and growth based on biological systems limited by constraints and resources. They saw growth as a purposeful response to external constraints.

Mintzberg developed a taxonomy of organizational structures in different categories of organizations – the entrepreneurial, bureaucratic (machine and professional), divisional, adhocracy, and matrix. He suggested that, as organizations grow. they undergo structural changes – from the entrepreneurial to bureaucratic. divisional, and finally matrix structures. An organization can be bureaucratic without being centralized. This happens when professionals are needed because of the complexity of tasks, but the tasks themselves can be perfected through standardized operating programmes. The result is the professional bureaucracy structure.

Structural changes, therefore, correspond to both internal requirements and environmental demands. They arc contingent on quite a large number of factors. Organizations must change and adapt to internal political conditions, to external changes in the environment, and to technological changes and the opportunities they create. Integration mechanisms are needed to achieve coordination and these needs also depend on situational variables such as the competitive market structure or the stage of the life cycle. Although empirical research has failed to lend unequivocal support to the hypothesis that strategy follows structure, the implementation of any strategy must be based on a certain structure and on systems, including rewards.

Organizations are basically information-processing entities, and must match the demand for information processing with the capacity of the firm to do it. The information required depends on the environment, on technology, and on other variables such as size and complexity. Nowadays, firms can create significant competitive advantage on the basis of sophisticated use of information systems.

New information technologies are facilitating new forms of organizations and different structures, allowing greater integration across national borders. The increased power of personal computers, for example, is profoundly affecting both structures and systems. Computers have also allowed service firms to achieve both low-cost positions and customized services. All these new developments arc allowing new types of structures, such as the "infinitely flat" organization.

New telecommunications capabilities have eroded the boundaries between firms and their suppliers, as well as between geographic territories; and organizations can run borderless networks connected by electronic data interchange (EDI) and electronic mail with very little formal hierarchy. Moreover, in a knowledge-based society, the ability to tap all possible knowledge to achieve the task is crucial.

Much of the needed knowledge cannot be maintained in books on standard operating procedures, but is tapped by professionals communicating with each other. Professional workers must be willing to cooperate across tasks, professions, and geography to implement the strategy of the firm. This kind of cooperation has been achieved by professionals such as engineers and consultants. However, when a firm needs to trim its staff, self-preservation, fear, and frustration may lead individuals to be much less cooperative.

The organization of the future is sometimes portrayed in terms of project management and flat structures. This type of structure is perhaps more appropriate to expert organizations such as consulting firms or CNN (Cable News Network), with their prima-donna "star" performers, than to organizations that can standardize their operation to allow a machine bureaucracy as the optimal mode.

Indeed, companies such as CNN, EDL, and McKinsey & Co. are organized around many small teams carrying out shifting project assignments. They employ mainly bright, aggressive, though not arrogant, individuals who are unwilling to abide by too many arbitrary rules and standard operating procedures, but are happy to do all it takes to get the job done. These organizations focus on solutions to customers' problems, which they achieve at a much greater speed than the older, hierarchical bureaucracy.

Much in the way of theoretical contributions and empirical evidence is available on the relationships between structure and contextual factors. A survey of the organization theory literature certainly shows a diverse and sometimes inconsistent set of rules related to the organizational structure of firms.

In many cases, the number of variables to be taken into account is quite large. Duncan, for example, suggested a decision tree for structures based on three possible dimensions of the environment: complexity, change, and segmentation. Robbins discusses environmental hostility, positing that greater hostility necessitates greater centralization. Perrow discussed the impact of technology, while considered the impact of size.

If one combines all these variables with Mintzberg's (1979) basic configurations (simple, functional, divisional, matrix, machine bureaucracy, professional bureaucracy, ad hoc), a very large number of possible combinations emerge. Organization theory guides managers in choosing those configurations that allow fit between the organization and various parameters, such as environment, strategy, size, technology, and management style.

These variables may or may not be different in an international context. Bartlett and Ghoshal in particular stressed the role of overseas operations (as well as the development and diffusion of knowledge) in creating unique configurations for international operations.

According to these authors, firms operating in many countries can be based on self-sufficient national units and a decentralized system ("multinational"), on a globally scaled centralized system ("global"), on a hybrid design in which only sources of core competence are centralized and the rest of the operations are decentralized ("international"), or in the transnational mode, in which functions are dispersed across the globe but integrated to achieve competitive advantage, with knowledge being developed in different parts of the system and shared by all of its parts. The transnational design, according to Bartlett and Ghoshal, goes beyond the matrix configuration (for somewhat similar configurations. Integration can be achieved by several means, to be discussed later.

The Organizational Structure of the Multinational Enterprise

The increasing importance of various forms of multinational enterprises spreading their activities across national boundaries has not escaped the attention of academics. A large number of treatises have been written, attempting to explain, inter alia:

1. The reasons for internationalization;
2. The reasons for the various forms of internationalization, such as licensing, joint ventures, strategic alliances, or wholly owned subsidiaries;
3. Factors explaining the competitive advantage of a multinational firm vis-a-vis its domestic rivals;
4. The ways multinational enterprises compete with other similar enterprises on a global basis;
5. The organizational structure of the multinational enterprises;
6. The relationships between the multinational enterprise and home and host countries.

Almost all of these works have aimed at explaining the extracting and/or manufacturing multinational enterprises. Until the beginning of the 1980s, it was assumed that services were nontradable.

Thus, internationalization has been studied mainly by the Uppsala school and has been viewed as a process in which the enterprise gradually increases its international involvement. Three decades of research on multinational firms since the seminal work of Hymer (1976) have led to the conclusion that a multinational firm must have some advantage to offset the additional costs of running its operation, compared with domestic rivals.

Different authors have proposed different types of advantages, most of which are assumed to be intangible and firm-specific. In a producing enterprise, most of these advantages are based on scale, specific knowledge, or brand names. John Dunning attempted to combine many of the explanations in his eclectic theory, while Ozawa (1979) proposed some differences between U.S.- and Japanese-based multinationals. With time, research evolved from a total reliance on economic factors to a focus on internal issues of firms' operations. It was only toward the end of the 1980s that researchers began to relate to management issues.

Again, much of this research is not always applicable in attempting to explain why some service-providing firms have become multinational and others have not. Thus, if reputation and brand names are important firm-specific advantages, why was the Harvard Business School unable to exploit these advantages when it tried to build an executive development programme in Mt. Pelerin, Switzerland?

In the past decade or two, most studies have stressed the globalization of operations. Within multinational firms, globalization means the increased integration of resources and capabilities, and it can be operationalized by the extent of transfer of these resources within the multinational enterprise. The resources crossing borders can be capital, products, or knowledge. In a "transnational" firm, the flows are two-way – from subsidiaries to headquarters and from headquarters to subsidiaries – and they are associated with increasing information flows.

Managing international interdependencies is inherently more complex than managing activities within a single nation. Firms must organize to derive, combine, and transfer resources. Thus, international management theory can benefit from the knowledge to be derived not only from economic theory or strategic management analysis but from organization theory too.

Yet very little research has been done on organizational structure. A notable exception is the work of Stopford and Wells, who were the first to show that firms adopt different strategies in different stages of their internationalization; while Egelhoff (1988) stressed information processing. Organizational structure is no longer considered a sufficient explanation of multinational operations, and an understanding of managerial systems and control mechanisms is perceived to be a necessary additional line of inquiry.

Organizational structure is nevertheless a major constraint on the strategic flexibility of the MNE. Once a certain structure has been adopted and functions, authority, and operations have been distributed among different units in different countries, any reorganization is both time-consuming and costly. It also often works against a firm's "administrative heritage". Thus, a firm that has enjoyed a long tradition of a multidomestic strategy will have to contend with serious challenges if it is to move swiftly to a global strategy, as the history of firms such as Procter and Gamble or Philips amply demonstrates.

In a multinational enterprise, the key decisions relate to the means of coordination, degree of integration of activities from the home centre, and the degree to which authority is dispersed across countries. The giant European (and a few American) multinationals of the pre-World War II era developed a very decentralized structure in which each subsidiary was allowed a great deal of autonomy and maintained its own production, marketing, and even development facilities.

Headquarters appointed key personnel, approved major capital expenditures, and received dividends. Each subsidiary was allowed a high degree of differentiation as well as local adaptation. Given the state of the managerial arts and the relatively high costs of transportation and communications, this structure seems to have been the most appropriate for its time.

The U.S. multinationals in the period after World War II were generally much more integrated and centralized, and all new technology and products stemmed from the home country. The greatest strength of these firms was their ability to internalize the transfer of technology and of management skills across national boundaries. The subsidiaries did enjoy a high level of autonomy, but their competitive advantage derived mainly from transfers of technology, know-how, and brand equity from the centre.

Many of these firms, which Bartlett called "coordinated federations," lost ground in the 1970s and the 1980s to Japanese competitors that used "centralized hubs" – a very efficient domestic hub and a global, integrated system based on economies of scale in manufacturing at the centre, with subsidiaries supplying mainly distribution and service functions, at least initially.

When scale is a key factor of success, global integration turns out to be very effective. Yet, local responsiveness – to the domestic conditions as well as to the different governments – is often required too. Many MNEs advocate both global integration and local responsiveness – what Bartlett termed "the transnational solution." Bartlett believes that, during the 1990s. firms will be forced to achieve both efficiency, through scale and integration, and local responsiveness, through catering to differentiated demands from customers and to pressures from governments for local content as well as other regulations. The simultaneous pursuit of these two requirements (global integration and local responsiveness) is also important in maintaining a high level of innovativeness.

This objective may be achieved by using different structures for different parts of the value chain, and often by outsourcing certain activities. Scale economies call for integration, but innovations are best encouraged by decentralization. The centre ceases to be the only source of ideas or new products. In contrast, each national unit is a source of ideas that are shared throughout the whole network, and each may achieve global scale by being the world source of a certain product for the whole system, with different subsidiaries having different roles. The centre, for its part, should foster "supportive organizational norms and values".

The experience of manufacturing MNEs shows that increasing internationalization may threaten their stability because domestic markets are no longer sheltered from the onslaught of intensified global competition. They are also broadening their global scope in many service industries. The new demands on multinationals have come about because of globalization and because of the enormous advances in information technology.

Many firms have achieved advantage by the use of proprietary software. Some were able to achieve "mass customization"; others created global networks that made it easier to share information with suppliers as well as customers and across geographical areas. Computers not only allow speed but enable the firm to install intangible assets and to trade in ideas. Only ten years ago, centralized mainframes comprised about three-quarters of all computing power, whereas today the figure is between 1 and 5 percent.

Sales of the personal-computer (PC) industry (both hardware and software), by contrast, grew from $2 billion in 1981 to $82 billion in 1990. In the new age of modern information technology firms can build and sustain a competitive advantage based on information systems. This is particularly apparent in services such as reservations systems and frequent flyer (or user) programmes of airlines and hotels.

Another anticipated change is a reduction in the importance of scale. The giant diversified firm of two or three decades ago is now trying to shape itself up and reduce its size. In 1954, the first year for which Fortune magazine published its "500" ranking, these firms represented 37 percent of U.S. GNP. By 1979, the share was 58 percent. Since then, they have been losing ground in the market. Their share was 42 percent in 1989 and 40 percent in 1991, which is equal to the 1959 figure.

It is argued that the only way giant firms can survive is by becoming less hierarchical, more decentralized, and organized on the basis of teams carrying out ever-changing projects. In short, manufacturing MNEs will have to learn from service firms. An idea of the corporation of the future that will operate in the borderless world may be seen in the professional business services and the many strategic alliances that already exist today.

Information technologies and other changes have allowed many new forms of organization.

The common denominator of all these entities is the form of the organization's various boundaries. The legal boundaries remain the same, as in strategic alliances, so that coordination has to be achieved among legally separate organizations. This active coordination means extensive expansion of the information boundaries and often of management boundaries. Thus. suppliers may be allowed to get into the computer of a firm and supply goods without a specific order.

In a network type of activity, the organization must be defined to include all the separate legal entities that comprise the network. The management boundaries are extended to the whole network to ensure coordination. Coordination itself can be achieved through different forms that may or may not be centralized. The process of coordination and integration may be formal- developing systems, policies, and standards; it may be effected through central processes – by the direct intervention and actions of an elite group based in a unit designed as headquarters in the management of each separate division; or it may be achieved through socialization.

The latter prevails when the task is unique, integrated, or ambiguous. Bartlett and Ghoshal (1993) argue that, in new organizations, each subsidiary is a self-contained unit that is part of a whole. These and other new forms of organization are more prevalent in service firms, particularly in professional service firms.

Globalization of Services

In recent decades, growth in the service sector in most countries has been very impressive, particularly in the operations of global service MNEs, which may or may not have become not only multinational but also global for the same reasons as the manufacturing firms. The accelerating trend of corporate internationalization has put a premium on the ability of service firms to serve their clients uniformly worldwide.

Financial institutions, accounting firms, law firms, and management consultants have all followed their manufacturing clients abroad. In addition, some leading firms have expanded internationally to create challenging work opportunities. Thus, McKinsey & Co. created its London office in 1959, and by 1990, 63 percent of its income was generated outside the United States. By the 1980s, the belief among service firms that they must follow their clients to other parts of the globe had become pervasive.

Moreover, the United States has gone further than any other country in deregulating its airlines, trucking, and telecommunications, compelling these industries to restructure and reengineer to meet competition by undergoing a wrenching overhaul of management systems. U.S. firms also recognized earlier that advantage lay in a lead in brainpower and innovation, and accordingly spent large amounts of money on R&D. Today, of course, the U.S. lead in brainpower is eroding with the increasing level of technological sophistication of firms from other countries.

All service organizations operate in several distinct markets and must satisfy at least three sets of goals: economic goals (profitability, growth). satisfaction goals (of staff, often desiring professional challenges and variety), and client goals. To achieve all or a subset of these goals, some firms opt to become global players, as part of a network of independent entities sharing common services or by managing a single global firm. Of course, the firm must organize its value-creating activities in a way that will help it achieve the greatest degree of success.

Studies of national accounting firms in North America indicate governance structure and primary task as important characteristics. Governance structure is based on partnership, with local offices as the principal place of business. Managers return to these offices after a temporary assignment in the top office. Local offices are independent, inter alia, because of professional norms of independence. Tasks are carried out by principal partners helped by associates, in proximity to the client. Greenwood et al. (1990) point out that these task characteristics are not amenable to central control. Control is achieved mainly through certain shared norms, agreed standards, and peer review.

Yip identified certain "globalization drivers" and global "strategy levers" that explain why certain firms (or certain industries) have become global. One group of globalization drivers are those based on market. A second group stems from cost. A third are government globalization drivers, and the fourth are what Yip terms "competitive globalization drivers." Johansson and Yip found that market and cost drivers were more significant than government or competitive drivers in their sample of manufacturing businesses. This finding may or may not hold for service industries, where government globalization drivers might be more relevant.

Yip also identified five global strategy levers, to measure international strategy on a scale of pure multi domestic to pure global. The global ends are as follows:

- Global market participation: countries are chosen according to their potential contribution to globalization benefits, not only on the basis of their stand-alone attractiveness.
- Global products/services: a standardized core product or service with a minimum of local adaptation or none at all.
- Global location of value-adding activities: the value chain is broken up so that each activity may be conducted in a different country.

- Global marketing: a standard marketing approach is applied around the world, even though not all elements of the marketing mix need be identical.
- Global competitive moves: these are integrated across countries. The same type of move is made in different countries at the same time or in some systematic sequence, or a competitor is attacked in one country in order to drain its resources for another country, or a competitive attack in one country is countered in a different country.

The same levers may be conceptually identified in service industries, though their importance may not be significantly different. In some cases, the levers relate to industries. In others, they relate to firms.

In services, Heskett, Sasser, and Hart used the concept of the "strategic service vision" (SSV) to analyze the alignment between target market segments, the service concept, the operating strategy, and the service delivery system. When target market segments are in different countries, the service delivery system is often guided by standard firm practices across countries, as in the case of American Express travellers' checks or McDonald's. Service firms must be able to guarantee standardized quality services across many countries.

Clearly, one advantage of a multinational hotel system is that it can promise "no surprises." By contrast, however, some global service firms, notably professional service firms that sell expertise, focus on diagnosis, and the projects they handle are customized and specialized. To address each local market with customized service, some firms find that they have to be much less integrative and to differentiate across market segments. The problem with such a choice is the greatly increased complexity.

The decision to serve vastly different customers in different geographic locations fosters a need to develop entirely different strategic service visions with all the added complexity this entails. In the extreme, if the firm is totally differentiated, it may find that it has no communality and therefore no competitive advantage over a domestic firm.

It may find it better to use a loose, ephemeral network of professionals who do not share all standard operating procedures or profits worldwide. Even within professional business services, however, there are cases where firms offer less creativity and more standard procedures. Thus, in auditing and information-systems consulting, the firm offers more standardized service. The blend of standardized procedures and customized solutions is different in different professions.

The more standardized the elements, the easier the integration, the less complex the structure needed, and the greater the probability of global operations.

Clearly, both the globalization drivers and levers and the key factors of success are different in different types of firms. Some sell expertise. others efficiency, and still others experience. In some types of business, the uncertainty in the mind of the client is very high – sometimes even after the service has been rendered (as in the medical profession). In others, it is not. Some are people-intensive, while others need scale and/or capital. All of these factors may have an impact on the organizational structure. The next section proposes a fuller taxonomy and advances some contingent factors in terms of organization structure.

Professional service firms are different from manufacturing multinationals in several important respects. First, they are people-intensive and demand minimal investment in fixed assets. In addition, key persons capable of creating value added do not have to work for a particular firm. They can move easily and can also work on their own – in other words, the firm becomes a "voluntary" organization. A corollary of the above is that, in some firms, the most critical assets walk out the door every night and a crucial success factor is the ability to recruit and retain the best and most imaginative talents.

These persons have to be carefully nurtured, motivated, and allowed to grow. They have to be trained and retrained and their values reinforced through indoctrination. Incentive systems need to encourage teamwork and cooperation. These factors, though important, are not crucial to success in travel-related business, for example. In some professional service firms, economies of location are important. That is, it is important to have a branch wherever the multinational clients have branches. Failure to participate in a certain strategic market can undermine global competitiveness.

For example, the fact that some European firms were unable to establish a strong base in Japan limited their ability to use economies of scale and reduced their exposure to new innovations; more importantly, it prevented them from creating a hostage for good behaviour on the part of their major Japanese rivals. It is hypothesized that this participation is less crucial in some service industries such as auditing than in others such as travellers' checks or airlines.

Professional service firms are marked by a "think versus grind" mentality. Professional business services that offer mainly expertise can leverage the time of senior professionals much less than even other professional service firms, not to mention hotels or restaurants. Their staffing requirements call for getting the best persons or top-percentile graduates from the best schools. Others that deal with familiar, often standard types of problems depend for their success on efficient performance.

The "think" expertise type is much more difficult to globalize, and it attracts clients by the reputations of its employees rather than by the firm's name. The more standardized the solution, the greater the importance of integration and of centralization, and the smaller the need for differentiation, the easier it is to offer global services and to enhance the ability of each location to serve clients by drawing on the firm's systems, its accumulated knowledge in databases, and the experience of the whole network.

A related factor is the degree of customization. The success of certain service firms (such as McDonald's) has been largely based on the ability to create standard performance based on routine and repetitious work. It is important to distinguish between routines and standardization. Audit work, for example, is based on routine and repetitious work, but there is a great deal of variability in the different audits performed for firms from different industries.

The degree of importance of information systems (e.g., reservations in hotels or airlines, databases of firms on systems' experience, or skills available within the firm) is another critical factor. The more important and developed the information systems. the easier it is integrate activities, even across national borders.

Another factor is the degree of the client's uncertainty before or even after the service has been rendered. Service firms need to be client-centreed. Clients may or may not appreciate the intellectual challenge of a solution or may even be unable to distinguish between competent and outstanding technical work. Often, a large number of contingencies cloud the ability of a client to assess the work (e.g., is a lawyer good even though he or she did not win the case?).

One result is that clients focus more on what they perceive as the quality of delivery than on the quality of the work itself. Clients are often shopping for peace of mind, reassurance, trust, or confidence. Maister says that, in the medical profession, people look for availability, affability, and ability-in that order. Because of all these considerations, clients often use proxies for quality, one of which is size.

Finally, the higher the uncertainty, the greater the willingness to pay for reputation and brand, and therefore the greater the competitive advantage of those firms that succeed in creating a major integrated global organization. These variables may be a vector in a matrix that explains firms' decisions to use different structures and systems.

In addition, an interim variable that will affect the choice is the form of entry: A firm may opt for a very weak form of a global network such as using correspondents (as in financial institutions), or it may refer the work to a trusted domestic firm; it may decide to create or to join a network of independent firms, as accountants often do; it may choose strategic alliances or joint ventures, or it may acquire or create a wholly owned subsidiary.

Another critical factor in the internationalization success of professional service firms is governance structure. Firms registered as corporations such as consulting firms – are often organized hierarchically.

Many other professional firms are partnerships, with ad hoc committee structures and therefore very weak central headquarters. In other words, the legal boundaries of service multinationals tend to be different from their management and information boundaries. In a strategic alliance or a network overall strategic direction is limited to certain functions agreed upon by all participants through a process of negotiation and consensus building. Successful implementation of the strategy depends on acceptance of the ideas by the different legally autonomous entities. No hierarchical relations exist, at least not formal ones.

In this type of firm, different sets of management skills are needed. The first relates to recruitment – or the way subcontractors, partners, or vendors are chosen. The right choices are crucial to the operational success of the network as a whole. Second, top management has to manage an array of independent persons who are not cogs in the wheels of a corporate hierarchy but a part of an autonomous organization. Since added value comes from knowledge, those with more knowledge will enjoy more power.

Third, the network must be flexible and flat: flexibility is important because very often changes cannot be anticipated; flatness is important because, if communications have to go up and down hierarchies, much time is lost. To achieve responsiveness to markets, communications must be unimpeded, and horizontal consultation has to be encouraged. In addition, initiative has to be encouraged or even mandated through a socialization process. Managing such a network is a rather delicate affair, since the system may run out of control.

From the conceptual discussion up to this point, particularly that relating to the very useful differentiation/ integration framework, the following rules for organization design in service multinationals appear to emerge.

First, the higher the degree of homogeneity among clients in different countries, the greater is the need for formal standard systems. Therefore, the more a firm serves global clients, the greater the pressures for common standards and centralized coordination and control. Global clients demand service of consistent quality and quick access to the best experts available. These demands increase the need for linkages across different entities, better integration, and more formal processes of coordination.

Second, the more complex and/or diversified the work performed for clients, the greater is the need for experts from across the network and formal integration.

Third, the greater the importance of scale, the greater is the tendency of the firm toward integration. Integration is also important when the economics of location are salient or when capital-intensive services are being provided. It is easier when the tasks being performed are repetitive. By contrast, the more expertise and thinking that are needed, and the greater the need for innovation or brain work, the more difficult it becomes to formally enforce standards and the greater the need for differentiation.

In the extreme, when the key factors of success are the expertise and superior minds of individuals who tend to resent formal processes, integration is almost impossible. The organization will be extremely flat and based on project management. The contradictory pressures for more central control and more independence are the major challenge of the global service firm, in particular, the professional service firm.

These firms are also constrained by their administrative heritage, based on an organization of independent partners. Enforcement may be achieved by moral suasion, by appeals to collegial loyalty, by socialization processes, by training, and even by indoctrination, to get what Maister termed "the one-firm firm," or by a constant flow of information and horizontal transfer of knowledge.

Fourth, coordination and integration among units are based less on traditional forms of organizational structure such as divisional or formal bureaucracy than on committees designed to achieve coordination in the flow of resources among the different units. These resources are capital. technology, persons, and information.

Fifth, while manufacturing multinationals allocate capital for investment and repatriate dividends, professional service firms hardly move capital across borders. The resources transferred are mainly persons and information, and, to a lesser extent, technology.

Sixth, some professional service firms will increasingly be organized as centralized bureaucracies if they are able significantly to increase the part of their work that is based on experience, with the availability of databases-of both past experience and available skills — a key factor of success. The greater the need for a network of scholars and professionals, the more individualistic they become, and the less central control the firm has over them. To be sure, advances in information technologies allow much more differentiation while, at the same time, tapping into centralized resources. However, old-fashioned centralization is detrimental to the work of the organization.

Seventh, information flows are difficult to manage because of their volume, complexity, and diversity. However, professional norms, as well as rules, roles, and responsibilities, may allow more effective horizontal transfer of knowledge. As one example, university professors devote a significant amount of time learning about the work of others through a word-of-mouth web of relationships.

Senior professors spend an inordinate amount of time refereeing papers or writing letters of recommendation for tenure or promotion at other, often remote' universities. This work is not remunerated financially, but is still meticulously carried out because of the commitment to professionalism and excellence. Academics know one another and socialize at conferences, where they receive instant feedback. Thus, the individual reputation stakes are very high.

Eighth, a major difficulty is the means of enforcing priorities for work done by an entity in one country for one in another country. Thus, the audit of a subsidiary of a multinational in a certain country can be of great importance for the auditors in the country where this multinational's headquarters reside.

Finally, bargaining and consensus building among committee members as well as ad hoc task forces and individual partners with high status provide alternatives to hierarchical structure.

Although the list of possible propositions connecting the contingency variables and organizational structure is much larger, the major lesson of this paper is that there is a need for much more research on alternatives to structure as a means of achieving coordination and integration.

A firm operating globally must manage the flow of people. information, services, and money across national borders. It must nurture and cultivate distinct competence that will allow it to offer better or more efficient services than the domestic firm, as well as the executive reward system and the systems of coordination and control that will nurture its strategy. Even more than in extractive and manufacturing firms, the success of the global service MNE depends on its ability to gain and to maintain clients. In addition, firms must make sure they are able to recruit and maintain the human and other resources needed to operate in the market of their choice.

A major constraint on the globalization of services is the ability to integrate all activities, particularly as most service firms need to have a high degree of local autonomy and flexibility. An important question is what kind of value-adding support does each subsidiary receive from headquarters?

Because of the speed of change in the marketplace, on the one hand, and better information processing on the other, globally operated firms can learn a lot from the way organizations are designed in the investment-banking business, or in the professional business services or in networks such as CNN or EDL.

The new knowledge-based organization in a brain-based economy will have to be organized more like professional service firms or institutions of higher learning, which have traditionally faced a more fickle environment of shifting temporary assignments. This paper proposes some variables that impinge on a contingency theory of organizational design of global service firms.

Chapter 3

Sharing and Service

HOSPITALITY SHARING AND SERVICE

The concept of Hospitality Services, also known as "accommodation sharing", "hospitality exchange", and "home stay networks", refers to centrally organized social networks of individuals who trade accommodation without monetary exchange. While this concept could also include house swapping or even time share plans, it has come to be associated mostly with travellers and tourists staying with one another free of charge. Since the 1990s, these services have increasingly moved away from using printed catalogs and phone trees to connect users towards Internet websites.

These have grown exponentially since 2000 and today it is estimated that well over 100,000 people are registered users of these networks. These vary in operational structure, place different emphasis on graphical vs. textual formatting, and cater disproportionately to specific geographic regions. In 1949, Bob Luitweiler founded the first hospitality service called Servas Open Doors as a cross national, non-profit, volunteer run organization advocating interracial and international peace. The next earliest began in 1965 when John Wilcock set up the Traveller's Directory, originally as a listing of his mutual friends willing to host each other when traveling.

This later became the Hospitality Exchange in 1988 when Joy Lily rescued the organization from imminent demise. Hospitality Club is the direct successor Hospex, the first

Internet-based service, operating out of Poland since 1992. It is currently the largest hospitality exchange network, growing rapidly. CouchSurfing is a newer but also rapidly growing hospitality exchange organization founded in 2004.

Just as all the individual services have their own individual creation stories and organizational histories (often including demise and resurrection), many also have specific niche markets that they cater to including students, activists, religious pilgrims, and even occupational groups like police officers. However, the trend in recent years points to a greater consolidation of users in networks without a specific group, value, or lifestyle affiliation.

In essence, these systems employ reciprocity - users gain access to other users' information only by posting their own. Required fields normally include name and contact information, though newer services encourage users to include more detailed personal material, including likes and dislikes, hopes and dreams, and even photographs. Of course, more information included tends to improve the chances that someone will find them trustworthy enough to host or stay with while traveling. It is very much akin to online dating services.

MONETARY SAVINGS

Staying in private homes means that travellers can save lots of money on accommodation that they would usually be spending on hotels or hostels. Used over a long period of time (2 to 4 weeks), this strategy can cut overall travel budgets in half, or even more combined with hitchhiking. These savings can then be passed on towards more generously patronizing local establishments or simply staying abroad for longer periods of time.

Local Economic Sustainability

Many tourist vacations today are sold in package form, often including flights, hotels, rental cars, sightseeing tours, and coupons for chain restaurants and bars. While this makes purchasing more convenient, it also puts more money in the hands of large multinational corporations exploiting the synergy strategy of marketing their products in the context of their subsidiary companies operating in other markets.

Many years ago, this might have been termed *collusion;* today, however, it is the norm. This comes at the expense of locally owned independent businesses. Accommodation sharing helps to break apart this monopoly and hopefully redirects some of the tourist revenue back to the local or national economy.

Ecological Sustainability

While this is especially important in more rural travel venues where hotels are often built in very picturesque, though fragile environments, every night stayed at a local's home means that much less demand for such hotel rooms. Also, if accommodation sharing does in fact increase the length of average stays, it may reduce the amount of trips to and from different locations and back home again, thus reducing the overall fuel expenditures in the process.

Ostensibly, one of the primary reasons we travel is to experience what life is like for people living in other countries. Making interpersonal connections and fostering understanding of different cultures may in the long run also be important to international relations.

However, even in our increasingly globalized world supposedly rife with diversity, in many popular travel destinations we find tourists milling around "tourist enclaves" where the companies they patronize back home have set up shop to cater to their desires while they are abroad. Sociologist George Ritzer has referred to this phenomenon as the "McDonaldisation of society" and the more recently, the "globalization of nothing".

The location of hotels near these centres only fosters more convenient envelopment of the tourist dollar. During hospitality exchanges, hosts want to show off their local knowledge and exciting "off the map" venues. Not only may travellers get a distinctly different experience, but they will also get a feel for the everyday lives of local residents.

Reciprocity

These systems foster richer and more convenient travel experiences not so much on the premise of altruism, but on the basis of social exchange theory. Implicit in the agreement to host travellers is the ability to ask to be hosted by them in the future. If one enjoys having interesting guests in their home, this works out well for both parties.

It works comparatively better if you are visited by travellers from a locale you find particularly attractive. Thus, hosting someone from New York City in Gainesville, FL seems to be an unbelievable opportunity. Moreover, if you are a Westerner visiting someone in a developing nation, your stay might be the only way that this individual or family could afford a trip to a rich nation. This may mean more than just a relaxing vacation for such disadvantaged parties.

Authenticity and Adventure

Tourism has always searched for these two qualities, but much like Midas and his golden touch, the reach of tourism has to a large extent destroyed the opportunity to encounter them in most places. Unluckily, the experience has been thoroughly commodified by everyone who wanted to secure their opportunity to make a buck in the process. Accommodation sharing offers a way out of this bind and a viable alternative to having one's desires manipulated by corporate conglomerates who never had the best interests of the place or the people foremost in their minds.

Lack of Guarantee

There is no contractual agreement between users in these systems. Reservations are made, but if they are for some reason broken, there is no higher authority to which one could plead for a refund or other compensation. The only repercussion will be the poor rating you give that user and your only consolation will be that your warning will deter others from visiting or hosting them. For those who feel insecure unless their travel arrangements are written in stone before departure, this system will not be comforting.

Potential Interpersonal Conflict

There is a chance that guest and host will not get along. Perhaps there will be scheduling or ideological conflicts. Maybe you will find that hosts or visitors have misrepresented themselves. Perhaps the experience will not live up to your expectations.

Intense interpersonal communications in advance and a flexibility once you have arrived is your best bet. These experiences require additional planning and courtesy towards the demands of your host. Thus, your living conditions, length of stay, and overall experience will be circumscribed by the living conditions you enter into.

Demographic Segregation

The average user is a young white person who speaks English and lives in a developed nation. While there are many users who do not fit this description, the more different they are, the less likely they will be involved. This is especially true for persons living in the developing world who likely do not have easy access .to the fundamental prerequisite for using these services: computers and the Internet. Thus, the sample population found in searches of these databases are really much less diverse than a geographical representation of worldwide users might suggest.

There is a distinct possibility that someone will abuse the system and that innocent users (especially women) will get hurt. All services include disclaimers that require users to waive their rights to hold anyone but themselves responsible for any harm that may come to them in using the system. They advise that the best defence mechanism is to only involve oneself with users that have extensive personal information and interpersonal networks within the system that have been verified by others.

It does seem entirely plausible that someone clever and patient enough might be able to invent an entire group of complex user identities and build histories convincing enough to fool even more cautious patrons. Still, the difference between these systems and the other social networking platforms popular nowadays on the web (such as MySpace, Tribe, Orkut, LiveJournal and Ebay) is that any agreement reached through the accommodation sharing medium is contingent on actually meeting other people face-to-face.

Other web scams are easier because interpersonal interactions rely so much on putative identities that are never actually verified in the real world. However, this does not diminish the greater risk to physical well being that this kind of traveling by definition must entertain. The best advice is to meet unknown persons in public spaces first, and try to meet some of their acquaintances in person before agreeing to a hospitality exchange.

An elaboration of certain elements of traditional Pacific communities which are also very much of the essence of the community of faith could benefit communities that have lost these tenets and thus also help to enrich our ecumenical life of sharing and service. A substantial number of Pacific islanders continue to live in such traditional communities, although they are being encroached upon relentlessly by modern development, Western political and economic systems, the mushrooming of small "paradises" (hotels, golf courses, sandy beaches) and thriving cities where traditional values are challenged, discarded and forgotten.

Over the last hundred and fifty years or so, colonial governments and churches have made marked inroads into the very being of the Pacific people and in many ways shattered the cohesiveness of community life, replacing it with capitalistic individualism. The Pacific people have been dominated for so long that they have become, to use Paulo Freire's term, "domesticated"; and at the same time they have lost their own identities.

A new wave of Pacific leaders, however, both in the secular world and in the churches, has awakened to the need for a Pacific island identity, rediscovering their own cultural heritage and attempting to protect their traditional communities. The Pacific people need to re-establish, nourish and grow a community that is truly Pacific and indigenous while maintaining its integrity in the world community. This has obliged the churches in the Pacific to reread the Bible and to engage in a theological process of contextualization, drawing upon aspects of their cultural heritage that can explain to them more about their life, their being and their relationships to the divine.

The following account seeks to unfold some traditional elements of traditional Pacific community. In recent years communism has collapsed in Eastern and Central Europe, and, while capitalism continues to assert itself, it is clear that this political and economic system cannot solve all the world's problems. Perhaps the world can look to the traditional communities of the Pacific as an alternative way forward for the next century.

Pacific Communities: Four Examples

As my friend and I sit cross-legged inside the maniaba, we are experiencing activities at the nerve-centre of sharing and dialogue. Traditionally in a Kiribati village, the maniaba is a central open house, built in the middle of the village. It serves as a meeting place for all the villagers, including the elders who make decisions for the village. For villagers and visitors alike it is a centre for meal-sharing, care-giving and entertainment.

Each family brings in their meal which they serve and share with other members of the village and visitors. After the meal, visitors are entertained with traditional dances and then garlanded with beautiful flowers and given gifts as tokens of the community's appreciation for the visit.

Nowadays the maniaba has also become the centre of village worship, where the whole community sings, prays and reads the word of God together. As a community and educational centre, it is a place for both intellectual and spiritual empowerment for the people of God and their mission. The maniaba serves as the centre of communion for the community. The shared meal becomes a point or a "table" where members of the families serve and share whatever they bring for the community gathering. It is the table where everyone is both guest and host – a point of reciprocal service and sharing.

During this meal different families and groups stand from where they are sitting and share their traditional dramas, songs and dances which relate biblical stories or traditional stories with Christian teachings or Christian applications. At this point the "worldly" and the "other-worldly" tasks are united, for there is no separation of the secular from the spiritual. Here people are reminded that the poor and the neglected are to be accepted and fed as equally important members of the community. Those members who are absent because of sickness or other reasons are prayed for and visited with food from the maniaba.

The Samoan fale. The fale or fale tele ("great house") is a symbol of Samoan village life and community. Its construction is geared towards community unity, relationship, participation and partnership. Its round or oval shape represents the unbroken chain (no beginning, no ending) for those who congregate in it, thus symbolizing unity. Its openness, a house with no wall, symbolizes inclusiveness: the extension of what goes on inside the fale to those outside in the community. What goes on in the fale reflects the life of the whole community and its concern for the wellbeing of all.

The fale tele is used for gatherings of the whole village or for district officials. It serves three functions: as the fono, a meeting place for different groups in the village for the welfare of the people; as the tapuaiga, a place for worship or supportive actions for any undertaking by the village community; and as the malaga, a place for entertaining villagers and guests, for the common meal which is brought in and shared among the members of the community.

In all three of these functions unity, fellowship and relationship are central themes. Only here can family members come to meet and discuss their differences, worship together or entertain and be happy together without feeling isolated or outcast. Perhaps one of its most important functions is as a place for reconciliation. The fale tele brings together or acts as the place of refuge for different parties.

The Tongan spreading of the mat.(5) It is the duty of the ancestral head to prepare and spread the mat for community gatherings for important occasions in Tonga. For this special ceremony a new mat is spread on top of the one used every day. As soon as the head arrives, the talanga or discussion begins. No one is allowed to say anything until the mat is spread. During an occasion of reconciliation, it is important that the two parties keep their stories until the mat is spread.

They may come with different ideas and conflicting views, but the mat on which they sit remains the common bonding factor; everyone sits on the same mat, which symbolizes the community. During the time of sharing and dialogue, everyone is free to speak about whatever has caused a problem. With the arrival of Christianity, the lotu mat was spread for the communion of the people, and it became the centre of Holy Communion, the serving and sharing of food (body and blood of Christ) for the community.

The spread mat on which everyone sits is a symbol of oneness, a clear pointer to reconciliation and sharing. The spread mat symbolizes the absence of boundaries. Everyone is welcomed to participate, either in dialogue or in the sharing of the meal prepared by and for the community.

The Fijian kava or yaqona ceremony is an occasion on which the whole village gathers to discuss matters of importance or to welcome an honoured guest. The presentation of the kava includes ai wase ni yaqona vakaturaga – the portion of food for the chief after the drinking of the kava. This food is eaten by the guests and people, shared equally among the people of the community, with no one left out. Even those people who are absent because of other engagements are given shares. There are special deacons to do this task.

This concept carries over to church gatherings in which food is shared among the people. During the kava ceremony the chief informs the people of any motions for discussion and the spokesman will then elaborate for further discussion. Affairs of the village, whether secular or spiritual, are discussed and resolutions are made by consensus. Traditional communities in biblical and theological understanding

When Jesus taught his disciples that he came "not to be served but to serve", he used the Greek word diakoneo, "to serve or to wait on tables", which refers to slaves who poured out wine for the guests. It includes giving food and drink, extending shelter, providing clothes and visiting the sick and prisoners. The maniaba, the Tongan spread mat, the Fijian kava ceremony and the Samoan fale are points of sharing, service, reconciliation, dialogue and participation and fellowship. These were the very essence of the first Christian community.

In the Fijian yaqona ceremony the servant sits at one point in the circle while the chief sits at the opposite point. Jesus saw in the word diakonia the essence of the dynamic that makes a servant and disciple: "Who is greater, the one who is at the table or the one who serves? But I am among you as one who serves". Luke was very selective in his choice of the word diakonoi to describe the ministry of Timothy and Erastus. The diakonos or servant is clearly identified as the person serving and mixing the kava.

The kava format, with its ceremonial words, has been used experimentally in the celebration of Holy Communion. The format is the reverse of the usual church celebration, in the sense that the minister or clergy sits at the servant point of the circle, not standing in the front as in a rectangular sanctuary. This is also an excellent format for Bible study, conversational sermons and church meetings, for on one occasion the same minister can be both the preacher and the officiator of Holy Communion.

When delivering the word, the minister sits in the position of authority (the chiefly seat), and when officiating at the celebration of communion he sits where the servant sits. The circle indicates that everyone included is important and should share in the dialogue and in the sharing of food — the elements of the Lord's supper.

The village community is already there, and the added concept of the faith community enhances its capacity as the basis of security and survival. The community should be engaged in what Freire calls conscientization or awareness-raising, an important effort to empower and motivate people to assert their own identity and develop their land as a source of livelihood. This empowering education enhances justice, peace and integrity of creation and helps the people to learn the art of participatory decision-making.

The pastors and village leaders need to sit where the people sit and be among them as community developers, not as community exploiters, which the colonial masters and missionaries often were. The people are encouraged through education to be more interdependent, to divert their energies away from being imitators of mission boards and oppressive pyramid structures in society at large and to develop more and more people-oriented structures for the sake of diakonia in their own locality and environment.

In the village community, people need leadership, conversion and incarnational preaching. They need to work on resolutions and actions here and now. The key to working towards the preservation of community in the village, the church or the oikoumene is the awareness that "koinonia community without the spirit of diakonia service is dead; and diakonia without the spirit of koinonia is also dead". These two concepts are part and parcel of each other and should be treated as such.

The concept of inclusiveness in the maniaba, the Tongan spread mat, the Samoan fale and the Fijian kava ceremony calls for an end to sexism in the community and in the kind of church brought to us by the missionaries. The church is so institutionally patriarchal that it is hard to believe a few personal transformations will make much of a difference to the systematic oppression of women and other minority groups. Christian symbolism is so deeply entrenched in people's subconscious experience and their culture that they can never completely walk away from its influence. Yet Christians also believe that the gospel is essentially liberating for all peoples at all times.

Sexism and women's liberation are two issues that have proved to be difficult in the Pacific. Certain aspects of patriarchal society and the church's identification with that structure have made it a hard wall to break down. But the hallmarks of the community as inclusive, serving and sharing, and belief in a liberating God who will raise prophets to sound the trumpet will in due time cause the wall of sexism to come tumbling down.

Re-development of the community of faith with a diaconal focus in the Pacific will consolidate and strengthen voluntary and self-supporting ministry. In the famous passage on spiritual gifts, Paul links the gifts of the Spirit with services, diakonia. Elsewhere Paul used diakonia when he referred to the collection for the saints in Jerusalem.

In other words, the collection was for Paul a ministry of sharing and service, the feeding of starving ordinary people who were followers of the Way in Jerusalem. In general, Christian diakonia refers to any service of genuine love. Christians have not exhausted the potential of creating new sharing and service ministries. The early Christians learned to regard diakonia as very significant in building up the Christian community. The church in the Pacific and the world can continue to do the same today.

Pacific islands are just dots in a vast ocean, trying to live alongside the megapowers of the world. I have already alluded to the negative impact of these forces. Today neo-colonialism is breeding dependent societies and creating disadvantages for the underdeveloped Pacific islands. Unfortunately, the governments of these island nations have gradually internalized the oppressive structures imposed by the superpowers, widening the gap between islands and creating new economic disparities. The rich grow richer and the poor become poorer.

No Pacific island can act alone. A concerted effort is needed to bring together the small positive concepts of each community so that they may serve as catalysts in our political, economic, religious systems and the environment. Smallness may of course create passivity, uncreativity, submission and dependency; but the other side of smallness is important and beautiful.

Both the Old and the New Testaments use the concept of smallness begetting big things: out of two persons, Sarah and Abraham, a nation was born; out of the Israelites, Moses was chosen to liberate God's people; out of Palestine, God incarnated himself in a small baby to be the light to Israel and to bring salvation to the people of the world. Jesus, too, uses the "smallness" concept: the poor widow's only small coin, given wholeheartedly, is as important as the great amounts put in by the wealthy.

Faith in God is like a small mustard seed which later grows into a big tree where the birds of heaven come to rest. Any great thing in life must always begin with the smallest beginning. E.F. Schumacher comments, "Our scientists incessantly tell us with the utmost assurance that everything around us has evolved by small mutations sieved out through natural selection...Even the Almighty is not credited with having been able to create anything complex."(8) Human beings cannot create complex things at one throw; we must go through a process, beginning with the small, to be able to create the important, the significant, the beautiful and the complex.

Pacific islanders have only one natural way to begin: with the small. In any Pacific village the elders will open or close a community meeting with a few words of encouragement. One of these basic community philosophies is "united we stand, divided we fall". Or, "bend one reed and it will break; put ten together and it will be difficult to break."

Those ancient words are very applicable to sharing and service in solidarity. Even in our small islands, working together in unity will create undreamed-of potential for asserting common identity in the competitive world of today. Jesus' prayer "that they may be one as we are one" is an invitation to unity and solidarity in sharing and service, promoting the gospel of Christ and maintaining our prophetic role amidst injustices in the Pacific and in the world.

Sharing and service, two important concepts of community living, issue a call for total liberation, a profound transformation, a redefinition of basic community that will radically and qualitatively change the conditions now experienced by the Pacific Islands. The concepts of dependency and of an endless cycle of submissiveness have become mythified. The only way to break the cycle is by demythologizing it through the concept of smallness. When the Lilliputians found Gulliver on their shores, they did not try to manhandle the giant alone. Instead, the small people got together, thought of a wise plan, then put it into action. Little by little, in their Lilliputian – and communal – way, they overpowered the giant.

The giants facing us today are from within and from outside the Pacific. They include aspects of the social system, sexism and other oppressive forces from within the islands, multinational corporations and the dominant political and socio-economic powers from outside. These oppressive powers cannot be overcome by one island alone. Small islands of the Pacific, both governments and churches, must stand together in solidarity and devise appropriate plans for action. Our own awareness of positive aspects of the Pacific communities will assist in curing the ills of oppression and oppressors.

Jesus' story of the landowner who hired people to work in his vineyard at different times during the day and paid them all the same amount no matter how many hours they worked(9) clearly sets forth the concepts of sharing and service in the community as comparable with the concepts of the kingdom as treasured by Jesus. I want to suggest with Letty Russell that this story illustrates God's "new maths" – a new, communal way of looking at reality. This new maths invites people to look at things not from the human perspective but from God's perspective, God's reality. As Paul said to the Corinthians, "we regard no one from a human point of view" but "if anyone is in Christ, there is a new creation".

Now people are looking at the world and their different vocations according to the standard of Christ and not through human standards. Paul had established a community, a community of faith in which there is mutual sharing and service like the maniaba, the Samoan fale, the Tongan spread mat or the Fijian kava ceremony.

Future shock. The hired workers in Jesus' parable knew from tradition what the daily wage was; and their grumbling can be seen as evidence of their loyalty to or longing for the past. They love tradition; they want to preserve the status quo, to stick to the conventional. Our forefathers were paid one denarius a day, so we should continue to be paid that amount today. But to their dismay and surprise the boss gave those who worked for only an hour the same wage as they received.

Those who suffer from future shock become disoriented when changes threaten their security. They seek to control their world by ordering their view of the world according to a set of static, already-established answers. Are Pacific people content with the political, economic, educational, church and other systems imported from Europe, from England, from Australia and Aotearoa-New Zealand and imposed on them? The rigidity of the present leadership and its insensitiveness to the tenets of Pacific community can cause political, economic, social and religious brokenness.

When people see from God's perspective, when they cease to regard things from the human point of view, then they can see the future from the present: this is where they are going – which is reflected in Matthew's introduction to this parable, "the kingdom of heaven is like this". It is futile to be content with the past and celebrate its perpetuity, but people should feel the inadaptability of the present, so they can always be on the pilgrimage to the longed-for future.

The early workers were self-centred and capitalist-minded. They wanted to move away from their roots in community life. They thought only of themselves, of "my thing", "my life", "my work", "my money", "my church". The possessor becomes the centre of relationship; others are sidelined and not counted. These "my thing" workers cannot see beyond their own selfish motives, whereas those who are rooted in community life place other things as priority: you, us, the world. These Christian concepts are pertinent to the life in the maniaba, the fale, the falaga and the yaqona vakaturaga.

As fellow citizens and servants people are here to indulge in sharing and service. They want to work in their own community with the world in mind. Pacific Islanders are trying to identify themselves as equal partners in a common bond with others in the world. Growth will not take place as long as people continue to focus on my things – whether race, people, religion or church. Growth will come when we look from God's perspective, God's reality, God's "new maths", and see the importance of others in Christlike love and humility.

The workers who started early were very conscious of their hard labour: "We have borne the burden of the day and the scorching heat". This is understandable. The problem is that these workers drew a circumference around themselves; they set their own boundary to mark themselves as the "chosen", thus forming an isolated group.

To take an example from the present-day Pacific, neither indigenous Fijians nor Indo-Fijians should see themselves as the elite group in Fiji; rather, their priority should be to live as a community, as the President pointed out in his speech opening parliament this year: one of the country's priorities is "to promote the harmonious relations between the different groups that make up our society".

The apostle Paul offered a vital and important definition of life: "For me living is Christ". Rather than drawing a circumference, a boundary forming an elite club, let Christ be the centre of people's life. People are wide open, as Jesus said, "for God so loved the world..." Christ became "the man for others", as Bonhoeffer said. As fellow servants, people exist for each other, since Christ is their very centre and they are always open.

Subtraction tables. The hired workers in the parable who arrived first knew their subtraction very well. They calculated their hours of work in the hot sun, minus the hours worked by those who came at 9 a.m., or noon, or 3 p.m., or 5 p.m. To put their reaction in contemporary terms: "Something is very wrong here! We settled here first. These people just came in 120 years ago; some of them just came yesterday."

The problem is that the early workers view persons quantitatively, so that everything is based on "how much" or "how little". Quantitative thinking is that of subtraction table, in which one person wins, the other loses. This kind of thinking is alien to the community concepts of the Pacific. The community includes the guests alien to the community concepts of the Pacific. The community includes the guests and the wayfarers. It is inclusive; everyone belongs to the community. The key ingredient for human relation is quality, not quantity. God in Christ shows this quality of love.

It is the quality of humility in relationship with people and God that counts. In people's relationship with others they must be conscious of the presence of Christ, who will give them the quality of love, faithfulness and justice; qualities that can grow only as they are given away and shared with others. That is God's "new maths", the community's maths.

The early hired workers had a superiority instinct: lacking humility, they act in ways that seek to maximize their own wage at the expense of the others. They grade themselves against the others to establish their own self-worth. They enhance their own authority, power and prestige as being first and having worked long hours by degrading others. In our world we have with us the oppressed and the marginalized of society, the squatters, the minority races. If Fijian Christians really want Fiji to be a Christian country, they should have a policy of inclusiveness: to be a community where all belong and no one is to be left out.

An old Chinese saying warns, "You cannot continue giving fish to your friend who asks for fish. Give him or her a fishing line and he or she will eat fish every day." If your neighbour continues to ask for tapioca, give him or her a basket of tapioca and some branch cuttings to plant. In the Pacific community, there is no spoon-feeding. The people know their servant role and what they can share for the community.

"We came first and worked hard; we deserve more wages. These others who came late should be given less." This is typical of looking at reality from the quantitative human perspective. It advances domination and subordination of others in a fixed structure of permanent inequality in church or society. The basis of unity is not this kind of equivalence but rather the willingness of the Christian to become a servant. God in Christ did this for the world. Paul stayed on and forgot about the serenity and comfort of life with Christ in order for the time being to serve the people.

What people need is a temporary inequality, to become servants for other people and for the community. In the community we do not belong to ourselves. Each one of us is a part of the community, and whatever one possesses is not his or hers but the community's. This is the message of Easter: self-denial and sharing of life. For Christ lived for others and died for others. This is very much related to the integration of the secular and the spiritual in the Pacific worldview.

The deacon or deaconess in his or her engagement in daily life continues to interpret the faith, and this process becomes relevant in the act of service within the life of the community, the church and other non-church activities. The commitment of the people to service and sharing in the community grows out of their belief that God has genuinely called them to these different services or ministries.

The peoples are servants of the community; chiefs are servants of the people; people are servants of the chiefs; those in leadership, including ministers, are the servants of the community of believers, the church. When people discover these clues in the midst of life – inclusiveness, reconciliation, unity, dialogue, participation, partnership, fellowship, sharing and service – then we are closer to that heavenly community, the kingdom of heaven.

Global Competitiveness

Cities have long held the privileged role of major centres of production and consumption of both economic and cultural activity. However, the precise nature of these functions has changed over time. Cities have changed from centres of manufacturing and mass production in the first half of the twentieth century to central places for a range of service industries by the end of the century.

Recently, globalization forces and the increased mobility of labour and capital have led to increased competition among major cities as they aspire to become centres of capital accumulation and foci for the knowledge based industries. Gertler argues that the foundations of economic success in an increasingly competitive world are the social qualities and properties of urban places as well as their 'cultural products.' The growth in cultural products and the development of urban cultural tourism as part of this phenomenon are instrumental in enhancing city images, attractiveness and competitiveness.

Cultural tourism is defined as "visits by persons outside the host community, motivated wholly or in part by interest in the historical, artistic, scientific or lifestyle/heritage offerings of a community, region, group or institution". This growth in cultural activity is particularly relevant to competitiveness in tourism marketing and tourism commodities in cities such as Toronto which are attempting to become 'global cities.' It is also relevant in that cultural products and amenities provide a high quality of life for existing residents and for the attraction of potential residents in growth and 'footloose' industries.

The purpose of this paper is to investigate in what ways one example of a cultural tourism product, a special event, enhances competitiveness in a major city.

It is hypothesized that a special cultural event has a number of functions in facilitating competitiveness: it increases linkages with the urban hinterland by attracting tourists; it temporarily increases the tourism resource base by increasing the range of attractions available; and it generates income both to the attraction and to the surrounding city functions as event visitors participate in other activities. In the broader sense, a special event contributes to the quality of life both for locals and tourists alike.

A case study approach is taken by secondary analysis of a data set of visitors to the Barnes Exhibit, an Art Exhibition of Impressionist paintings, that were shown for a limited time at the Art Gallery of Ontario in Toronto in 1994-1995. This exhibition can be considered a 'hallmark' event in that these rarely seen paintings came from a private collection and were displayed in only a few major cities. Other secondary sources in the form of news media reporting comprise a further means of qualitative inquiry used in this study. The following objectives provide the basis of the research:

a. To examine the urban fields created by the event in order to show the interconnectedness of Toronto to surrounding regions at different scales. Here the research focuses on a comparison of the Ontario (not Toronto) and US markets and the distance decay functions of these visitors.

b. To compare the characteristics of visitors from different origins. Here a spatial segmentation approach is taken and visitors from Ontario (not Toronto) are compared by their socio-demographics and trip characteristics. This will investigate what type of visitors are attracted. It will identify if the event is elitist or whether it appeals to a wider audience.

c. To examine the characteristics of the visitors that are attracted to Toronto specifically to attend the event compared with those who were in Toronto for other reasons. This question isolates the role of the event as an 'attractor' and demonstrates its importance in attracting additional visitors to the city and enhancing competitiveness.

d. To investigate the event as a generator of economic impact and the improvement of competitiveness by revenue generation. Such contributions are difficult to measure but demonstrate the 'value' in hosting a special event to urban residents and planners.

e. To examine the linkages between the event and visitor attendance at other tourism products in the downtown cluster. This objective shows the potential synergy among urban attractions which leads to improved competitiveness.

These objectives explore in detail the 'value-added' nature of an urban special event both for recreational and tourist travel. The competitiveness of the city is hypothesized to be enhanced by: an increased connectedness with surrounding regions; the types of visitors attracted; their economic impact; and their increased synergy with other attractions.

Thus, this study of the spatial and economic impact of an event indicates its role in improving the competitiveness of its host city. Empirical evidence is used to show the relationships between global cities, urban competitiveness and cultural tourism products. This case study is a response to the second part of Ashworth's call for more theory in urban tourism studies. Ashworth argues:

Urban tourism requires the development of a coherent body of theories, concepts, techniques and methods of analysis which allow comparable studies to contribute towards some common goal of understanding either the particular role of cities within tourism studies or the place of tourism within the form and function of cities.

These objectives are investigated as far as possible, given the limitations imposed by secondary data analysis.

Global Cities and the Cultural Economy

Globalization forces have resulted in a world economy with quicker and denser transactions between its sectors due to better communication, cheaper transport, a new international division of labour, the activities of transnational corporations and the effect of more liberal trade and capital flow policies. This has resulted in the development of 'global cities' in response to the intensification of the transactions and interactions between different segments in the world economy. In addition, international transactions are concentrated in certain cities whose significance resides more in their global rather than their national roles.

Global cities are the sites of immense concentrations of economic power and command centres in the world economy, whereas many traditional manufacturing cities have suffered decline. Sassen argues that cities that are now strategic sites in the global economy tend in part to be disconnected from their region or even their nation. This view argues against the traditional urban systems approach of cities which are postulated to be territorially integrated into regional and national economies. Flows of people, information and products link cities to their regions in such urban systems. Urban tourism provides one way in which these flows and linkages can be maintained.

As well as economic changes, there is a very marked convergence between the spheres of cultural and economic development. For instance, Scott states that "capitalism is moving into a phase in which the cultural forms and meanings of its outputs become dominating elements of productive strategy and in which the realm of human culture as a whole is increasingly subject to commodification i.e. supplied through profit making institutions in decentralized markets."

The concentration of the production of cultural products in cities makes them leading centres of dynamism and growth. Such products are heterogeneous, ranging from products from manufacturing (clothing, furniture, jewellery, apparel, footwear), services involving personalized transaction (tourism, advertising) and a hybrid form (music recording, book publishing, film production). The 'Arts,' comprising of attractions such as museums, art galleries and live theater, are examples of high cultural tourism products.

The competitive success of cultural products relies on their originality, distinctiveness, creativity and imagination. Scott, and Hall have contended that cities have long been major concentration centres for the production of cultural products and as their production increases in importance so too does the cultural economies of cities.

However, these researchers concentrated on cultural products which did not focus on tourism. For example, Scott performed an in depth analysis of cultural products using SIC categorized segments of urban industry but excluded tourism products (perhaps because they do not have a separate SIC classification). In fact, there is a dearth of theoretical research on urban tourism. It seems that those interested in the study of tourism "have tended to neglect the urban context in which it is set, while those interested in urban studies... have been equally neglectful of the importance of the tourism function of cities". Urban tourism is a complex phenomenon and its scale, importance and significance is often underappreciated.

Urban Competitiveness

Urban cultural attractions offer leisure opportunities for the recreation of local residents, domestic tourists and international tourists. Appealing to all three markets enhances a city's competitiveness in a number of ways. To be successful players in the global economy cities need to produce, attract and retain those talented workers who play a leading role in knowledge based industries. This highly mobile market tends to be attracted to cities but such cities need to offer a high quality of life and diversity in leisure opportunities.

Sophisticated and prestigious cultural products are important in attracting such workers. They also tend to attract the business traveller, the convention planner and the elite tourist of high income and advanced education. Capitalizing on cultural tourists is a sound strategy for urban areas. Previous research in Canada and the United States indicates a common pattern in which the cultural tourist:

- Earns more money and spends more money on vacations
- Spends more time in an area while on vacation
- Is more likely to stay at hotels and motels
- Is far more likely to shop
- Is more highly educated than the general public
- Includes more women than men
- Tends to be in older age categories.

Cities by definition are the homes of large numbers of permanent residents whose demands combine with those of tourists to sustain a variety of high order urban functions. Large cities which occupy central places in urban hierarchies with large spheres of influence are able to support higher order functions according to the marketing principle of Christaller's Central Place Theory. Museums and art galleries and other high order functions, have high thresholds since large numbers of attendees are required to make them viable. They also have high ranges, since people are willing to travel long distances to attend such service facilities.

Hence, these services are used by local urban and rural recreationists and act as magnets for tourists as part of their tourism experience. Tourists are only one group of users of an urban cultural facility, and usually not the most important, but they can enhance its economic significance to the urban community and help maintain its viability and competitiveness. To a performance, museum or gallery that already exists, the tourist is a clear gain at least until physical capacity is reached.

Interest in cultural products and cultural tourism is growing and represents an opportunity in the Canadian economy. This type of tourism represents a source of significant economic and social benefit to urban areas. Recent reports reveal that cultural experiences are of increasing value to tourists in North America.

In 1993, a Lou Harris Poll for Travel and Leisure Magazine found a significant increase in the level of interest in culture. For example, in the 1990s, 88 percent of respondents stated that they considered understanding culture to be very important when planning their trips, compared with only 48 percent in the 1980s. Furthermore, cultural tourism was expected to grow significantly with the number of trips with a cultural component projected to increase by 15 percent per annum to the year 2000.

The Role of Event Tourism in Urban Competitiveness

Event tourism is a particular form of urban cultural tourism which has experienced considerable growth in recent years. In contrast to permanent tourism attractions, "events are temporary occurrences, usually with a particular theme which aim to attract people (spectators, visitors, residents, guests) to a local point of short lived, organized activity in which visitors may participate, watch, view, learn from and enjoy". The event may be an attraction in its own right or may take place at an established attraction, adding a temporary extra dimension and appeal.

Such special events act as 'enlarged magnets' which may attract local, regional and international travellers. The staging of special events with unusual attractions will alter the 'urban field' of an existing attraction by its effect on temporary visitor movements. Events may also be effective as a means of appealing to the short break and special interest educational tourist. As the standard of living rises for the individual, life becomes more than just meeting basic needs and buying essential goods.

Non-essential consumption becomes more important and produces demand for education and entertainment products. Events within cities are well placed to meet those needs, especially if the events are unique and distinctive. Such events improve the image of the city and may attract new visitors.

However, they may be more effective at consolidating and reinforcing the core audience. Horne described the cumulative effect of an ongoing series of events in the small city of Brandon, Manitoba. Together, these events provided national and international exposure which was sufficient to improve the image of the city as a tourism destination.

They also created a variety of recreation experiences for the local and regional market. The revenue from tourism and potential tourism when special events are staged increases the attractiveness of such facilities and enhances the visibility and viability of those institutions. Where events are staged deliberately to encourage tourist interest, particularly in the off season or the shoulder season, local residents benefit from the variety, high quality and uniqueness of the events.

The influx of the tourism dollars helps in the funding of the event and extends the length of the tourist season. Without anticipation of the economic benefits from tourism, grants and sponsorship to launch such events are unlikely to be forthcoming. As outlined by Myerscough, tourism brings audiences and substantial income to the Arts, whereas the Arts creates attractions for tourists and opportunities for the tourism industry. Both the Arts and tourism have an interest in extending the season, and bringing them together represents a means of doing so.

Event Tourism as Part of the Urban Tourism System

Many visits to urban areas are multipurpose and provide opportunities for visits to a wide array of attractions, facilities and events in a tourist opportunity spectrum. As previously discussed, the opportunities which form the tourism product overlap with the recreation opportunities which urban areas provide. These opportunities include museums, art galleries, theatres, cinemas, restaurants, specialized shopping facilities, public buildings, sports stadiums and parks which tend to be clustered in relatively small areas.

With such a wide range of attractions it becomes difficult to disaggregate the relative pull of individual cultural facilities and events, and to study their visitor markets in isolation. However, in an analysis of economic impact for a special event, for example, it is important to identify visitors who were attracted as a direct result of the event, i.e. it is their main purpose. It is also likely that visitor characteristics will differ according to the main purpose of their trip.

Despite the growth in cultural products in urban areas, the role of urban cultural tourism in enhancing city competitiveness has been relatively unexplored. Special events appeal to locals and tourists and produce spatial impacts in the form of urban fields. Such events form part of the attraction mix within the tourism system and produce a variety of economic impacts. Furthermore, different types of visitors are likely to influence competitiveness in different ways.

The following case study of the Barnes Exhibit in Toronto provides the opportunity to investigate the role of this event in enhancing urban competitiveness. It illustrates the importance of isolating trip purpose and origin as market segmentation tools, following Jansen-Verbeke and Van der Well's suggestion that inner city tourists are best segmented by place of residence and motive for visiting the city.

The Barnes Exhibit Case Study

in Toronto, the Art Gallery of Ontario (AGO) has hosted a number of special events, for example, the Tutankhamen Exhibit from November 1 – December 31 1979, closely followed by a Vincent Van Gogh exhibition. Previous studies have shown the wide catchment areas that these events produced. More recently, from September 17, 1994 to January 1, 1995, the AGO hosted a major art exhibit 'From Cezanne to

Matisse: Great French Paintings from the Barnes Foundation.' The so-called Barnes Exhibit was promoted as a once in a lifetime event and received widespread media attention. This indeed was a rare event in that only a few cities were chosen to host the travelling collection of 83 impressionist and post-impressionist paintings from a private collection in Pennsylvania.

Along with Toronto (Canada), the paintings were on display in sequence in 1993-1995 in Fort Worth (Texas), Washington DC (USA), Paris (France), and Tokyo (Japan). Overall the paintings were seen by 4.5 million people with 540,000 of them in Toronto. The tour was allowed only after a Pennsylvania court overturned the will of Albert Barnes, the eccentric collector who created the foundation. This tour was required to raise money for repairs to the Foundation's suburban Philadelphia home. In fact, $10 million US in total was raised by the tour, so this roving exhibit might be considered a hallmark or 'block buster' event.

The hosting of the Barnes exhibit by Toronto was timely since it followed closely on the recommendation of the 'Strategic Directions for Planning and Development and Marketing of Ontario's Attractions, Festivals and Events' in 1993, which stated:

> In view of the compelling evidence concerning the growth of the cultural tourism sector, thought and planning should be given to investment by the tourism sector in the development of cultural product. This may be most appropriate for the unique 'block buster' type of art exhibitions which have been extremely successful tourism generators throughout major US cities and in Montreal but have been notably absent from Ontario's major cities in the past 15 years.

Subsequently, a grant from the Province of Ontario of $3.75 million to the AGO was instrumental in funding the exhibition. The Barnes Visitor Survey Methodology.

The Ministry of Culture, Tourism and Recreation of Ontario commissioned Research Resolutions and Econometrics

Research Ltd. to conduct an economic impact study of the Barnes Exhibit. This study involved a multi-stage research design. Interviewing periods were randomly selected throughout the 15 week period and 25 separate time slots varying by day of the week and time of day were selected as interviewing periods over the course of the exhibit.

Visitors from Quebec and the United States were oversampled and the data adjusted later to reflect the true proportions of out of state visitors. The true proportions were recorded in a brief tally interview, in which visitors upon entering the Barnes Exhibit were asked about origin, party size and age characteristics. 13,335 household parties were interviewed in the tally process and data from this survey was considered accurate within [+ or -] 1 percent of the 95 percent level of confidence.

After the tallies, adult representatives from the selected household visitor parties were asked to participate in exit surveys. Exit surveys were completed by 1595 household party representatives. This sample size is considered accurate within [+ or -] 2.5 percent of the 95 percent level of confidence. The exit survey included demographics, trip characteristics, origins of visitors and spending patterns. Follow up telephone surveys were conducted for a sample of visitors from Ontario (outside Toronto), Quebec and the United States to validate expenditure data.

While the main purpose of this survey was to assess the economic impact of the Barnes Exhibit, an interesting data base of event visitors was developed during the research process. This data base was made available to the author for a secondary analysis of visitors. Spatial segmentation and trip purpose segmentation are the focus of this secondary analysis. Segmentation is a form of research and analysis that seeks to identify groups of people who have similar patterns of preference and/or consumption and are distinct from other groups. A priori segmentation is used in this study as a basis for defining and classifying event visitors.

This method assumes that criteria can be defined in advance and that visitors classified in this way will form meaningful and different groups. Previous studies have shown a priori segmentation using trip origin has identified significant differences between event visitors. Similarly, segmentation according to trip purpose and degree of interest in attending a cultural event or facility have been identified as an important variable to be used in describing cultural tourism markets.

Findings

This section addresses objective (a): to examine the urban fields created by the event in order to show the interconnectedness of Toronto to different regions at different scales; and objective (b): to compare visitor characteristics from different origins. The Barnes Exhibit had a large impact on visitor movement and created a number of urban fields related to visitor origin. First, visitor origins of all visitors to the Barnes Exhibit are described, then a comparison is made between out of town visitors from Ontario and the USA.

During the fifteen week event at the AGO, the Barnes Exhibit attracted almost 600,000 visitors. Almost half of these visitors were residents of Metropolitan Toronto (48%); approximately one third, (32%) lived in Ontario but outside Toronto; and the remainder came from Quebec (6%), other Canadian provinces (3%), the United States (9%) and other countries (2%), (Research Resolutions 1995). The Exhibit generated almost 20 percent of its visitors from out of province and had a significant effect on the movement of day trippers and tourists within Ontario.

The total percentage of Canadian visitors was 89 percent. This was very similar to the visitor proportions for the Tutankhamen exhibition in 1979 which drew 88.8 percent of its visitors from Canada, 10.7 percent from the United States and 0.5 percent from other countries. The pull of special cultural events is clearly large and widespread.

Visitors from Ontario (other than Toronto) and the USA were chosen for comparative analysis as they both represent meaningful tourism market segments for Toronto. Respectively, they made up 32 percent and 9 percent of the Barnes Exhibit visitor market. They fulfill Kotler et al.'s (1996) criteria for viable market segments: measurability, accessibility, substantiality and actionability.

While there are many definitions of what constitutes a tourist, this study takes a wide definition of a tourist as being "anyone coming from outside the host community". Such visitors are perhaps better referred to as 'out-of-town' visitors. Domestic visitors from Ontario and international travellers from USA were compared on a number of variables: distance decay effect; trip purpose; socio-demographics; and expenditures.

DistanceDdecay Effect

They illustrate the extent of the 'urban field' of the Art Gallery of Ontario, Toronto for this special event. The mapped data show the influence of the distance decay effect i.e. that less visitors are drawn from greater distances. These findings are in keeping with Getz's observation that most events must rely on the local and regional (day trip) markets and that tourists coming from a greater distance and staying overnight are not likely to be the largest component.

Out-of-town visitors numbers from Ontario and the United States were clearly influenced by the distance decay effect: and by emissiveness factors with large cities like Ottawa and New York contributing a high percentage of visitors. To test out the effect of origin emissiveness and distance from the Toronto attraction, separate gravity models were developed for the Ontario (other than Toronto) and the United States submarkets. Distance in km from Toronto and census population data (for cities in Ontario, or states in the United States) were used as independent variables.

For US states, distance to the major population centre in the state was measured. This difference in methodology used between the provincial and US data was necessary since US data was only available at the state rather than the city level. The Ontario model showed a high goodness of fit in predicting number of trips. The US model was less successful although still significant.

This Ontario model suggest that a distance decay model performs well in modelling day trips and overnight trips over short distances within Toronto's urban sphere of influence. However, a similar model for the US seems less appropriate in considering trip predictions from longer distances and internationally across the US border. The findings from this exploratory analysis suggest that different distance decay curves exist for different types of visitor markets.

It is realized that poorer prediction of the US model may be the result of data coding limitations and aggregation. Many US visitors to Ontario come from border towns in Michigan and New York state and not from the main population centres. Nevertheless, despite the crude nature of the US model, the distance decay function is still significant. The size and intensity of the urban fields illustrate the 'pull' of this special event. Such tourists from outside of the Toronto region bring in basic income to the city economy and enhance competitiveness.

Trip Purpose

The Barnes Exhibit was a strong motivator for travel for out of town visitor parties from Ontario and USA. In this analysis two groups were identified: a) Barnes (as main purpose), those for whom seeing the Barnes Exhibit was the main purpose of the whole trip, and b) other visitors, those who took a pleasure trip that included a visit to the Barnes Exhibit, but said their main purpose was visiting friends or relatives or other pleasure purposes.

It is not surprising that Ontario visitors had a higher percentage of people than American visitors stating that the Barnes Exhibit was the main purpose for their trip. Seventy eight percent of the visitors from Ontario specified Barnes as their main purpose, while 7 percent were on business, 2 percent on holiday or vacation, 9 percent were visiting friends and relatives and 4 percent were visiting other events and attractions. Other data shows that Ontario visitors coming specifically to see the Barnes Exhibit are more likely to be on a day trip whereas US visitors with Barnes as their main purpose are more likely to be staying overnight and visiting other attractions.

Visitors coming from further distance are likely to be less aware of the Exhibit before they arrive in Toronto. Forty-seven percent of US visitors described the Barnes Exhibit for the main reason for their trip. However, once an event is staged and visitors become aware of it while in the region, it can attract business travellers (17%), those on holiday or vacation (12%), the visiting friend and relative tourist (12%) and those in the city for other events and attractions (12%).

Demographics

The findings on the demographics of the Barnes Exhibit visitors are consistent with previous studies, in that the Exhibit was typically a middle-aged adult event, favoured more by females than males. Ontario out-of-town visitors tended to be older than US visitors. This finding was consistent for the two main purpose categories. Male and female proportions were similar over all categories with females accounting for roughly two thirds of the visitors.

The Exhibit attracted visitors with considerable affluence and many years of formal education. In fact, all Barnes visitors were more highly educated and with higher incomes than the general population. However, the US Barnes visitors who were in Toronto specifically to attend the event were somewhat less affluent and had fewer university degrees than the US visitors who were in Toronto for a different purpose. The reverse was true for Ontario visitors.

US visitors had more formal education and income than Ontario visitors for both Barnes (as main purpose) and visitors who had a different main purpose. It seems, therefore, that a cultural attraction such as the Barnes Exhibit draws a sophisticated market from a longer distance but draws a much wider range of socio- economic groups from a closer surrounding area. This fits with the concepts of Central Place Theory, which suggest that people are prepared to travel long distances for higher order goods.

However, this conclusion is complicated by the fact that most US visitors were attracted to Toronto for reasons other than just attending the Barnes Exhibit. Some visitors were attracted to Toronto, as it is a major tourist destination with many attractions and higher order functions to explore. Other visitors were drawn to this city for business reasons, reflecting Toronto's position as a major commercial centre and a competitive centre in the global economy.

Trip Expenditures

Out of town visitors spent almost $46 million in Ontario over the course of the trip that included visits to the Barnes Exhibit. Of this, $28 million was directly attributable to the Barnes Exhibit. A breakdown of expenditures shows less per party spending per trip for Ontario visitors than US visitors and less per party spending per trip for Barnes (as main purpose) compared with other purpose visitors. However, spending at the AGO itself was higher for Barnes (as main purpose) than for other visitors.

Souvenirs were important to visitors whose trip had been motivated mainly by this special event. US visitors spent considerably more than Ontario residents on souvenirs possibly reflecting, for some travelling from greater distance, the novelty value of their trips and the greater need for trip markers and memorabilia. US visitors had higher incomes. They also benefitted from a favourable exchange rate and the ability to claim back GST (goods and service tax) expenses accrued in Canada on their return to the US.

Aggregate Characteristics of all Visitors

The following discussion uses aggregate data from all visitors and focuses on objectives (c), on page 311 above, to examine the characteristics of the visitors that are attracted to Toronto specifically to attend the event compared with those who were in Toronto for other reasons; objective (d) to investigate the event as a generator of economic impact and the improvement of competitiveness by revenue generation; and objective (e) to examine the linkages between the event and visitor attendance at other tourism products in the downtown cluster.

Main Purpose of all Visitors

On the Barnes Exhibit Exit survey two questions were used to investigate the importance of the Barnes Exhibit in the decision to visit Toronto. This focus isolates the role of the event as an 'attractor' and demonstrates its importance in attracting additional visitors to the city and enhancing competitiveness. Approximately half of the visitors had the Barnes Exhibit as their main purpose for the overall trip (56%) and would not have visited Toronto if the Barnes Exhibit was not there (50%).

As these two questions were phrased differently, they yielded slightly different responses but do still give convergent validity. Question 1 also reveals that 14.5 percent were on business and 15.4 percent were visiting friends and relatives. This data shows that business travellers and the friends and relative market have much potential for art gallery target marketing.

Economic Activity Attributable to the Barnes Exhibit

To arrive at the economic activity that was generated by the Barnes Exhibit, the Research Resolutions Economic Impact study (1995) provided a reasonably conservative estimate. The study focused on only the spending that occurred for approximately half of the visitors who were in Toronto solely or primarily to see the Barnes Exhibit.

This estimate of the direct impact of the Exhibit was $38 million (direct consumer spending), as well as additional benefits in jobs, wages, salaries and tax benefits created by this direct spending to produce a total of $71 million of goods and services (value added) to the Ontario economy. If spending by all visitors was considered regardless of their main purpose, the figures were $75 million (direct consumer spending) and $137 million (value added).

As previously discussed, out-of-town visitors spent almost $46 million in Ontario over the course of the trip that included visits to the Barnes Exhibit. Of this $28 million was directly attributable to the Barnes Exhibit. This provides yet another way of defining direct impacts which, in this case, is attributed to tourism spending.

These lower figures are more realistic of the true impact since they provide information on 'basic' money drawn into the local economy by the event. However, it is interesting to note that the figures quoted by the press err on the high side: "AGO visitors spend $75 million generating $137 million in goods and services".

The Special Event as Part of the Tourism System

The clustering effect of attractions in urban areas like Toronto has some spin off effect for the art gallery. 5.5 percent of visitors were in Toronto specifically to attend other events and attractions but also visited the AGO for this special event. In fact, other questions on the survey revealed that many visitors to the Barnes Exhibit, especially those from out of town, took advantage of shopping opportunities, high quality restaurants, sightseeing, night life and cultural performances. This finding is consistent with the idea of the tourist opportunity spectrum in cities.

Visitors who stated that a visit to the Barnes Exhibit was their main trip purpose had less time and opportunity to participate in other activities. However, many of them used the high order functions of the large city, particularly the shopping and restaurant dining functions. 32 percent of visitors whose main purpose was stated as being in Toronto specifically to visit the Barnes Exhibit were also visiting friends and relatives.

They were taking advantage of cheap accommodation. It may be argued that they were perhaps responding in an expected way to the question about main purpose. However, the closeness of response between question 1 and 2 on main purpose as discussed earlier makes that bias in the data collection unlikely.

The positive economic ripple effects were felt in the gallery and in the surrounding city. At the gallery, membership increased by 40 percent, visitors made souvenir purchases ($5.5 million) and food and beverage purchases ($1 million). Restaurants in the immediate vicinity of the gallery reported increased business of as much as 30 percent.

Hotels and other forms accommodation sold about $5 million in lodging and entertainment and recreation facilities had $7.7 million in receipts because of the Barnes Exhibit. Not surprisingly, the US visitors had much higher accommodation and food and beverage expenditures than the Ontario visitors. As a result of the popular appeal of the event it drew many people to a cultural activity who otherwise would not have engaged in one.

In Ontario, it had the effect of encouraging repeat visitors (perhaps who had not visited for some time) to the AGO to experience the 'new' product offering (ibid.). It also may have encouraged new visitors to the art gallery who would not have otherwise visited. This is illustrated by a comment overheard from an uninformed visitor leaving the AGO, "That Barnes must have been some painter to have worked in all those different styles".

This visitor was obviously no expert on the French Impressionists. The event increased the pull of Toronto for day trippers, many of whom were coming especially to see the exhibit. Therefore, the event acted as a major draw to the city, supplementing revenues received from visitors during the shoulder season and off season.

As a catalyst to city dynamism and global competitiveness, the Barnes Exhibit was a great success. This study has shown that this special event facilitated competitiveness in a number of ways. it increased linkages with urban hinterlands by attracting different types of tourists. It temporarily increased the tourism resource base and generated income both for the AGO and for surrounding city and regional facilities and attractions. This was a very popular event. By attracting so many visitors who might not have otherwise participated in a cultural activity, it drew in a wide range of visitors. Furthermore, because of its international prestige and uniqueness, the event contributed to quality of life and urban attractiveness for local residents.

Toronto's position in the global economy is reflected in its ability to attract this hallmark event. Toronto was chosen to host the exhibit from more than twenty cities around the world. AGO director, Glenn Lowry was quoted in saying that "This is a cultural event of international significance. It'll bring prestige to the gallery, the city, and the country".

Cultural events are recognized now as important economic development tools. Anne Swarbrick, Provincial Minister for Tourism, Recreation and Culture claimed that "Bringing events and exhibitions of this stature to Ontario is essential to economic stimulation and job creation and it is an important component of our provincial tourism strategy". The previous discussion of economic impact showed significant returns on investment for the AGO as well as spin off effects in the city and provincial economy. As AGO president, John Rotman stated "It proves the tangible benefits from investment in the cultural industries".

Like all special events, the Barnes Exhibit represented a temporary change in 'attractiveness' of a facility within the supply side of recreation and tourism. The event's success was based partly upon increased demand for recreation and tourism stimulated by this improvement. Consequently, the urban field of the AGO was temporarily changed by this special event. The event because of its significance may have attracted visitors who would not normally patronize art galleries. The challenge for the AGO is how to retain the first time visitors and infrequent visitors as repeat visitors to the gallery on a regular basis.

It is likely that "an Exhibit such as the Barnes can extend the 'cultural umbrella' to cover people who otherwise would not have experienced a cultural activity". Thus, a cultural activity which is normally associated with elitism may be democratized with a popular, unique and significant event.

For the visitor from the United States, especially from New York and Michigan, it had an 'attractor' effect for both day and overnight visitors. However, more distant travellers from parts of the United States, as a consequence of lack of awareness, were more likely to experience the event as an additional attraction within the product mix of Toronto. Such a cultural event would appeal, for example, to a business traveller of high affluence and educational level.

This opportunity may bring about a more positive image of the city as a place to live, invest in, and visit. The high number of business travellers attracted to the event reflects Toronto's importance as an international commercial centre. In addition, segmentation according to trip purpose revealed that Barnes (main purpose) visitors differed demographically, in trip characteristics and in spending patterns from the other purpose visitors. Furthermore, differences were observed between the US and Ontarian Barnes (main purpose) visitors.

This study is limited to a study of the Barnes Exhibit, which took place at a specific time, in a specific place and with an extensive marketing and promotional campaign. Toronto is a gateway city for communications, well placed within the 'Golden Horseshoe' with easy access to Montreal, Ottawa, and Hamilton in Canada and Buffalo, Syracuse and Detroit in the United States. The extent to which the composition of visitors attracted to the Barnes Exhibit is similar in other centres or at other times is not known. Neither is data available for comparative purposes of AGO visitors in the same season.

A previous study of AGO visitors by Wall was completed during the summer and records a lower proportion of

Canadian visitors (73%), reflecting, not surprisingly, a higher tourism component in the visitor profiles. However, this study does provide some generalisations for event managers as to the types of visitors which special cultural events generate.

It reinforces the idea that a priori segmentation of visitors according to trip origin and trip purpose is a valid method, revealing important differences between visitor segments. The high levels of expenditure in hosting such a 'blockbuster event' were more than justified by visitor expenditures stimulated specifically by the event being held. In addition, useful marketing information was gathered for predicting the impact of similar events upon the accommodation and service sectors and other attractions.

This reinforces the contention that urban tourism is a multifaceted and multipurpose activity but that it is possible to isolate specific economic ripple effects generated by special events. The success of the Barnes Exhibit stimulated investment in other events of similar types.

For example, the Renoir Exhibit at the National Gallery in Ottawa in 1997 and the Vincent Van Gogh Exhibit at the Art Gallery of Ontario in 1999, mirrored the success of the Barnes Exhibit and further illustrated the importance of cultural special events in contributing to urban economies.

As a study of a cultural tourism product and its significance for city competitiveness, this research contributes to our knowledge of the spatial and economic impact of such events. Despite the limitations in the use of secondary data, it provides evidence for an assessment of the role of cultural tourism in destination competitiveness. By linking an empirical analysis to a framework of urban globalization processes, this research provides an initial step in answering Ashworth's call for more theory in urban tourism studies.

Findings from this study could be compared with future studies on similar cultural tourism products to examine consistencies in the impacts and visitor characteristics of the products. The conceptual framework also offers opportunities for extension to other cultural products (built attractions, heritage landscapes, other types of special events and festivals) in other areas and contexts and at different scales of analysis.

While the emphasis in this research has been on competitiveness measured in terms of spatial and economic impact of a 'one off' major event for a city, smaller events and festivals should not be ignored as all may contribute to overall urban competitiveness.

Chapter 4

The Idea of Quality

QUALITY AS AN ABSOLUTE

A possible reason for the enigmatic nature of quality is that it is a dynamic idea. The emotional and moral force that quality possesses makes it difficult to define accurately. In fact, there is an argument against attempting too precise a definition. There is the danger that much of the vitality of the concept can be lost if it is subjected to too much academic analysis. Westley and Mintzberg make the point that this happens to many important concepts that are freely used in practical settings:

> A strange process seems to occur as concepts such as culture and charisma [and we can add quality] move from practice to academic research. Loosely used in practice, these concepts, as they enter academia become subjected to a concerted effort to force them to lie down and behave, to render them properly scientific. In the process they seem to lose emotional resonance, no longer expressing the reality that practitioners originally tried to capture.

While heeding this advice, nevertheless it is important to take a tour of the concept. There is so much baggage attached to the idea of quality that without some understanding of its philosophical underpinnings it is difficult to build the management structures necessary to achieve the goal of improving the education of students.

Quality has a variety of ambiguous and contradictory meanings. Much of the confusion over the meaning of quality arises because it can be used both as an absolute and as a relative concept. Quality in much everyday conversation is used as an absolute-this is a thing of quality. The word quality comes from the Latin qualis meaning what kind of. The quality of something can be said to be a part of its nature.

People use quality freely when describing expensive restaurants and luxury cars. Used as an absolute quality it is similar in nature to goodness, beauty and truth. It is an ideal with which there can be no compromise. As an absolute, things that exhibit quality are of the highest possible standard that cannot be surpassed. Quality products are things of perfection made with no expense spared. They are valuable and convey prestige to their owners.

Quality cars, for example, are hand-built and expensive and have interiors of walnut and leather. Rarity and expense are two of the features of quality in this definition. Quality in this sense is used to convey status and positional advantage, and the ownership of things of quality sets their owners apart from those who cannot afford them. Quality is a concept with class. It is synonymous with high quality or top quality. To quote Pfeffer and Coote on the subject, 'most of us admire it, many of us want it, few of us can have it'.

Used in the educational context, this concept of quality is essentially elitist. By definition only a few institutions are able to offer such a high quality educational experience to their learners. Most learners cannot afford it, and most institutions cannot aspire to provide it.

The Relative Notion of Quality

Policy-makers and academics have always maintained a keen interest in reviewing and debating the link between skills, knowledge and organisational performance at national, sectoral and firm level. The extent though to which policy-makers, in particular, are willing to admit anything other than the need to aspire to a putative high skill, high wage, high quality route, means such debate can remain somewhat static. Quality in the technical sense is largely a relative concept.

The relative definition views quality not as an attribute of a product or service, but as something which is ascribed to it-'the quality of your essay varies between good and excellent'. Consequently, they argue that there is a need to shift the debate from concentration on supply side issues in relation to skills provision and instead concentrate as well on demand side concerns. Thus, other issues need to be considered such as skill deployment, the relationship between skills, job design, career and employment structures, work organisation and product market strategies.

A further aspect of this concern to develop a more searching analysis is the need to develop a comparative focus across sectors. The emphasis on this sectoral focus can be seen in relation to things like the impact of sectoral institutions on strategy, training and the labour market in that sector. Based on the foregoing, hospitality, as an employing sector, becomes a particularly interesting focus of research. As a sector it is heterogeneous, both in relation to the predominance of small and medium-sized enterprises (SMEs) but equally in relation to the way that organisations adopt differing routes to competitive advantage.

Notwithstanding that latter point hospitality is generally considered as a sector which has traditionally erred on the side of adopting a model of competitive advantage which has been premised on a low skills model or 'poor' human resource management (HRM) practice. Given this situation there is a need to understand some of the pressures pushing firms to pursue such an approach and why this model is more likely to win out in particular organisational settings.

Equally, though, there is a need to recognise the increasing importance of the rhetoric (and reality?) of quality service and the implications of this for hospitality organisations. In particular, there is a recognition that certain product markets in the hospitality sector must be seen to be offering quality service, which in turn is reliant on a sophisticated approach to HRM, for example the upper/luxury market of the hotel sector. In many respects this dichotomy between 'poor' HRM and the ever increasing rhetoric of quality service could rather crudely be characterised as a debate between whether HRM strategies in hospitality should be, to use Boxall and Purcell's (2000) descriptors, 'best fit' or 'best practice'.

On the one hand, the 'best fit' school argues for an approach to HRM which is fully integrated with the specific organisational and environmental context and argued most strongly by the likes of Schuler and Jackson. On the other hand, proponents of 'best practice', such as Pfeffer, argue for a universalistic approach to HRM wherein all firms who adopt a prescribed range of HR policies and practices are more likely to create a high performance/commitment workplace.

As a corollary the notion of 'best practice' is also dependent on employers adopting a high cost, high skill employment strategy, as organisations aim to compete on the basis of high quality and productivity. The need to find a way between much of the ideal types described to this point is to seek to review a number of issues within a specific sectoral context to examine how these issues are played out within that context.

Pursuant on this situation the key aim of this monograph is to:

- Determine the influence of companies product market strategies, in-company and external structural factors on skill levels, work organisation, job design and people management systems.

More specifically the paper has a number of secondary objectives:

- To develop active definitions of service quality and its specification and review operators' conceptions of different dimensions to quality.
- To review the different elements of the product and service that make a given offering 'high spec' or 'low spec' in relation to issues such as physical capital, equipment, décor, ambience and the role of people.

- To assess the contribution of employees to the dimensions of quality; modes of involvement and type of staff involved; skills involved by type (technical, aesthetic, social, emotional); and level.
- To analyse the relationship of skills 'fit' to broader system of work organisation and job design and the relationship of high/low specification operations to forms of work organisation using a variety of models such as that provided by Lashley and Taylor.
- To assess the extent to which people management systems support or hinder the delivery of quality.

  Where possible, and particularly on the question of HRM outcomes, these considerations will be illustrated by empirical data gathered from a number of different sources. It is recognised here that the use of this data is merely illustrative and should be recognised with due caution as to its generalisiblity. In this sense the data sources utilised for this monograph include:

- A small number of interviews with small business owners or managers and managers in a large international hotel chain.
- Interviews conducted with five managers and two focus groups with employees from several Pret A Manger shops.
- Interviews conducted with 'significant others' such as representatives from local enterprise networks, the employers organisation for the hospitality industry, the British Hospitality Association (BHA), and a consultant working with the Excellence Through People (ETP) initiative.

In a wider sense the review of the hospitality sector is particularly important as traditionally there is a paucity of work considering the implications for HRM within service work settings.

Service work comprises a large and growing part of the workforce in the advanced societies, with knowledge work in both goods and service production making an increasingly important contribution to economic growth. The absence of debates about alternative ways of organising and supporting service work indicates that service work and its HRM implications has not received the attention they deserve. The heterogeneity of service work, including the settings in which it is undertaken, suggest a wide field of exploratory research. On the other hand, there is a need for theorising that will define the direction in which cumulative empirical research might progress.

This review of the hospitality sector aims to add to this theorising in offering a comprehensive picture of a sector which is particularly important in the wider service sector. The importance of the sector is evidenced by recognition that it is one of the largest employers within the service sector, with the largest overall employment growth of all sectors in recent years.

In order to assess some of these issues we will firstly engage with the debate about the 'uniqueness' which is often ascribed to the service sector generally and how this is likely to impact on the product market strategies of firms. Related to this point we will review definitions of quality and suggest that the lack of a definitive consensus on the issue of service quality has implications for the differing approaches to product market strategies and HRM adopted by organisations.

Following this, the next section will further develop some of these issues by reviewing a number of important models, most obviously Schuler and Jackson (1987) and Lashley and Taylor (1998) which have sought to theorise the relationship between competitive strategy and HRM. From this general discussion attention will then turn to the particular dynamics of the hospitality sector. An integral point to emerge from descriptions of the hospitality sector is the SME dimension.

Often overlooked in wider debates about skill acquisition and usage there is the need to be aware that the SME sector can offer specific challenges to both policy-makers and owner-managers. This is especially true in the hospitality industry due to the preponderance of SMEs in the sector. Recognising this point, the paper specifically considers the impact of the SME dimension. The description of some of the key characteristics of the sector, including the SME dimension, and the likely impact on HRM approaches provides the framework to offer a considered view of two potentially antithetical responses from organisations.

These responses are characterised, rather crudely, as the 'pessimistic' 'poor' HRM approach and the 'optimistic' high quality approach. To develop these positions we will draw heavily on the extant work which has sought to address the issue of HRM in the hospitality sector, as well as our own illustrative empirical material. Consideration of these approaches also allows for the description of putative 'best practice' approaches. The paper will then move on to consider some of the methodological issues generated by the discussion, and particularly how the future research agenda reviewing the nature of HRM in the hospitality sector is best carried forward.

In sum, this monograph seeks to synthesise a number of different themes to offer a comprehensive picture of the hospitality industry. In doing we aim to understand the pressures which push organisations to adopt particular routes to competitive advantage and ultimately recognise that the high skill, high wage and high quality route is one which remains rare in the hospitality industry. This process can be considered as a reflection of what Segal-Horn (1993) calls the 'hard', more tangible, elements of service that may be more responsive to standardisation.

This is a useful distinction that allows us to examine the strategies adopted by service organisations in relation to the 'hard' or 'hardware' and the 'soft' or 'software'. Hardware can be broadly conceptualised as the physical product (for example, the interior and exterior of a hotel, its rooms, meals, beverages and leisure services). The software consists of the more amorphous notions of service quality, service delivery and the emotional interaction between the producer and consumer. Thus, it could be suggested that both the hardware and the software comprise the overall product and in the normative view held by much of the services marketing and management literature must successfully coalesce to ensure organisational success.

Nonetheless, it is widely recognised that within the notion of intangibility, service organisations which offer a product that is, in the words of Lashley and Taylor (1998), 'intangible dominant', increasingly seek to differentiate themselves on the basis of the software aspects such as seeking high quality and 'authentic' service interactions for the increasingly discerning customer.

The identification of the main services characteristics, the study of service encounters and service experience suggest that service quality is more complex to evaluate than in the case of goods. Services are more difficult to measure and standardise and consequently establishing an instrument attempting to measure quality has become a central challenge for the delivery of good service quality and service companies' success.

The challenge of evaluating service quality has been motivated by recent research and debate, as noted above, which increasingly demonstrates the significance of service quality as a central factor of business success. Service quality has consequently become a focus of any management and marketing strategy and high levels of service are seen as a means for organisations to achieve a competitive advantage and position themselves more effectively in the market place.

Customers are also becoming more aware and critical of the alternatives on offer and rising standards of services, prompted by competitive trends, have increased customer expectations. However, as Hoque notes whilst service quality may well be increasingly critical to competitive success, 'defining what exactly is "service quality" is somewhat problematic'. Generally service quality cannot be objectively measured as can technical quality for manufactured goods and it therefore remains an elusive and abstract construct. The characteristics of intangibility, heterogeneity and inseparability presented earlier also constitute a challenge for managers because they do not allow for an easy process of quality evaluation.

More importantly, a customer judgement of a service depends as much on the service process as on the outcome, therefore customers' quality evaluation can be seen as depending on the production of services as well as on their consumption. The services marketing and management field has displayed different views of how this construct might be assessed.

For example, Akehurst and Harrington in a review of managerial perceptions of service quality in UK hotels note two schools of thought - American and Nordic - which have sought to address this issue. Though they differ in the detail of their approach, both schools of thought largely adopt a common approach in seeking to group a range of quality items into dimensions.

Quality in this sense is about being measured against criteria. It is not an end in itself, but a means by which the end product is judged as being up to (or not up to) standard. Quality products or services, in this relative or ascribed definition, need not be expensive or exclusive. They may be beautiful, but not necessarily so. They do not have to be luxurious or special. They can be ordinary, commonplace and familiar. Overhead projectors, laptops, ballpoint pens and the school catering service may all exhibit quality. Any product or service can aspire to the label quality.

They do not have to be exclusive. While the absolute notion is elitist, the relative notion is potentially egalitarian. What allows the label of quality to be ascribed to any product or service is that it meets the standards set for it. It must do what is claimed for it, and do what its customers expect of it. In other words it must be fit for purpose, as the British

Standards Institution defines quality. In this relative sense quality is about measuring up to predetermined standards and meeting those standards time and time again.

Two Concepts of Quality

The relative definition of quality has two aspects to it. The first is concerned with measuring up and ensuring conformity to a predetermined specification. The question that is asked is 'Does this good or service do what is asked or expected of it?' This is fitness for purpose. This is sometimes called the producer definition of quality or the procedural concept of quality.

In an industrial setting quality is achieved by products or services meeting a predefined specification in a consistent fashion. Quality is demonstrated by a producer having a system, known as a quality assurance system, that supports the consistent production of the good or service to a particular standard or specification.

In this definition popular cars as well as luxury models can be quality products. Luxury, beauty, exclusivity and price do not enter into the equation. It does not matter whether they are Fords or Rolls-Royces so long as products conform to manufacturers' specifications and standards. Both can be quality products. A product exhibits quality so long as it consistently meets the maker's claims for it. This view of quality is sometimes called quality in fact. Quality in fact is the basis of the quality assurance systems devised in accordance with the international standard.

The procedural concept places considerable emphasis on working to defined systems and procedures. This is seen as the method most likely to produce a standardized or quality outcome. Quality is achieved by putting systems and procedures into operation and ensuring that those systems are efficiently and effectively operated. It is the audit trail approach to quality.

Today much quality work is concerned with finding appropriate evidence about the way particular activities within the institution have been carried out. The procedural concept is about proving that things have happened in accordance with predetermined specifications. It ensures that activities conform to requirements, although critics of the approach argue that it can stifle creativity and innovation.

Proving, approving and reporting are the key descriptors of this largely instrumental approach to quality. It is an accountability or audit approach that is concerned to ensure consistency and conformity. It is based on the predominantly hard indicators of measurable performance. In education hard quality indicators include public examination league tables for schools and colleges.

Transformational quality is different. It has less to do with systems and procedures and more to do with continuous improvement and organizational transformation. This concept views quality as a complex process with a wider canvas. It focuses on the softer and more intangible aspects of quality.

These softer concepts include care, customer service and social responsibility, and often go to the heart of the difficult and intangible issues of customer satisfaction and delight. It is often said that while the procedural notions of quality are essential and necessary they are by themselves not sufficient to ensure customer loyalty. The things that bring customers back time and time again and hold their allegiance are often centred on personal service and customer care.

Transformational quality is achieved not through adhering to systems and procedures, but through the exercise of leadership. It is leadership that establishes a vision that translates into customer service and builds the structures and organizational culture that empower staff to deliver a quality service.

Whereas the procedural concept is about proving, the transformational approach is about improving. It is about doing things right, not just doing the right things. It is a state of organizational mind that sees continuous improvement at the very heart of the quality process. Transformational quality blends the aspirations of customers with the empowerment of staff. It takes a wide and more eclectic view of quality.

It puts the customer first and seeks to expand their horizons. In an education setting the transformational culture is a function of staff motivation and academic leadership in a setting that is student centred.

Transformational transformational quality aims for excellence and is satisfied with fitness for purpose. This is not to confuse it with the absolute definition of quality. Excellence is an aspiration, a striving. What transformational quality is about is aiming high and ensuring that there is a quality improvement agenda in place.

The important part of making the distinction between the procedural and the transformational ormational aspects of quality is not to label one right and the other wrong. Both concepts play a key role in understanding quality. The point of the distinction is to recognize that there are different approaches to achieving quality.

The pursuit of quality is an exercise requiring not only well-developed and understood systems and procedures but also a customer-oriented transformational culture where individuals are given the responsibility for the quality of the work in their area and can contribute fully to its achievement.

The Consumer's Role in Quality

Any discussion about the nature of quality has to centre on the crucial role of the consumer. Who should decide whether a school or college is providing a quality service? The answer will tell us much about the values and aspirations of the institution. It is essential to have a clear idea of who is ascribing the attribute of quality. The views of producers and consumers are not always identical. It does happen that consumers reject perfectly good and useful products and services. Providing a service to specification does not guarantee success.

Organizations that follow the TQM path regard quality as being defined by their customers. They are the final arbitrators of quality and without them the institution will not exist. The institution that champions TQM as its philosophy has to use all means at its disposal to explore their customers' needs. As Edwin L Artzt, the Chairman and Chief Executive of the Procter and Gamble Company, has put it:

Our customers are both those who retail our products and those who ultimately use them. Total quality means knowing them in ways and depths never fully explored before and using this knowledge to translate needs into innovative new products and business approaches.

Quality can be defined as that which satisfies and exceeds customers' needs and wants. This is sometimes called quality in perception. Quality can be said to be in the eyes of the beholder. This is a very important and powerful definition, and one that any institution ignores at its peril. It is the consumers who make the judgements on quality.

Tom Peters in a discussion of the pivotal role of the consumer in quality (1987) argues that the perceived quality of a business's product or service is the most important single factor affecting its performance. He argues that quality as defined by the customer is more important than price in determining the demand for a majority of goods and services. As he says of his researches over the years:

(1) Customers-individual or industrial, high tech or law, science-trained or untrained-will pay a lot for better, and especially for best, quality; moreover,

(2) Firms that provide that quality will thrive;

(3) Workers in all parts of the organization will become energized by the opportunity to provide a top quality product or service; and

(4) No product has a safe quality lead, since new entrants are constantly redefining, for the customer, what's possible.

Quality Control, Quality Assurance and Total Quality

As well as providing a definition of quality, it is necessary to understand the difference between three other important quality ideas. These are the distinctions made between quality control, quality assurance and total quality. Quality control is the oldest quality concept. It refers to the detection and elimination of components or final products that are not up to standard. It is an after-the-event process concerned with detecting and rejecting defective items.

As a method of ensuring quality it may involve a considerable amount of waste, scrap and reworking. Quality controllers or inspectors usually carry out quality control. Inspection and testing are the most common methods of quality control, and are widely used in education to determine whether standards are being met.

Quality assurance is different from quality control. It is a before and during the event process concerned to prevent faults occurring in the first place. Quality assurance is about designing quality into the process to attempt to ensure that the product is produced to a predetermined specification. Put simply, quality assurance is a means of producing defect- and fault-free products. The aim in the words of Philip B Crosby is 'zero defects'. Quality assurance is about consistently meeting product specification or getting things right first time, every time.

The quality of the good or service is assured by there being a system in place, known as a quality assurance (QA) system, that lays down exactly how production should take place and to what standards. Quality standards are maintained by following the procedures laid down in the QA system. Quality assurance is the responsibility of the workforce, usually working in quality circles or teams, rather than the inspector, although inspection can have a role to play in quality assurance.

Total quality management incorporates quality assurance, and extends and develops it. TQM is about creating a quality culture where the aim of every member of staff is to delight their customers, and where the structure of their organization allows them to do so. In TQM the customer is sovereign. It is the approach popularized by Peters and Waterman (1982), and which has been a constant theme of Tom Peters' writings ever since.

TQM is about providing the customer with what they want, when they want it and how they want it. It involves moving with changing customer expectations and fashions to design products and services that meet and exceed their expectations. Only by delighting customers will they return and tell their friends about it (this is sometimes called the sell-on definition of quality). The perceptions and expectations of customers are recognized as being short term and fickle, and so organizations have to find ways of keeping close to their customers to be able to respond to their changing tastes, needs and wants.

The Educational Product

It is always necessary to ask two fundamental questions when trying to understand quality in any situation. The first is 'What is product?' The second is 'Who are the customers?' These questions are equally applicable to the discussion of quality in education.

The product of education is an area of difficulty. There are a number of different candidates for it. The pupil or the student is often spoken about as if they fulfil that role. In education we often talk as though learners are the output, especially with reference to the institution's perceived performance over discipline and behaviour. Terms like 'the supply of graduates' make education sound like a production line with students emerging from the end of it. The problem with this definition is that it is difficult ficult to square it with much educational practice.

For a product to be the subject of a quality assurance process the producer needs firstly to specify and control the source of supply. Secondly, the 'raw material' must pass through a standard process or set of processes, and the output must meet predetermined and defined specifications. Such a model does not easily fit education, although there are those who might wish it would. Such a model would clearly require an initial selection of learners to be made.

Some sectors of education do this, but many, following the comprehensive principle of open access, do not. However, it is from there on that the analogy begins to fall apart. While processes such as the national curriculum and the specification of standards and competencies in National Vocational Qualifications (NVQs) in the UK have improved the standardization of the process, nevertheless the process of education is anything but uniform.

It is impossible to produce pupils and students to any particular guaranteed standard. As Lynton Gray has put it in his very useful discussion of the issue:

Human beings are notoriously non-standard, and they bring into educational situations a range of experiences, emotions and opinions which cannot be kept in the background of the operation. Judging quality is very different from inspecting the output of a factory, or judging the service provided by a retail outlet.

The idea of the learner as the product misses the complexities of the learning process and the uniqueness of each individual learner. What then is the product? Rather than answer this directly it is more helpful to view education as a service rather than a production line. The distinction between a product and a service is important because there are fundamental differences between them that have a bearing on how their quality can be assured.

Service Quality

Service quality characteristics are more difficult to define than those for physical products. This is because they include many important subjective elements. The causes of poor quality and quality failure are materially different for services and products. Products often fail because of faults in raw materials and components. Their design may be faulty or they may not be manufactured to specification.

Poor quality services, on the other hand, are usually directly attributable to an organization's behaviours or attitudes. They often result from lack of leadership, care or courtesy. Indifference, lack of training or concern are the principal reasons for a breakdown of service. Services differ from production in a number of important ways.

There are major differences between delivering a service and manufacturing goods. The first difference between the two is that services usually involve direct contact between the provider and the end-users. Services are delivered directly by people to people. There is a close relationship between the customer and the person who delivers the service.

The service cannot be separated from the person delivering it or from the person receiving it. Every interaction is different, and the customer in part determines the quality of the interaction. The quality of the service is determined both by the person delivering and the person receiving the service. Unlike products, there can be no absolute consistency or homogeneity in service delivery. The consistency of the service can only be within boundaries.

Time is the second important element of service quality. Services have to be delivered on time, and this is as important as their physical specification. Additionally, as a service is consumed at the moment of delivery the control of its quality by inspection is always too late. The close personal interactions found in services allow multiple opportunities for feedback and evaluation and these provide the main, but not the only, means of judging whether customers are satisfied with it.

The third difference is that, unlike a product, a service cannot be serviced or mended. A poor meal is a poor meal. It cannot be repaired. For this reason it is important that the standard for services should be right first time, every time. Paradoxically, it is the high possibility of human error and failing that makes it difficult if not impossible to achieve the right first time standard. Nevertheless, this should always be the aim.

Fourthly, services face the problem of intangibility. It is often difficult to describe to potential customers exactly what is being offered. It is equally difficult on occasions for customers to describe what they want from the service. Services are largely about process rather than product. It is usually more important how an outcome is arrived at than what the outcome is.

The fact that services are usually rendered directly to customers by junior employees is the fifth distinguishing feature of a service. Senior staff are generally remote from customers. Most customers never have access to senior managers. The quality of the initial interactions colours the view customers have of the whole organization, and so the organization has to find ways of motivating front-line employees always to deliver of their best.

This is why training and staff development are of crucial importance. While senior managers may not serve at the front in service organizations they must lead from the front and convey to their staff their vision of the service and the standards they want set for or it. Lastly, it is very difficult to measure successful output and productivity in services.

The only meaningful performance indicators are those of customer satisfaction. Intangibles or soft measures are often as important to success and to the customer as are hard and objective performance indicators. Soft indicators such as care, courtesy, concern, friendliness and helpfulness are often uppermost in customers' minds. Intangibility makes it very difficult to turn round poor service, because it is sometimes impossible to convince dissatisfied customers that a service has changed for the better.

Consumers judge quality by comparing their perceptions of what they receive with their expectations of it. Much of this is also true for education. Reputation is crucial to an institution's success, but the origin of that reputation often defies analysis and measurement. What we do know is that reputation has a great deal to do with the care and concern shown to pupils and students.

For the purposes of analysing quality it is more appropriate to view education as a service industry than as a production process. Once this view is established the institution needs to define clearly the services it is providing and the standards to which they will be delivered. This needs to be carried out in conjunction with all its customer groups, including discussions with governors, parents, and with industry directly or via local education business partnerships.

Education and its Customers

We have defined education as a provider of services. Its services include advice, tuition, assessment and guidance to pupils and students, their parents and sponsors. The customers-the stakeholders of the service-are a very diverse group and need identifying. If quality is about meeting and exceeding customer needs and wants, it is important to be clear whose needs and wants we should be satisfying.

It is important to say something about the idea of a 'customer' in the context of education. To some educationalists 'customer' has a distinctly commercial tone that is not applicable to education. They prefer to use 'client' instead. Client, with its connotations of professional service, is seen as more appropriate. 'Stakeholder' is another term often used in this context.

Others reject all such language and would rather stay with 'pupil' or 'student'. Language is important if an idea is to be acceptable. Some people would make a distinction between clients, who are the primary beneficiaries of the education service, and customers, who pay for it but who may be once removed, such as parents, governors, employers or government.

The diversity of customers makes it all the more important for educational institutions to focus on customer wants and to develop mechanisms for responding to them. It can be helpful to make distinctions between:

- Primary customers-who directly receive the service;
- Secondary customers-such as parents, governors, sponsoring employers of vocational students, all of

whom have a direct stake in the education of a particular individual or in a particular institution;

- Tertiary customers-who have a less direct but nonetheless crucial stakeholding in education, such as future employers, government and society as a whole;
- Internal customers-who are the employees of the institution and who have a critical stakeholding in the organization's success.

The needs and views of the various customer groups, whether they are internal or external, do not always coincide, especially in large and complex institutions, although the conflict can equally be present in small ones. Potential and actual conflicts of customer interest will always exist. One of the best methods of resolving different interests is to recognize their existence and to look for the core of issues that unite the various parties.

All stakeholders need to have their views listened to and to be treated fairly. Quality and justice go hand in hand. This is particularly the case when dealing with complaints, which are instances of those critical incidents where it is possible to judge how committed an institution is to a customer-first approach. It is often difficult to ensure that the primary customers' views are paramount.

There are strong forces pulling against it, not least those that can be exerted by funding processes and mechanisms. Where the needs of the learner and funding mechanisms collide, it is very difficult for an institution to put its learners first. This is particularly the case where funding mechanisms emphasize efficiency that can only be achieved at the cost of quality.

For example, a staffing cut may lead to a higher pupil-teacher ratio; or a funding cut may lead to a reduction in service that may not accord with what customers are feeding back. This is a very difficult issue to resolve and TQM does not provide ready answers to it. What it does is to ensure that the institution's processes keep the learners' views centre stage.

In industry, benchmarking involves analysis of the best products and services available in a particular marketplace, or comparing best practices across industry sectors. These products or services become the targets or 'benchmarks' that the organization strives to meet. In education, benchmarking focuses on what are considered to be best practices and organizational features of special merit.

A benchmark is a standard against which to measure present performance. It is usually undertaken by seeking the best of the competition and understanding the way they produce quality. In manufacturing, benchmarking is a powerful tool in new product development. It involves evaluating any new product against that of the industry leader.

It can be taken a stage further so that not only the product, but also the systems used to produce the product are compared. The essence of benchmarking is about comparing the performance of critical processes against those of leading performers to identify how they achieve their results. Benchmarking is the means of establishing a competitive advantage. It is about finding out who is the best and seeking to better it. Benchmarking provides a means of learning from and doing better than the market leader.

It can considerably speed the development of a new curriculum and assure that quality standards are built in at the planning stage. The point of benchmarking is to ensure that your standards are at least as good if not better than those of your competitors. As such it is a systematic approach to organizational improvement by undertaking the exercise the best practice is sought and new processes are put in place to go beyond the benchmarked performance.

In education there are various simple means of benchmarking which can be carried out as staff development exercises. Teachers can simply visit other institutions in their area and see how things are done. They can discover best practice and ensure that theirs matches it, and then seek to improve on it. The importance of benchmarking is that it saves reinvention. There is almost always someone somewhere who has solved your problem.

The history of benchmarking goes back to the late 1970s, and like many quality technologies it has its origins in manufacturing. The Xerox Corporation is often credited as the first company to use the technique in a systematic manner. It initially involved an in-depth study of what competitors were doing as well as the reverse engineering of competitors' products and technology. This literally involved taking things apart and trying to learn how they were made.

Through such processes companies learnt more about themselves and about the best practices of their competitors. However, the process soon went beyond manufacturing because it became clear that after-sales service, marketing, sales and other functions of the competitors' business could also be benchmarked. In a word, benchmarking moved from an activity undertaken in relative isolation to become a mainstream part of organizational strategy.

Learning from the Best

Benchmarking can be defined as a systematic process for measuring and comparing the performance of one organization against those of others. The goal of benchmarking is to learn the lessons of others and to use them to make improvements in one's own organization. It is therefore a process whereby internal performance is compared to that of other organizations, particularly those with superior levels of performance. The aim is to look for what makes the difference in those higher-performing organizations and to learn their secrets of success.

This has led to the idea of world class, whereby companies model or benchmark themselves against the best global standards of performance. This can apply equally to education as to the manufacturing or the service sector. Too often education does not measure itself in global terms, but the possibilities opened up by information technology make it easy to find information about other institutions adopting best practice models, and finding ways to cooperate with and learn from them.

Benchmarking is an important and useful quality tool not only for continuous improvement but it also provides the necessary comparisons for accountability purposes. However, it is one that should be considered once an organization has taken some steps to improve quality. It is a proven tool for quality improvement and can be of considerable assistance with the process of quality improvement.What benchmarking is not:

- Copying or trying to catch up;
- A panacea or a quick fix;
- Spying or educational espionage;
- Educational tourism;
- A cost reduction exercise.

What benchmarking is:

- About learning from and trying to surpass the best;
- Identifying gaps in performance;
- Closing the gap between present quality and expectation;
- Seeking fresh approaches so that it aids innovation and new thinking.

Benchmarking has close links with knowledge management and with the idea of becoming a learning organization. A well-structured benchmarking exercise is a learning experience for the institution and a means of making the best use of the ideas and knowledge available to that organization.

Internal Benchmarking

Benchmarking does not have to be about comparing yourself with another school or university. Internal benchmarking, comparing and learning from the performance of different departments or subjects, can be an effective exercise, and is often a good place to start. There are no issues of confidentially or problems of accessing sensitive data.

Few organizations systematically study themselves or know much about the practices and processes in other parts of the organization. Exercises such as systematic lesson observations, information-sharing forums and knowledge-sharing communities are all means by which people can learn from each other. It may be that the answer to a problem or the means of achieving what seems like an unrealistic goal lies within the organization.

One interesting method of internal benchmarking can be learnt from knowledge management. This form of internal benchmarking makes use of the learning story. In this technique the story or history of a particular part of the institution is written up, filmed or videotaped in such a way that the salient features of success come to the fore.

In such a technique it is important that the team themselves have an input so that the authentic voice of success is apparent to the listeners and viewers. The learning story is not just a report about actions and results. Its power comes from its ability to convey the reality of the situation and allows the reader to undergo a learning experience from reading it. The learning story can be used as part of a staff development or quality improvement session.

Functional/Competitive Benchmarking

Comparing your institution's performance with other schools, colleges or universities who are competitors can be a very effective means of benchmarking. This is often called functional benchmarking. It provides like-for-like comparisons with other educational institutions and gives a very good idea of your overall institutional performance.

It is important in this exercise to compare against institutions that are leading performers. It is important to be clear what you want to compare in the exercise. Many countries, like the United Kingdom, publish league tables of school examination results and detailed comparisons of university performance indicators. While these can be very useful, there may be a wide range of issues that can be compared, and it is important to be clear about what aspects of performance are being compared.

Functional benchmarking can be of two types: competitive or collaborative. The problem with competitive benchmarking is finding out how the rival does it. Often the key information is difficult or impossible to obtain, and it is important that benchmarking does not become an exercise in spying. As a result, many commentators prefer collaborative benchmarking where the organization being benchmarked actively collaborates in the exercise. This has the advantage of a mutual benefit as any organization has lessons to gain from another.

The Educational Travel Club

To carry out inter-institutional benchmarking it is often useful to visit other schools to see how they do things. Often thought of as a type of educational tourism, it is an important exercise to see how others do things and to learn lessons from them. Of considerable value is being able to visit educational institutions in other countries and to make international comparisons.

This is particularly important if your institution has ambitions to become world class. Good sources of information are conferences and seminars, but much good data on other information can be obtained from official sources, annual reports, inspection reports and from the educational press.

Generic Benchmarking

It is often beneficial to make comparisons with organizations outside of education. This can often be of value in areas such as management systems, teamwork, information technology, human resources management, quality assurance processes, and customer care. Making comparisons with outstanding practice, regardless of the industry, is a very powerful means of quality improvement. This often has the advantage that it is easier to carry out than competitive benchmarking and there is a large two-way benefit to be had from the exercise.

Most organizations are willing to share information providing that the approach is made in a professional manner. It is usually seen as a learning experience and one that can be challenging and purposeful.

How to Set up a Benchmarking Exercise

Once you know whom you want to benchmark against, it is important to have a clear idea of what questions to ask and the performance measures you intend to use when setting up the benchmarking activity. There are a number of fundamental questions that an educational institution should be asking itself when undertaking a benchmarking exercise. These are:

- How good do we want to be?
- Are there standards available that we can benchmark ourselves against?
- How well are we doing in comparison with the best?

Chapter 5

Hotel Service for Overnight Rooms

EASE PRESSURE

What's the first thing that comes to your mind when you think of the word hospitality? Is it a semi-clean home with an open-door policy? Is it a chicken spaghetti casserole on its way out the door for a sick friend? Hospitality can be all of above and none of the above. Often hospitality is confused with perfection. Perfection seeks to impress; hospitality seeks to put another's needs before your own.

The word "hospitable" is derived from the word hospital, which means a charitable institution, a repair shop, a hospice or a shelter. Hospitality provides a shelter for the soul, a healing for the spirit. Ultimately this is what we offer when we open our home in the true spirit of love or when we offer our time, gifts or talents outside of our home to reach others. If hospitality comes down to love and kindness, one of the ways we are kind to ourselves is by doing our best to stay healthy.

If you're like most women, you probably don't sleep enough. You eat the crust off the peanut butter and jelly sandwiches as you feed your kids and run in a frenzy to "keep it together" each day. We have too much to lose by not being our best selves. Be kind to yourself so you have the energy to be kind to others. Keep in mind that home sometimes can be the hardest place to extend hospitable kindnesses.

Often at home, we're tired, overworked and grumpy. When we let our hair down, it has lots of tangles! Our goal is to freely give love and kindness to others, and our starting point is at home. Work together to solve issues, plan together to serve and listen to each other's concerns. Personal care of you+family+friends = the foundation for hospitality. For many of us, our friends are like our extended family. Life without them would just be dull.

We need that connection to ease our soul. A deep heart-to-heart talk with a cherished friend feels as comforting and soothing as a super-soft, oversized sweatshirt on a chilly day. Friends are important. A good friend is one who understands your world, the difficulties and triumphs. Thinking of my favourite friends always makes me smile because of all the love, laughter, tears, prayers and cherished moments.

Hospitality begins with us sharing our hearts. It blossoms by us loving our families and cherishing our friends. The key to accomplishing hospitality is easier than you think: an open door, a cup of coffee and listening ears. Happy hospitality. Often our planned visits revolve around food.

We meet at restaurants, at each other's homes for dinner or at a yogurt shop for a treat. Life loses its richness without the opportunity to live it with friends. Have you scheduled time with friends lately? They offer joy, share the burdens and lighten the load. Patients who travel to Aberdeen Royal Infirmary for an operation the next day, or who need to stay for long-term treatment, will all be able to make use of the facility. NHS Grampian believes the hotel, which will be built in the hospital grounds, will ensure better treatment for those who need it.

Dr Roelf Dijkhuizen, medical director with the health board, said: 'We want a facility where people who make use of hospital services can stay overnight. The most obvious example would be someone who comes from the islands and is waiting for a flight home.

'Another would be a cancer patient who needs treatment that is only available in the hospital over three consecutive days. At the moment, we have to ask them to stay in hospital for those days, but with a hotel we can provide much more convenient and private accommodation at a much lower cost.'

The hotel will be built in partnership with a private contractor. Aberdeen Royal Infirmary is seen as the perfect site for the development because it takes in patients from such a large area. At present, anyone travelling from Orkney and Shetland for a non-urgent operation is put up overnight in a fully staffed ward. Health bosses are growing concerned that this is taking away beds from patients who desperately need treatment. They feel the freeing-up of the beds will ensure better levels of care for patients on the wards.

The facility will operate in the same way as a normal hotel but people using Aberdeen Royal Infirmary services will be put up free of charge. Patients with relatives could also make use of it, as well as visiting health officials. Dr Dijkhuizen added: ' If we invite colleagues from the U.S. to visit for a conference, we don't have to give away all the profit to another hotel. We could put them up here.

'This would be good for the hotel company and good for the NHS if we put the contract together properly.' But Aberdeen MSP Brian Adam is sceptical and has raised his concerns with NHS Grampian. He said: 'I am not sure developing a hotel is the greatest use of NHS land, property or energies. 'I think the fact they are calling it a hotel shows that these days the health service is all about privatising as many services as possible.'

Reported customer tips averaged about half the cash earnings of waiters and waitresses in hotels and motels studied by the Bureau of Labour Statistics during July through September 1983. The survey, covering 23 metropolitan areas, found employer-paid wages making up the balance. In most areas, these wages averaged between $2 and $3 an hour, largely reflecting the tip allowance employers can apply toward meeting the Federal minimum wage of $3.35 an hour.

Customer tips also contributed substantially to the earnings of several other occupational groups. For waiter and waitress assistant, tips commonly averaged 16 to 22 percent of their earnings, 44 to 57 percent for bell persons, 25 to 40 percent for public bartenders, and less than 20 percent for service usually had the highest employer-paid wages, ranging from $3.99 an hour in Dallas – Fort Worth to $10.16 in Las Vegas. Public bartenders, receiving tips to a greater extent than service bartenders, had wages averaging from $3.55 an hour in Miami to $9.83 in San Francisco-Oakland.

Although service bartenders, who prepare drinks for waiters and waitresses to serve, usually averaged more in wages than public bartenders, this pattern was reversed when tips were included in the comparisons. Similar patterns occurred between other occupations, including waiters and waitresses and their assistants. For example, table waiters and waitresses in full-course restaurants averaged less in wages than their assistants in each area surveyed – usually by 30 to 60 percent. When tips were included in the comparisons, waiters and waitresses averaged more – usually by 40 to 70 percent.

Paid holidays, most commonly 6 to 8 days annually, were provided to at least three-fourths of the nonsupervisory, nonoffice workers in each area studied. At least nine-tenths of the workers in each area were also covered by paid vacations, typically 1 week after 1 year of service, 2 weeks after 2 years, and 3 weeks after 10 years. Life, hospitalization, surgical, basic medical, and major medical insurance (for which the employer paid at least part of the cost), were available to three-fourths or more of the workers in nearly all areas. Retirement pension plans were available to a majority of workers in 10 of the 23 areas. Also, food and beverage service workers typically received at least one free meal a day.

The 2,050 establishments within scope of the survey employed a total of 356,000 workers during July through

September 1983. Of this total, nonsupervisory, nonoffice employees represented five-sixths of the work force. Nearly one-half of these workers were concentrated in Las Vegas, Atlantic City, New York, Los Angeles – Long Beach (20,500), and Chicago. Corresponding employment in the remaining 18 areas ranged from about 14,000 in Dallas-Fort Worth, San Francisco – Oakland, and Washington to 1,750 in Buffalo.

Nearly three-fifths each of the food service and other nonoffice workers were employed in hotels and motels with collective bargaining agreements covering a majority of such workers. The proportions, however, varied widely by area. For example, virtually all of the workers in Atlantic City were covered by labour-management agreements, but no establishment visited in Houston or Memphis had union agreements covering a majority of their workers. The Service Employees International Union and the Hotel and Restaurant Employees Union, both AFL – CIO affiliates, were the major unions.

Service Encounter

As the services sector becomes a larger component of our national economy, it becomes increasingly critical that the management of service operations is addressed systematically. One concern is the interaction of service employees and the technology making up the job design. Effectively matching job design and technology leads to effective service encounters, while mismatches cause short-run or long run problems for the organization.

Organizational mismatches between job design and supporting infrastructure, specifically the information technology (IT) selected, can give rise to the use and exercise of judgment and discretion by service encounter employees that from the viewpoint of the organization or the customer is extraordinary, conflicted, or perverse. Perverse judgments debilitate the organization and degrade the quality of the service encounter.

Conflicted and extraordinary, judgments ultimately debilitate the organization and may degrade the quality of the service encounter if some customers should perceive others as having received preferential treatment. This paper explores dynamics in managing operations, technology, and human resources that give rise to the exercise of such judgments with the intent to construct a conceptual framework that will explain such judgments and the behaviours that issue from them.

The importance of the service encounter to a service organization is well documented in the operations management and marketing literature. This encounter is often the only point of contact the customer has with the organization. It is the context in which the organization provides the customer with what is presumably of value.

The customer assesses the value of what the service organization provides on the basis of how adequately it provides explicit and implicit benefits that meet customer needs and expectations. It is thus incumbent upon a service organization to insure that its customer contact personnel are sufficiently supported through appropriate job design, training, and supporting infrastructure that can include an appropriate information technology (IT). This better insures that the organization's customer contact personnel represent it in the best possible way to its customers.

Job design defines the extent to which customer contact personnel must exercise judgment in meeting customer needs. Ideally, the organization's infrastructure is sufficient to support the conformance of job design to customer needs. This paper will explore dynamics in managing operations, technology, and human resources that give rise to the exercise of problematic judgments with the intent to construct a conceptual framework that will explain such judgments and the behaviours that issue from them.

The authors have identified three types of problematic judgments that they label perverse, conflicted, and extraordinary judgments. Perverse judgments debilitate the organization and degrade the quality of the service encounter.

Conflicted and extraordinary judgments ultimately debilitate the organization and may degrade the quality of the service encounter if some customers should perceive others as having received preferential treatment. A conceptual framework that provides an adequate understanding of the dynamics that prompt such judgments being made permits more effective planning of the service encounter, the discovery and analysis of the nature of service quality gaps, and suggests actions that can be taken to close those gaps.

In cases where these judgments occur, remedial actions can be taken that have both operational and strategic implications. Such a framework can benefit both the organization and the customers it serves. This is divided into five parts. This review provides the motivation for critiquing the quality of service encounters as a technology management and subsequent organizational design issue.

This part will touch on the increasingly important role of services in societal economies, the focus on the training of customer contact personnel at the expense of attending to the organizational infrastructure that supports those encounters, and how the introduction of IT into a service organization impacts its infrastructure.

The Role of Services in the Economy

The evolutionary course societal economies appear to follow involves a movement toward increasing organizational complexity. Technological innovations result in increased productivity and diversity in the extractive (including agriculture) and manufacturing sectors of an economy which result in shifts of the labour force into other sectors. This shift is made possible only because of a simultaneous accompanying increase and expanding diversity of business, trade, infrastructure, social/personal, and public administration services.

Without the direct and indirect linkages that exist between the material goods producing sectors and these service sub-sectors, increased productivity and diversity in the goods producing sectors would not be viable. Adequately performing this increasingly complex function has resulted in the percentage of the U.S. workforce allocated to services steadily increasing at a modest exponential rate in this century. Since the 1960's, services have accounted for more than half of that labour force with no indication that the continued growth in this proportion has passed an inflection point.

By 1995, service industries accounted for 75% of GDP and 78% of employment. Therefore, it becomes increasingly important that services be the focus of critical attention for the purpose of evaluating their functional effectiveness and efficiency. If not clone, our understanding of services for this time and the future may prove inadequate.

Eventually, this inadequacy will lead to their practical mismanagement and the degradation of the effectiveness and efficiency required of services to contribute toward the realization of healthy activity of an evolving economy.

Focus on the Service Encounter

Addressing the concerns for service quality and effectiveness has been done in several different ways. The most basic way is to analyze the service encounter, the interaction between the customer and the service delivery or customer contact personnel. Research on service encounters may focus on perceptions of the persons involved in the exchange.

Hartline and Ferrell devised a model that addressed the management of service encounter employees based on the perceptions of the three groups that had previously been studied separately; managers, employees and customers. Their literature review and the literature search this paper's authors conducted inductively suggest that the preponderance of studies exploring service quality and effectiveness have limited themselves to issues related to micromanaging service encounters.

Global Views of Service Quality and Effectiveness Management

In addition to service encounter models, more global views of the management of service performance have been addressed. Bowen and Lawler stress that decisions concerning how to manage service employees should be based on five contingency factors. They state that an organization should consider its basic business strategy, the nature of the relationship to the customer (transactional versus relational), technology (routine versus nonroutine), business environment (predictable versus turbulent), and types of managers and employees. Thus, management of services is based on a set of variables that constitute settings in which service encounter perceptions are formed. Singh and Deshmukh advocate the application of Total Quality Management (TQM) principles to the management of services.

They stress that TQM is a systems approach to organizations in which every element interacts with every other element. Like Bowen and Lawler, they argue that service quality is not simply a function of what the manager wants the employee to do, or what the customer perceives, or how well trained the employee is. The success of a service organization is predicated more on the interaction of many its aspects. One systems approach to achieving service quality and effectiveness is found in Hauser's and Clausing's "house of quality." Applying the "house of quality" to the service encounter, Fitzsimmons and Fitzsimmons show how marketing, design, engineering and manufacturing (delivery) must be coordinated in order to actually meet the customer's desires.

A global or systemic view is critical in managing an organization's adoption of a technology, particularly when that adoption directly involves the organization's operations. The manufacturing management literature of the 1980's and early 1990's, for example, is replete with discussions that advocate this perspective. This is so because its contributors found that the repercussions of introducing a new technology into a manufacturing concern ran through virtually every aspect of that concern's organizational structure.

They further found that unless that concern accommodated the adoption of its new technology by reorganizing itself so as to effectively exploit its new technology's capabilities, the end result was far more likely to be counterproductive and deleterious than beneficial.

Both Sciulli and Rodger and Paper argue that what has been said about manufacturing organizations and their adoption of new technologies holds true for service organizations as well, and their adoption of IT, in particular in both the banking and healthcare industries.

Their argument is in part supported by the work of a committee of the National Academy of Sciences that identified a phenomenon that it labeled the "information technology paradox." This paradox refers to the lagging growth in service sector productivity when compared to the growth in investments in service sector IT. The committee provided a list of several explanations for this paradox. At the top of its list was the mismanaged employment of information technology. This pursues research of the sort anticipated in the efforts of those cited in the previous paragraph.

It does not however, discount the importance of the service encounter, that is, the interaction between customers and customer contact personnel. Rather, it regards successful service encounters as resulting from a coordinated convergence of organizational factors; customer contact personnel training, job design, the reward/punishment system, empowerment, and the manner in which IT is integrated with the rest of these factors forming an organizational infrastructure supporting those encounters.

By rigorously analyzing service operations and the encounters they produce as a function of the effectiveness with which technology and its adoption are managed, it may be possible to discover a basis for identifying types of service failures resulting from infrastructure design flaws integrating IT.

Business Strategy

Organizational strategy begins wish the organization's mission statement that identifies what service the organization provides. This implies an interaction between the target market segment and the service provided and an interaction between technology and personnel employed to produce and deliver the service and how the service package is designed.

The design of a job consists of what customer encounter personnel are expected to do based upon their skills and qualifications and organizational constraints. These expectations cannot, however, be divorced from the technology through which customer encounter personnel act.

A service is produced as a response to an existing market that it can opportunistically enter, as an instrument that calls new kinds of markets into being, or as a combination of both. The Internet auction company, eBay, is a recent example of such a combination. On-line auctioning existed prior to eBay's appearance.

However, eBay took on-line auctioning several steps beyond what already existed to an interactive environment and redefined customer expectations. As a result, eBay has virtually monopolized the on-line auctions industry and has dramatically expanded the industry's market in which it is the dominant player, attracting new customers while holding its old ones.

The nature of services is such that their production and consumption is simultaneous. Consequently, the production and delivery of a service constitute its encounter with the customer whose expectations are standards against which the efficacy of the service is evaluated. How the production and delivery of the service are designed into the service package is therefore, critical. The technology selected for the service package plays a part in that design. On the one hand, the service package is first designed to which a suitable and available technology is then attached.

Such is the case, for example, with fast foods where IT systems are employed to open transactions and communicate customer orders to the back room. IT may be employed in the back room to monitor operations and bring the transactions to a close. On the other hand, technology may restrict how decision makers would like to design their service packages or it can open up the design of a package so as to include heretofore infeasible possibilities by which competitive advantages can be pursued. Such is the case, for example, in tele radiology. Recent developments in IT (particularly compression and transmission technology) and standardization in the way imaging equipment generates its images has made it technologically possible to physically decouple radiologists from the images they must read.

As a result, access to radiological services has become decidedly more timely and widespread for potential customers (especially those in remote locales) than heretofore thought possible. Such developments have created opportunities to redesign the initial service package and revise customer expectations by reinforcing initial diagnoses with second and third opinions and exploiting subspecialization skills while at the same time, reducing the turn-around time to patient (customer) consultation.

Service Package Design

The widely accepted means of categorizing service organizations is through the use of typologies. One of the most widely used typologies is Lovelock's (1983) that strategically profiles a service package. Of particular interest to the authors of this Study is Lovelock's typology that juxtaposes customization of services with [+ or -] exercise of judgement and discretion by customer contact personnel in meeting individual customer needs.

A barber, for example, is expected to provide the customer more customized services than a home pest exterminator who has a finite set of programme modules from which to select and much less judgment to exercise. Like the barber, an attorney also performs a customized service but the attorney must use and exercise judgement and discretion that exceeds the judgment and discretion a barber uses and exercises and certainly exceeds the judgment and discretion the home pest exterminator must use and exercise.

It is expected that similar services will position themselves similarly in Lovelock's typologies. Technological innovations in service production and delivery can, however, lead to typological repositionings of a service operation and a consequent revision and redesign of its profile and service package. One must assume that such redesign of the service package is done to derive some competitive advantage or at least prevent the service operation from being competitively disadvantaged. The various technologies an organization chooses to employ therefore interact with all the typologies that strategically profile it and contribute to the design of the organization's service package.

The specific interaction between the employment of IT and the extent to which customer contact personnel are empowered or not empowered to use and exercise judgment and discretion to meet customer needs during the service encounter is this study's object of analysis. Working down the main diagonal of Lovelock's typology of customization and discretion, the more standardized the service, the less use and exercise of judgement and discretion by customer contact personnel is necessary. The more customized the service, the more use and exercise of judgement and discretion by customer contact personnel is necessary.

In most cases customer contact personnel are the sole points of contact customers have with an organization providing them the service they seek. Their evaluations of it and decisions about future patronization of it are largely determined by how customer contact personnel manage to present the organization during service encounters.

Thus, how the judgment and discretion customer contact personnel are empowered or not empowered to use and exercise and the IT they employ interact in the design of the service encounter can be decisive if the organization is to attract and hold its customers.

The extent of judgment and discretion customer contact personnel are expected to use and exercise understandably varies from service to service. However, what about situations that do not precisely conform to a given service for which the technology has been designed? Judgment and discretion used and exercised by customer contact personnel in such situations is important for at least two reasons. First, decisions including judgment and discretion or the lack of them may affirm or contradict organizational objective or policies.

Furthermore, unacceptable decisions issuing there from will result in positive or negative encounters from the customer's viewpoint. These decisions may be particularly important in achieving a service recovery when a service failure has occurred or is imminent. A service operation employs IT in order to increase and improve service efficiency and effectiveness in a way that is consistent with its competitive strategy.

Fitzsimmons suggests that IT accomplishes this by creating another entry barrier, generating revenue, creating a database upon which empirically based decisions can be made, and enhancing productivity. Customer contact personnel draw on and contribute to such a resource when they access IT to support their service encounter activity. Their access to the IT system can, however, vary. They may be restricted with respect to the range of information they can browse.

They may also be restricted with the respect to the range of information they can input. Fast food customer contact personnel can browse virtually no range of information and the range of information they input into the system is restricted to the orders they take. Their job can be characterized as being almost completely circumscribed by the technology associated with their job. A customer wants, for example, a taco with allowable modifications.

A predetermined closed set of intermediate steps is synchronic with the outcome. The employee merely selects predetermined and technologically constrained choices, as one would push a stop or start button on a machine. Airline ticket counter personnel must, on the other hand, be able to browse routings, schedules, and ticket information for the entire industry in order to input the orders they take.

The outcome of the order (a customer being at point B after having been at point A) is something separate from the subset of intermediate steps that achieve it (getting to point B from point A). Airline ticket counter personnel must create that subset (construct a routing). They use IT to expedite the construction and creation of that subset. The IT they employ does not therefore, so nearly circumscribe their jobs as with the fast food order taker.

Job design for service employees has been categorized as a "production line" approach or an "empowerment" approach. The production line approach, as its name implies, is based on a Tayloristic view. It is based on four tenets – simple tasks, clear division of labour, substitution of equipment and systems for employees, and little decision-making discretion of employees. This design seeks to gain customer satisfaction through efficiency, consistency, and low costs.

The empowerment approach, on the other hand, allows employees to make decisions that in the production orientation would be reserved for higher-level management. In such settings, jobs are less simple and more broadly defined and employees are given more latitude. In order for employees in such a design to be effective, they must have access to needed information, knowledge about how to use the information, and sufficient power to meet customer requests during the service encounter.

The production line approach gains its low costs through consistency, which can be translated into lack of personal service. This means that as the service encounter is standardized, the choice of actions possible by the service provider is limited. Attempts to provide personalized service in such a setting would drive up costs and violate the competitive advantage of the firm. In addition, while the customer receiving the personal service may be more satisfied, other customers who are receiving slower service because of it may be disgruntled.

The empowerment design is slower, less efficient and more expensive to operate. It requires careful selection and extensive training of employees. This design could put a firm at a competitive disadvantage from a cost standpoint servicing encounters of a routine form. Companies must clearly define their business strategy and know the environment and the customer base they pursue in making a decision concerning job design for their employees.

Interaction of Job Design and Information Technology

It is imperative with the production line job design that IT is installed as a part of that design so as to facilitate matching it to the service encounters anticipated. The number and nature of the options from which the employee chooses should then be limited to matching the constraints on their decision-making authority. Any access to additional information would not only be of no use; it would actually deter efficiency.

For example, if all hamburgers are prepared to the same degree of doneness, giving a customer encounter person the option of asking a customer how he/she would like the meat cooked would slow down the process. In fast food, cash registers (which also communicate orders to the backroom) prompt order-takers through the decisions that are allowable.

Thus, the more standardized the service the more easily circumscribed technologically it can be because the reality of the encounter is simple and presumed to be more easily captured than encounters in which provided services are customized and the outcome of any one such encounter is variable. The more circumscribed technologically the service is, the more efficiently the service can be performed but the more dependent upon the circumscribing technology customer encounter service personnel become.

In the case of the empowerment job design, use of judgment and exercise of discretion on the part of employees demands access to information. If the employee is to provide personalized service, the IT system must provide access to information concerning options and their availability. Thus, if the service can be customized and the service provider has discretion, the information must be provided to enable that discretion to be used.

This means that the less standardized the service the less easily circumscribed technologically it can be because the reality of the encounter is too complex and varied in individual outcomes to be easily captured. This does not mean however, that these customer contact personnel are any less dependent upon the technology that less extensively circumscribes their job than their counterparts who provide standardized services. Rather, their dependence is different. They cannot effectively use and exercise judgment and discretion that, by definition, are parts of their job without IT.

A Typology of Service Organizational Mismatches

One may assume that for any given range of actions provided to customer contact personnel, protocols exist that prohibit, obligate, and permit selections of alternatives that depend on the encounter circumstances. Within this normative framework, the exercise and use of judgment and discretion can be extensive or limited to the point of being virtually nonexistent.

Where their use and exercise are extensive, it is to presumably match and conform the job to the needs and expectations of specific customers. Where their use and exercise are virtually nonexistent, the job as it is designed and its supporting organizational infrastructure are presumably adequate to also match and conform the job to the needs and expectations of specific customers.

Organizational mismatches, therefore, arise between the job design and its supporting organizational infrastructure when customer contact personnel are confronted with a service demand that cannot be met without their being at odds with how they are to do their job and/or with the goals and objectives of the organization.

This section provides a typology of such mismatches based on job design and IT as the significant infrastructural component of interest providing the contexts in which judgement and discretion are used and exercised. Violations of the job design can occur in a number of ways. First of all, do customer contact personnel follow courses of action that fall outside what the technology circumscribes for them? Examples of such behaviour are abundant.

One can imagine an employee breaking open a cash register to make change for a customer because there is no sale with which to ring it open or no access to a key with which to unlock it. One can also imagine a situation where a hotel guest is permitted to take a free muffin from the breakfast line because the cash register is not programmed with a "muffin" key.

As job violations go, breaking open a cash register to make change is certainly more extreme than giving away muffins. Both cases, however, suggest that the customer contact job as it is technologically circumscribed may be inadequately designed to satisfactorily address every encounter for providing service that might come its way.

Such design inadequacies typify mismatches. Such mismatches could lead to service failures that in some cases only the extraordinary use and exercise of judgment and discretion can repair. Thus, the exercise of extraordinary judgment is a legitimate topic to examine.

The job design/service package is totally circumscribed, consisting of other organizational inputs including customer encounter personnel who have no leeway whatsoever using or exercising judgement and discretion in their conduct of the service encounter. As long as these encounters are routine, i.e., match the job's design, encounters are successful and customers are satisfied. Non-routine encounters, on the other hand, do not match the job design.

From the viewpoint of the organization, such an encounter is a non-event. It is certainly not a success but neither is it a failure, for the organization has not defined the customer's need as something the job was designed to satisfy. From the viewpoint of the customer seeking satisfaction, however, it is hard to argue that the encounter can be anything but a failure. The customer encounter personnel may, however, be able to satisfy a non-routine need and achieve a service encounter success attended by a mix of other results, but they must do so by abandoning altogether the use of the technology that is a fundamental functional part of their job's design.

Violations can occur within the job as designed and technologically circumscribed. These violations involve judgments that disregard organizational protocols and lead to particular technologically-doable ends that the technology installed is not intended to support. Such judgments may be conflicted or perverse.

The exercise of judgments that are conflicted may result in a service encounter success in the view of the customer and probably the customer encounter service person as well. Take for example, a customer who wishes to make a last minute change to his/her discount fare airline ticket at an airport airline ticket-counter. Penalties for making such changes are part of the terms to which the customer agrees when he/she purchases such a ticket.

Yet, the customer encounter service personnel at airline counters in airports rarely assess such penalties. Not only will they change flights for discounted tickets, they will even change airlines. They are perfectly capable of assessing such penalties, taking money, even making change. They have the IT available to do it, but they rarely do despite the fact that airline management directs them to the contrary.

Apparently, such personnel are empowered to exercise a great deal of individual judgment and discretion in such matters as they weigh such issues as customer flow, acceptable aircraft load factors, and customer goodwill. The authors regard conflicted judgments as being made in situations where the customers can be better served even though providing such service could prove detrimental to the service organization.

The job design/service package consists of a partially circumscribing IT and other organizational inputs including customer encounter personnel who have substantial leeway in terms of the judgement and discretion they can use and exercise in their conduct of the service encounter. Given that non-routine/custom service encounters are within the realm of possibility, success certainly occurs when customer contact personnel use and exercise judgement and discretion only insofar as they choose to strictly adhere to organizational guidelines and policies.

Thus an airline customer contact person could change a customer's discount ticket and assess the prescribed penalty and neither party would have any reason to regard such an encounter as anything but successful, for the desired change was made and the customer was assessed only the agreed-upon change fee. Such customer contact personnel can, however, use and exercise their judgement and discretion and not adhere to policies by choosing not to assess a customer a penalty for changing a discount ticket.

This also results in a successful service encounter from the point of view of the customer. It is, however, one that is lavish compared to assessing the customer a penalty for making the change. Furthermore, such a choice on the part of the customer contact person does not involve abandoning: the technology that is a part of his/her job design but putting it to use. The exercise of perverse judgments and the behaviours that ensue are often motivated by a perceived need on the part of various employees to "beat the system" and almost invariably jeopardize the success of the service encounter and well being of the service organization as well.

A study the authors did of a well-known fast-food service franchise, referred to as Flex-Mex, serves as an example. Flex-Mex's market qualifiers were a number of competitive priorities, "mass customization" of its product and speed of service. Its employment of IT contributed to a great extent in making this possible.

Flex-Mex's cash register(s) transmitted orders through a computer to display screens located in its back room where ingredients were assembled into menu items and orders filled. The assembly employee who completes the last step in filling the order removes it from the display screen. The screen then displays the next order in the queue.

Screens may hold many orders at a time and rarely do they become overloaded. This is due in part to screen capacity and in part due to the fact that an order can be "bumped" (erased from the screen) at anytime. Assembly personnel, therefore, do not necessarily need to wait until a customer physically receives his/her order to remove that order from the screen.

IT, however, performed more than an order communication function for Flex-Mex. It was used to monitor order delivery speed performance and foodstuffs wastage. Crews were rewarded for above-standard performance with half-price menu items for their meals and were denied half-price menu items for their meals and/or penalized individually with demotions or dismissal for sub-standard performance. As a result of this additional set of functions IT performed, assembly personnel would often "bump" an order before it was filled because that would stop the timer on that particular order.

Thus, assembly personnel were able to insure that no one order ever took an excessive amount of time quite independent of whether a customer had to wait an excessive amount of time for his/her order. Such a practice also resulted in misfilled orders since employees often carried as many as five different orders in their short-term memory. Several other downside phenomena accompanied these service failures. First, the correct order had to be refilled.

This took additional time but IT was not timing this activity. Second, the shelf life of these menu items is very short once prepared, less than five minutes in most cases. Thus, a certain amount of foodstuffs had to be scrapped if no new customer came along shortly ordering the same item. The assembly crew could only compensate for this waste by shorting other orders by small amounts of the ingredients.

The job design/service package consists of a partially circumscribing IT and other organizational inputs including customer encounter-personnel who have no leeway whatsoever in terms of the judgement and discretion they can use or exercise in the conduct of the service encounter. What is noteworthy is that it is not an encounter with a customer that elicits a perverse use of the technology of which the job design is in part constituted, but the encounter with limited measures of employee performance upon which a system of rewards and punishments is based. The encounter with the customer is irrelevant.

Analysis of these cases can establish the utility of a conceptual framework to explain the use of judgment by customer contact service personnel when acting within the technology paired to their jobs. Thus, what would otherwise be anecdotal information can be processed into knowledge about the management of operations, technology, and human resources. Such knowledge will permit decisions to be made as to the extent to which customer contact service personnel should use judgment and exercise discretion to the benefit of both the customer and the servicing organization.

The first case involves two examples in the use of extraordinary judgment. One is the example of breaking open the cash register to give a customer change. The other is the hostess who gives away breakfast muffins. Both examples suggest that the involved customer contact personnel are committed to effectively serving the customer. Both, however, constitute organizational mismatches that derail the organization's pursuit of its goals.

The circumscribing technology has not adequately comprehended all the different kinds of service encounters involving customer needs. Given that service operations management does not recognize needing change or wanting only a muffin as legitimate customer needs, the protocols in place are not adequately conceived. The ends of the organization and the ends of its customer contact personnel are at odds because the technology as employed by the organization is divisive.

Given the conceptual framework the authors have constructed several alternative courses of action that can be proposed. There may be very good reasons why customer contact service personnel are not allowed to make change. If management wishes to continue that restriction, the protocols must be very clear that customer contact service personnel are not so empowered.

If the failure to make change results in needless loss of goodwill, the most obvious alternative course of action would be to give the operator the cash register access key. Such a change in policy would invariably require additional protocols as to whom change can be given and when it can be given, thus empowering the register operator to use his/her judgment and exercise discretion in applying those protocols.

Concerning the muffin give-away example, the most obvious failure is that the technology inadequately captured the range of service encounters.

This failure should be easy to rectify by merely programming the register with alternatives to selling just the buffet. This would further circumscribe the register operator's job and remove the need for extraordinary judgments from time to time. Given that part of the hotel's breakfast line consists so often of a breakfast buffet, there may be little incentive to go to that kind of trouble since little control would be exercised over breakfast buffet customers as to how many muffins they might take in the first place.

Be that as it may, over time, the practice of muffin give-away could prove costly and, while the cost of operating a breakfast buffet line is partially subsidized by hotel registrations, there is little reason to carelessly add to its cost.

Despite upper management level directives urging airline ticket counter personnel to assess penalties more frequently, they continue to use and exercise their judgment and discretion in this matter and assess them much less frequently than upper management would prefer. They do this without fear of sanctions. This is a case of conflicted judgments and could of course be resolved by technologically circumscribing the process by which those changes are made.

It would be an easy matter to programme for such changes so that the change could not be finalized until the penalty was assessed for the change. This would take the control of assessing such penalties out of the hands of the airline ticket counter personnel. Such programming has not however, been done. The reasons for not doing such programming could be several, the most likely one being that airline ticket counter personnel have as a primary task facilitating the movement of traffic through the terminal.

Anything contributing to impeding that movement must be regarded as undesirable and costly. Airline ticket counter personnel are, therefore, left to use judgment and exercise discretion in such matters since assessing penalties could prove time consuming. On the other hand, changing discounted tickets disrupts the yield management schemes designed to optimize flight revenues.

Changing discount tickets involves a cost for which airlines can make a compelling argument. Penalties are assessed to offset this loss. This conflict between what is practiced and the protocols in place suggests that from the standpoint of the conceptual framework the airline ticket counter personnel have not been sufficiently empowered.

They certainly have been sufficiently empowered in terms of their use and exercise of judgment and discretion. They have not, however, been sufficiently empowered to have a say in how the protocols are devised and applied. The higher levels of airline management would do well to so empower them. Working together on equal footing, both parties might be able to agree on protocols that would garner more revenue through penalties that would offset the organization's yield management shortfalls while keeping the traffic moving at an acceptable rate.

The case of Flex-Mex provides a true-life example of the judgments service personnel (in the case, back room personnel) make that are perverse. Unlike extraordinary and conflicted judgments that work for the most part to the benefit of the customer but are potentially debilitating to the service organization, perverse judgments are debilitating to the service organization including the quality of the customer service it provides. The conceptual framework the authors have constructed provides a basis for identifying the factors that contributed to the Flex-Mex mismatch and proposing alternative courses of action to remedy it.

First, the extent to which technology circumscribed the jobs of the Flex-Mex employees, particularly those in the back room, was not extensive enough. This resulted in Flex-Mex's reward/punishment system and its performance measurement method that were intended to motivate high performance actually leading to the contrary.

In addition, Flex-Mex's employees were not sufficiently empowered for management to be receptive to their observations concerning their dysfunctional work setting or suggestions they might submit as to how that work setting could be made more functional. Thus alienated, they acted in a way to protect their individual interest that put them at odds with some of the organization's goals and objectives.

The conceptual framework constructed suggests several alternative courses of action Flex-Mex could pursue to remedy this mismatch. First, it could extend the application of its IT to more completely circumscribe the tasks of its employees. This could include timing an order from when it is placed with the order taker to when it is placed on the customer pick-up portion of the front counter and not electronically permit back room employees to "bump" orders from their screens.

The IT system could also be reengineered to account for redoing misfilled orders. Such changes in IT's application would certainly restrict the extent to which employees could make perverse judgments. It would also, however, undoubtedly further intensify the hostility of the work environment and could lead to other undesirable results.

Flex-Mex could also consider empowering its employees in ways that could possibly even dispense with any need to reengineer its IT system. Revising the incentive and performance measurement systems would be a start. Tying their rewards to the success of both their local operation and the organization at large might do better at gaining the loyalty and dedication of Flex-Mex's customer service personnel than providing them half-price menu items.

This would be especially so if these personnel had some say as to what those rewards would be and how their performance should be measured. This does not necessarily mean that the use of judgment and the exercise of discretion in doing their jobs would be increased. These jobs require the use and exercise of little judgment and discretion. Rather, it would mean that Flex-Mex's customer contact service personnel had a stake in how well Flex-Mex does.

This paper has provided a conceptual framework for exploring the dynamics that arise in managing the integration of operations, technology (primarily IT), and human resources. It has focused on how mismatched combinations of operations, technology, and human resources impact the use and exercise of judgment and discretion by customer contact service personnel and how these organizational anomalies can be eliminated.

The few examples presented in this paper hardly provide sufficient data to empirically validate this framework and the kinds of organizational mismatches it identifies. Furthermore, the off-diagonal categories have not been addressed.

Therefore, further work empirically validating and perfecting this framework or developing one to more accurately categorize types of service organizations in order to better isolate types of intra-organizational mismatches is in order.

Beyond that is the issue of determining from among a set of alternative courses of action the framework specifies which alternative is the most appropriate to pursue in eliminating organizational mismatches.

Thus, it will be necessary to identify, select, and develop measures as well as techniques to process these measures to rigorously determine the appropriate alternative course of action.

This programme of applied research is both fruitful and valuable inasmuch as it addresses potential service operations ineffectiveness and inefficiency resulting from failures integrating technology and human resources and could contribute to sorting out the factors that have resulted in the "information technology paradox."

1. This empirical observation, the Clark-Fisher hypothesis, explains employment shifts toward sectors of lower productivity.
2. According to Cook, Gho, and Chung (1988), researchers have developed different typologies to answer specific questions w a pragmatic consideration. Therefore, the authors believe that they have sufficient warrant to employ one of Lovelock's typologies because of its implicit usefulness to the question at hand.
3. A competitive advantage can be achieved by providing a low-cost speedy standardized service to a large market segment with similar needs or by providing customized service to a segment whose needs are dissimilar. In the first case customizing services would be inefficient, strategically contradictory, and possibly annoy customers delayed by the preferential treatment they perceive others receiving. In the latter case, such customization would be strategically necessary because it would be what was expected.
4. A totally circumscribed job design is one in which every organizationally sanctioned course of action

customer encounter personnel can take as a part of their job is executed through the IT system.

5. The extent to which a particular service is technologically circumscribed, if at all, depends of course on factors other than the mere fact that it can be done. Certainly the benefits gained and the costs incurred to so circumscribe a set of tasks are major considerations.
6. From conversations with Delta, USAir, and TWA airport ticket/check-in counter personnel.

Chapter 6

Sustainable Competitive Advantage

ON BEING SERVICE ORIENTED

The core of any product is essentially a commodity. Competitive advantage comes from services as product enhancements made to the core. To compete on service, firms need to understand the opportunities and challenges presented by the special nature of services. Sustainable competitive advantage comes from an ability of the firm to compete through service.

A bewildering array of terms and confusing acronyms make it nearly impossible to remain abreast of the information technology (IT) industry. Just as things settled down after the dot.com-era, along came Service-Oriented Architecture - more commonly known as SOA. The important question is "does SOA have the potential to significantly and positively affect hospitality industry IT?" The answer is a resounding "yes."

There is no universally accepted definition of SOA, but as the term implies, it is not a particular technology, but rather a structural design used to build and implement a technology solution. SOA is the technology architecture that adheres to the principles of service-orientation. When realized through the Web-services technology platform, SOA establishes the potential to support and promote these principles throughout the business processes and automation domains of an enterprise. SOA is particularly relevant to the hospitality industry because it was conceived to address precisely the types of challenges the industry faces.

The hospitality industry is dependent upon mature and relatively expensive core central reservation, global distribution and property management systems. Similar to trying to widen a major roadway during rush-hour traffic, constant and everyday usage makes modernizing these mission-critical systems expensive and risky. In addition, the industry is legendary with regard to the sheer volume of proprietary interfaces needed to connect small point solutions built on disparate and non-interoperable platforms.

Lastly, the hospitality industry is in a constant state of flux. This natural dynamism is being exacerbated by the rapid growth of e-commerce, strategic M&A, distribution channel optimization and a host of other factors – all of which place a growing importance on organizational agility.

SOA addresses the above and other industry challenges by delivering a number of tangible and quantifiable business benefits, including among others:

- **Agility** – SOA produces loosely coupled applications based on a standardized way of orchestrating the interaction among the largely separate presentation, business, application and database layers of an application. This attribute enables the rapid creation of highly functional and flexible composite applications based on the dynamic combination of unique Web services that will run in virtually any IT infrastructure.
- **Reusability/Speed to Market** – SOA promotes the use of encapsulated Web services that can be reused in a variety of separate applications. The ability to assemble new applications from standardized, reusable components can dramatically decrease development costs and increase the speed to market.
- **Vendor Diversity** – The fully encapsulated nature of SOA-designed Web services allows them to run in virtually any environment, giving companies the option of migrating to a cheaper platform and

changing their terms of trade by reducing their dependency on any single technology vendor.

- **Business Involvement/IT Alignment** – SOA requires the active involvement of business as it is based largely on combinations of the company's business processes. This not only enables a much tighter alignment between business and IT but over time allows business to take greater control over applications' functionality.
- **Accurate Metrics/ROI** – SOA enables new cost recovery and allocation models because its very nature requires the monitored usage of individual Web services. This allows companies to calculate and monitor ROI more precisely and constantly improve the effectiveness of their business processes.
- **Legacy Modernization** – SOA enables interoperability between disparate applications and platform. As such, it allows for the graceful modernization or retirement of often expensive legacy systems through the controlled and cost efficient extraction of selected functionality - "truly fixing the airplane while in flight."
- **Application Integration** – Point-to-point integration is notoriously complex, time-consuming and risky - all of which contribute to high costs. SOA provides for "build once and run anywhere" interoperable applications that reduce costs by eliminating the need for point-to-point integrations.

Of course, these benefits do not come without a price - primarily from the increased overhead associated with the planning, design and ongoing operation of a potentially more complex IT architecture. In addition, depending on the implementation strategy, this overhead tends to be incurred at the outset of the transformation project, as much care must be taken in not only the design of the individual Web services, but also in mapping out the business processes, business rules and the various layers of the SOA.

This requires the extensive involvement of the business and a good understanding of SOA principles and technologies. A successful implementation of SOA will likely be a multiyear effort that will require a secure, committed and predictable funding and more hands-on IT governance structure. Organizations should build a strategy and business case before embarking on an SOA-enabled transformation journey.

Recall that the very nature of SOA promotes the "reuse" and "platform independence," thereby reducing the need for each company to reinvent the wheel. And, because so much rides on the initial planning and design, many companies seek the assistance of an experienced outside IT services providers to help them accomplish this.

Others have also opted to further reduce cost, complexity and time-to-market by leveraging the existing SOA infrastructure of an outside company. Lastly, given the obvious criticality of such an infrastructure, companies must choose their partners very carefully.

A common misconception is to view services as being synonymous with customer service. "Services" are not limited to customer service. Customer service is only one of the services that enhance products. Managers who are product focused and not customer focused usually see services as meaning customer service. They see service as something that is done when a product fails or invoked to prevent it from failing. Others who see service as "freebies" that you toss in with the product are probably sales focused. Firms with such a product or sales orientation actually do a disservice to the customer in the name of service.

Their tendency is to offer a refund or return policy, which is often enough structured to favour the firm rather than the customer. These firms may offer a customer service toll-free telephone number, which is usually set up to be a frustrating encounter for the customer service personnel as well as the customer who may have been calling in for retribution. Such is often the unfortunate consequence in firms that are not customer focused. In customer-focused firms, customer service is not just an add-on, a little something extra to keep the customer happy. Customer service is an integral part of the total product.

Service is not what you do to the product, it is what you do for the customer. The customer-focused firm looks at the core product as an incomplete solution for customers. These firms supplement the core product with services that help customize or otherwise enhance solutions for customers. Such product enhancements add value for the customer.

The Aramark employee being on location at Sears adds value to the core product of catering for Sears. It allows Aramark to be more customer focused by obtaining first-hand customer information and being able to deliver on it. By being on hand, Aramark can be immediately aware and responsive to the customers' needs. Service-based product enhancements are an imperative for the customer-focused firm.

This chapter establishes the frame of mind required for the customer-focused firm to be service oriented. You will see what the inherent characteristics of services are, and thus the challenges and opportunities you need to recognize when you incorporate services into the value you create and deliver to the customer.

The Service Orientation Imperative

The traditional view of services is to treat products dichotomously, in two categories – either services or (physical) goods. Sometimes the term product is even used interchangeably with packaged goods but not with service. Not only has this usage caused unnecessary confusion, but it has also encouraged the flawed approach that services and packaged goods are separate and mutually exclusive entities. Scholars have gone as far as to suggest that "most product manufacturers and service providers alike are largely service operations."

They asserted that the role of services is critical for any organization in providing value in the form of "technological improvements, styling features, product image, and other attributes that only services can create." The fact is that all products come with some services. As a matter of degree some products have more services than others and are therefore more intangible than others.

Picture a continuum ranging from products that are most tangible (and least intangible in proportion) at one extreme to products that are most intangible (and least tangible in proportion) at the other extreme. At one end of the continuum, services such as education, consulting, and financial services have very few physical goods that customers take title to. At the other end, packaged goods such as a bar of soap or table salt come with no apparent service unless, for example, the customer initiates a customer service phone call.

In the middle of the continuum are products such as fast food restaurants and custom-made clothing that have an almost equal proportion, with no real predominance of tangibles or intangibles. In products that are predominantly intangible, where the customers don't take title to anything physical, such as in banking services, the service provider might use tangibles such as documentation, statements, and billing. The value for the customer is in the information contained in them.

As a proportion of what the customer is getting in the total product, the predominant source of customer value is from the intangibles in the total product. For physical goods, services enhance the core product and provide opportunities for competitive advantage. Thus, any product has some proportion of services attached to it, and this part of the product has a special nature that needs to be handled differently. If all firms provide some proportion of service components as part of the total product, it behooves them to have an understanding of the nature of services.

Only with such an understanding can we truly get into the service-orientation frame of mind. Take for example, the table salt manufacturer, Morton's. For this firm to look at itself as a packaged goods firm and therefore not concerned with services is a mistake.

The fact that Morton's makes the product available at the retail store through the appropriate distribution channels is a service to the customer. Morton's has essentially outsourced its distribution and retailing to channel intermediaries. To be truly customer focused, Morton's needs to view all the value-added it provides the customer, over and above the product of the production process – the salt – as services it provides to the customer. Morton's cannot manage its service components in the same way that it manages the production of its table salt.

Most B2B manufacturing firms intuitively recognize the importance of the service component in enhancing its product. Caterpillar, the earth-moving equipment manufacturer, recognizes that prompt and reliable service is critical to its success and organizes the whole firm around customer locations. You need a service orientation to see such product enhancements as service dimensions that add value to the core product. Service orientation is

- A philosophy or frame of mind reflected in the firm's culture,
- An attitude to serve the customer reflected in the firm's treatment of its customers, and
- A view of services as necessary enhancements to any core product to make a complete solution.

To provide complete and competitive solutions to the customer, one needs to understand and adopt the service orientation. The service-oriented frame of mind requires a grasp of the fundamental nature of services (whether as the product or a component of a product). Once the inherent characteristics of services are clear, it becomes apparent that their implications for the customer and the provider offer a number of opportunities and pose a variety of challenges.

As a preface to a discussion of these issues, it would be useful to note the evolution of interest in the concept of service.

Prompted by the frustrations of practitioners in the service sector who were finding that marketing practices from the packaged goods world did not make sense for services, scholars began to get interested in the problem. In the late 1970s and early 1980s, for a number of reasons, the academic research community in business disciplines, particularly in marketing, operations, and human resources, began a serious intellectual debate as to whether products that were services, compared to products that were packaged goods, needed to be studied differently.

For example, could you study the marketing of hospitality services the same way as you would the marketing of toothpaste? Some scholars maintained that marketing is marketing regardless of what you are marketing. Either way, they argued, one had to go through the tasks of segmenting the market, positioning a product, and making product, pricing, distribution, or promotion decisions.

Others argued that although that might be true, one would need to approach these tasks very differently; and they proceeded to offer the rationale for this argument. There was a great deal of interest in this effort, especially among those who recognized the tremendous growth of the services sector.

Around the same time there were environmental changes in the economy and in the competitive landscape. Services sectors such as airlines, telecommunications, and, later, banking and insurance were going through deregulation in the United States. Manufacturing was moving to cheaper labour markets in the Far East and in Latin America. Meanwhile, by the late 1980s in the United States, even professional services such as health care and legal services began to recognize the need to employ marketing practices.

Not surprisingly, even manufacturing firms were being forced to add service components to their product offerings. As these changes occurred and services were being established as an integral aspect of doing business, the United States had become a service economy. Ultimately, the debate over whether services were really different from physical products produced the rationale that the skeptics demanded. The evidence and essence of this argument epitomizes the service orientation.

Characteristics of all Services

There are certain fundamental characteristics that are inherent in all service products and in the service components of any product. Let us begin by defining service as a deed, performance, or action. Thus, by definition, services are intangible. The product that is a service or that component of the product that is a service cannot be seen, touched, or felt. As a deed, performance or action, a service is consumed as it is produced, such that the acts of production and consumption are inseparable. Thus, services are also perishable, in that they cannot be inventoried or produced and stored for later use.

Nor can they be produced without some level of customer interaction. Since services are produced and consumed in real time, they are inherently variable – from customer to customer, from provider to provider, and from time to time for the same customer and/or the same provider.

These statements describe features that are fundamental and are inherent in products or components of products that are deeds, performances, or actions, and may sound very simplistic until you delve into the meanings and consequences of these inherent characteristics to the customer and to the provider. It is generally accepted that services are different from physical goods along four fundamental characteristics labeled as intangibility, simultaneity or inseparability, perishability, and variability.

These characteristics are conceptually inherent in all services or in the service component of any product. Although this framework is more useful as a pedagogical vehicle rather than a framework for research or practice, it is powerful in fully capturing the concept of service orientation and accomplishes the objective of placing the reader in the necessary frame of mind.

This mindset is grounded in the appreciation of the fundamental nature of services necessitating appropriate managerial decisions and actions. The fundamental character of services and the associated consequences may play out for the manager. A service orientation requires a thorough understanding of how these inherent characteristics of services are manifested for the customer and the manager.

Intangibility – Services Are Intangible

Services are performances. Services cannot be seen but they can be experienced. The product is a process. As a service provider, you cannot show your product as you could if you were the marketer of a packaged good. Yes, services are the result of value-creating activities, just as physical products are, and may employ tangibles or physical products in producing the service. However, the product being purchased is an experience and not a physical good. Customers cannot take ownership or title to a service.

For example, hotels provide the service of overnight stay as their core product. The customer does not take title to the room that is being rented. The hotel provides the use of the room for the duration of the time that the customer has paid for. Similarly, customers don't take title to anything in air travel or in entertainment. When office copiers come with service, there is no ownership involved with the service component unlike with the copier itself.

When your automobile comes with free service under warranty, unlike the automobile itself there is no real ownership of the service component. Now, as a manager, you might say: "All this is well and good, but if it doesn't change the way I manage the product, its production, or its marketing, whether it is a packaged good or service, why should I care? Services are intangible and service components in products are intangible – yes! But so what?" Let us examine this question from the customer's point of view.

For customers, one immediate consequence of the intangibility is increased perceived risk. When you cannot see the product or what you are going to get before the purchase, customers have to acknowledge a certain amount of risk they are taking. While there is perceived risk in the purchase of a packaged or physical good, you cannot return a vacation as you can a defective lawn mower.

Thus, you accept a certain amount of risk as unavoidable in the case of a service. When you book your vacation, do you really see the product? If you have previously been to the locations, you may have seen the facility, but your product was the experience. Complicating the perceived risk is the fact that the evaluation of services or the service component of the product is inherently subjective. Compared to packaged goods, customers find it harder to evaluate services before the purchase.

Table: Fundamental Issues Common to All Services

Fundamental Characteristics	*Managerial Implications*	*Managerial Actions*
Intangibility	Product is a process and difficult to evaluate; Perceived risk is high.	Find ways to reduce perceived risk, e.g., service sampling and guarantees.
Simultaneity	Customers are resources and co-producers; Customer participation needs to be managed.	Shape individual customer behaviour during consumption, behaviour during consumption, e.g., diagnostic questions for service specifications.
Perishability	Product cannot be inventoried; demand management is key to profitable capacity utilization.	Smooth fluctuations with segmentation and marketing mix, e.g., discounts during low-demand periods.
Variability	Product varies across frontline providers, customers and over time. Quality control is difficult.	All frontline personnel are marketers as well, e.g., training in customer interaction skills.

In some cases, services are harder to evaluate even during and after their performances. In the case of health care, for instance, you use several proxy elements, such as the cleanliness of the facility, the medical professional's "bedside manner, " and the process you had to go through. What you are evaluating is a lot more than the core product, the medical treatment itself. Being intangible, services cannot be produced until you have purchased (whether you pay before, during, or after) the service.

Simultaneity – Services

The acts of production and consumption occur simultaneously in services. This is primarily because services are produced and consumed in real time. There is a great deal of interaction before, during, and/or after the service between provider and customer. Some sort of customer interaction is necessary even if customer physical presence is not. At the very least, customers have to specify their needs and their need situations. In most if not all cases, it can be argued that production and consumption cannot be temporally separated. (Thus, this characteristic is also termed "inseparability.") A related complication for services is that in services, the provider is part of the product.

As a customer, the frontline personnel you interact with are a part of the product. In professional services, for instance, the lawyer is part of the (legal service) product, the doctor is part of the (medical care) product, the professor is part of the (education) product. Comparing this to packaged goods: Do you have to interact with Procter & Gamble and the shop floor employee who made your particular tube of Crest toothpaste? You do interact with the retailer of the toothpaste, but remember that the retail store that makes the toothpaste available to you is a service. What you are consuming from the retailer as it is produced by the retailer is a service. In fact, you interact with the provider of the service component of the packaged good. If you interacted with P&G, it was with customer service.

Once again, let us confront the question: "So what?" To understand what difference it makes for the manager, the customer-focused firm must examine the consequences to the customer from the customer's perspective. The customer has to interact with the provider at some stage or at all stages of the production process.

The customer is in the service factory in the case of an amusement park. Sometimes the service factory comes to the customer, as in the case of the landscape contractor. Sometimes the interaction is at arm's length, such as in the case of an online travel agent like Expedia.com. In each case, there is some interaction that the customer usually initiates. Thus, there is some effort on the part of the customer for the product to be produced. The customer takes on a role in the production process. To perform the expected role, customers have to be educated and sometimes socialized into the process.

For example, at a fast food restaurant, the customer needs to get familiar with the process of ordering and picking up the food. When you call your long distance phone company for a question on your bill, you need to have some information ready for the service to be performed. These days you have to be familiar with complex automated voice menus before you can get anything done over the telephone. Since consumption and production are simultaneous, the customer is consuming as the product is being produced. The product cannot be produced ahead of time and then consumed. This means that the product cannot be inventoried.

Perishability – Services cannot be Stored

Since services cannot be produced and stored for later use, as physical products can, services are said to be perishable products. What actually perishes? In fact, what perishes is the productive capacity of the service, or more precisely, the opportunity to produce a product. A hairdresser's time is wasted or unproductive when he or she is not serving a customer. The customer service personnel ready to handle customer enquiries is not producing a service unless there is a customer to serve. An empty airline seat perishes without a passenger in it on takeoff. The factors of production such as labour, facilities, equipment, and billable time are the value-creating assets for the service provider.

The opportunity to produce the product from these assets perishes without the adequate number of customers for which the capacity is designed. And the service provider needs to maintain a certain level of capacity that is not easily adjustable. Some services are more capacity-constrained than others. A hotel cannot reduce the number of rooms in its facility when there are not enough guests. A management consulting firm with fulltime employees would be hard pressed to release its staff when there are not enough clients to fill the capacity.

For the customer, service products need to be available and accessible when and where they are needed. When the productive capacity is sometimes not able to meet the demand, customers are likely to have to wait in queues or find another provider. Whether it is on the phone for customer service, at the doctor's office, or in line for a ride in an amusement park, customers will have to get used to waiting.

In some services, customers need to plan ahead of time and place reservations. That is how managers instinctively manage the utilization of capacity in the operation. Conversely, when there is more productive capacity than there are customers to be served, service providers have to look for other customer segment opportunities for their value-creating assets. Service providers have to manage that balance between capacity and demand. They employ methods to anticipate and manage the pattern of demand and to manage the capacity accordingly.

Variability – Services Vary from Production to Production

Service products as experiences vary from one experience to the next, from customer to customer, as well as for the same customer from one occasion to the next. In fact, this variability is compounded with differences among frontline personnel. When there are several steps in the service process where the customer interacts with several different personnel of the service provider, there could be variation from one interaction to another. In some cases, customers will prefer specific frontline personnel with whom they have become familiar and comfortable. Since services are produced and consumed in real time, it is clear that customers will likely see a great degree of variation in product quality.

Customers can receive a different experience each time, even at a standardized operation like McDonald's. Service managers attempt to deliver consistently high quality with frontline training and technology and to customize where possible and standardize where necessary. Customers expect customization even when it is not feasible. Managers have to balance the economics of standardization with the quality issues around customization.

Thus, the fundamental characteristics of services force their implications on the customer. The manager of services and products that involve a significant degree of tangibles are forced to orient themselves to these implications. The complexity of managerial situations as a consequence of these characteristics is manifested as opportunities and challenges. Consequently, the services manager must analyze these consequences and be prepared to take some actions to address them.

Challenges in Providing any Service

The implications of the fundamental characteristics of services suggest that managers need to examine how they would adapt their business processes to take advantage of the opportunities and to address the challenges. The following is a discussion of some of the key managerial challenges and opportunities.

Table: Managerial Challenges with Services

Impact of the Fundamental Nature of Services on the Customer	Managerial Actions
Intangibility – What aspects of the intangible product cause the customer to perceive risk in	What are the risk levers for the customer? Are there risk relievers that we can provide

committing to a certain service provider? What do customers use to anticipate and evaluate what they are likely to receive from the service provider?	to alleviate the customer's concern? What can we do to "tangibilize" our service?
Inseparability – Where, when and how do customers interact with the production and delivery process? What roles do or should the customer play in the production or consumption of the service?	How can we improve the customer's role so that the quality of the product can be improved? Are there opportunities for increased margins or reduced costs through customization or customer self-service?
Perishability – What are the demand patterns? What influences customers to purchase or use the service at the times that they do?	How can I influence demand patterns? Am I missing opportunities by not providing the service when and where customer wants it?
Variability - What aspects can be standardized and what needs to be customized in the customer interactions? What do the customers expect the frontline personnel to be able to do?	

Reducing Customers' Perceived Risk

With products that contain a significant proportion of intangibles and where the core product is a service, managers of services need to continuously monitor and understand the risk customers feel when they purchase the service. What is the nature of the risk? How do you lower this risk? Professional services providers such as lawyers and doctors have certifications prominently displayed on their walls. Consulting firms provide lists of clients, mutual funds companies show off their performance charts. What would be most appropriate for you to do to reduce customer perceived risk?

To determine this you begin by understanding what those risk levers might be. What is the source of the anxiety that customers feel? To what would you attribute the risk that they feel? Only when this is clearly understood can you think about the possible ways you might reduce their perceived risk. To understand the risk, you need to break down the service into the features that contribute value toward the total solution.

Which service features produce benefits, and how can the risk associated with each feature-benefit connection be reduced?

The degree to which the customer feels assured that expectations of these benefits will be met would depend on how you can instill confidence in the customer that you have the ability to deliver on those expectations. Christopher Hart is credited with the concept of service guarantees that works to reduce perceived risk. L.L. Bean's famed "100% satisfaction guaranteed" goes back to 1912, when the founder was marketing the Maine hunting shoe. Service providers who understand their customers' perceived risk seek to address it.

Customization Versus Standardization

One of the powerful implications of the fundamental characteristics of services is that they are not produced ahead of time. The service is designed, created, and delivered to customer specifications. While customization is possible, some standardized parameters are also necessary to derive economies of scale. There is opportunity to standardize as well as to customize. Where there is low margin from a service component and the volume provides the profits, perhaps ways to standardize the production process would be appropriate. On the other hand, if there is opportunity for high margin, customization and low volume is the way to go.

Consider the difference between automated telephone-based customer service and a fee sometimes charged for customers who want individual attention. Professional or knowledge based services are generally customized and are high-margin, whereas dry cleaning services are low-margin services and require considerable standardization and the required volume. The opportunity is to increase margins by providing customized experiences and the challenge is in standardizing the process to reduce costs and maintain consistent quality.

Quality Consistency

A related issue to the opportunity to customize is the accompanying challenge posed by the variability of the product. Since services are produced in real time, and they have a high degree of variability, the challenge is to ensure a consistent quality in the service. Managers must assess the sources of variation. Sources of the variability are typically associated with the people delivering the service.

Every interaction with the customer provides or facilitates some aspect of the product bundle, and therefore the quality of the product is dependent on each and every interaction between the service provider and the customer. Therefore, selecting, training, and motivating frontline personnel become very critical.

For example, service firms such as Walt Disney amusement parks and the Ritz-Carlton hotels have a specific profile in mind when they hire people for the front line. These firms provide extensive service training for their frontline employees, and they motivate employees to provide customer satisfaction. FedEx rewards employees who take care of customers in service failures. Empowered frontline personnel are more likely to deliver quality service.

Demand and Capacity Management

Since services are perishable, productive factors that are in place may be idle at low demand times and stretched to capacity at high demand times. The demand is fluctuating, and it might be impossible or at best a serious challenge to stretch or contract capacity. Therefore, smoothing demand and managing capacity become a constant endeavor for the managers of services. The key to managing this challenge is to understand the demand patterns and to figure out the flexibilities in your capacity.

To the extent that the demand patterns can be predicted with a good understanding of customer behaviour, service providers can manage demand as well as capacity. Pricing is commonly used in smoothing demand. Early bird specials, matinee prices, lower fares if you stay over Saturdays are all different ways by which service firms use pricing to manage demand. Reservations and appointments are another way for service managers to smooth demand.

Different segments and markets are served at different times and prices to fill capacity. Hotels depend to a great extent on the lucrative conferences and meetings market to ensure capacity utilization. Such capacity-constrained services rely more on managing demand than on managing capacity primarily because it is harder to adjust capacity. Product mix crease margins by providing customized experiences and the challenge is in standardizing the process to reduce costs and maintain consistent quality.

Quality Consistency

A related issue to the opportunity to customize is the accompanying challenge posed by the variability of the product. Since services are produced in real time, and they have a high degree of variability, the challenge is to ensure a consistent quality in the service. Managers must assess the sources of variation. Sources of the variability are typically associated with the people delivering the service.

Every interaction with the customer provides or facilitates some aspect of the product bundle, and therefore the quality of the product is dependent on each and every interaction between the service provider and the customer. Therefore, selecting, training, and motivating frontline personnel become very critical. For example, service firms such as Walt Disney amusement parks and the Ritz-Carlton hotels have a specific profile in mind when they hire people for the front line.

These firms provide extensive service training for their frontline employees, and they motivate employees to provide customer satisfaction. FedEx rewards employees who take care of customers in service failures. Empowered frontline personnel are more likely to deliver quality service.

Demand and Capacity Management

Since services are perishable, productive factors that are in place may be idle at low demand times and stretched to capacity at high demand times. The demand is fluctuating, and it might be impossible or at best a serious challenge to stretch or contract capacity. Therefore, smoothing demand and managing capacity become a constant endeavor for the managers of services. The key to managing this challenge is to understand the demand patterns and to figure out the flexibilities in your capacity. To the extent that the demand patterns can be predicted with a good understanding of customer behaviour, service providers can manage demand as well as capacity. Pricing is commonly used in smoothing demand.

Early bird specials, matinee prices, lower fares if you stay over Saturdays are all different ways by which service firms use pricing to manage demand. Reservations and appointments are another way for service managers to smooth demand. Different segments and markets are served at different times and prices to fill capacity.

Hotels depend to a great extent on the lucrative conferences and meetings market to ensure capacity utilization. Such capacity-constrained services rely more on managing demand than on managing capacity primarily because it is harder to adjust capacity.

The nature of these manifestations in different services implies different situations for the customer and the manager. While all services are fundamentally intangible, inseparable, perishable, and variable, services differ from each other along dimensions peculiar to their category. These category characteristics provide the manager with an insight into the specific situations that they have to deal with in their particular service category.

Christopher Lovelock demonstrated that this sort of categorizing is necessary and powerful as a means of understanding the managerial situations specific to each type of service. Service managers should look toward other services that share similar characteristics and expect to find similar challenges and transferable solutions to those challenges.

Consider for example that hospitals provide executive-style rooms for the businessperson who is a patient.

They learned this from hotels that have executive-style suites for the businessperson. Now consider the service characteristics that are shared between hospitals and hotels. In both cases, the customer comes to the factory and frequently requires an overnight stay. In both situations, the executive is likely to be away from an office with all its business support for an extended period of time.

Both services are similar in the type of customer interactions, even though they are in two completely different service sectors. An analysis as depicted the benefits of learning from the successes of services that share certain specific service characteristics.

Managers of services can understand the specific challenges and opportunities presented by the characteristics of their product and corresponding situations by examining a number of characteristics that profile a service category. Here are a few characteristics to examine:

- Tangible or intangible act
- Person or thing as recipient of the act
- Type of interaction between provider and customer
- Service delivered by people or equipment
- Extent of customization or standardization

What are the tangible and intangible acts involved in the services that you are providing? Is the service act delivered on a person or a thing?

For example, if you are an entertainment electronics repair and service provider, you perform tangible acts on a DVD player and intangible acts with the customer as you obtain information on what problems the customer has experienced with the DVD player. Now, examine the nature of the acts and the impact on the customer. When you are working on the DVD player, the customer needs not be present and the process that you employ need not be visible to the customer. However, you do interact with the customer at a number of points, from the initial customer call to the final interaction at delivery or pickup of the DVD player.

Similarly, you might analyze your service about the nature of interaction of with the customer. Is it face-to-face or arm's length, via telephone or the Internet? Do you visit the customer or does the customer visit your premises? How much technology is involved in the interface with the customer? Sometimes the customer does not even interact with a person. How much standardization is built into the service? Are there options provided to customers who require a customized interaction? What benefits does this analysis provide the manager?

The challenges and opportunities discussed earlier as fundamental are common to all service managers. By understanding the characteristics of their specific category of services, the manager can find ways to take advantage of the opportunities and address the challenges of their specific situation. Additionally, in understanding how the fundamental characteristic of intangibility manifests itself in their particular situation, managers can understand customers' perceived risk and use the tangibles in the customer experience to reduce the risk that customers perceive.

By understanding the nature of the interaction, managers are in a better place to manage the roles of customers and recognize opportunities for customization and standardization to improve the customer experience and, therefore, customer value. What is most interesting is that you may find that service businesses in a different industry sharing certain characteristics may offer you innovative ideas to meet these challenges and capitalize on opportunities to better serve customers in your business.

The Customer Focused Analysis

In order to understand how the required service-oriented frame of mind needs to be handled in the customer-focused firm, the firm analyzes the various services with which it augments the product. Each service is analyzed from a fundamental and category perspective. The fundamental nature of services requires an analysis of the implications of the intangible, inseparable, perishable, and variable nature of services for managerial action.

The analysis of category characteristics specific to each type of service should deal with how these consequences of these characteristics manifest themselves in that situation. As shown in Table, the customer-focused analysis should cover the nature and the recipient of the act, the nature of the interaction, and the fluctuation of the demand.

Table: Framing the Customer-Focused Analysis

Characteristic of Service	*Customer-Focused Analysis*
Nature of the Act	Is the act tangible or intangible? Who or what entity in the firm performs the acts? How does the nature of the act affect the perceived risk of the customer?
Who or What Is the Recipient	Which acts are directed at a tangible such as a person's body or a thing? Which acts are directed at the person's mind or intangible assets? How is the customer's perceived risk shaped by the recipient of the act?
Nature of the Interaction	What are the various ways in which the customer interacts with the firm? What are the roles of the customer and the firm in each interaction? Are there opportunities for economies of standardization or premium from customization? What other delivery options are feasible for the interactions?
Fluctuation in Demand	What is the impact of the fluctuation of demand on the value-creating assets and their revenue potential? What is the versatility of the value-creating assets in producing different solutions and catering to different segments?

Productive factors of the process are represented by capacity in the number of customers that can be served by the people, equipment, and facility. With activity-based costing methods, their costs can be assessed against their contribution to customer value. Firms attempt to keep costs down based solely on financial criteria. Indeed, any adjustments to capacity that must be made to keep costs down must be based on their impact on customer value.

Consider how some common practices to adjust capacity might effect customer value. Firms attempt to shrink capacity during low periods of demand. Practically speaking there is a limit to this – hotels cannot shrink or expand the number of rooms, for example. But it can close off rooms and other physical facilities and equipment for maintenance and reduce the staff during low periods. Customer-focused managers will consider the impact of these actions on customer value for patrons being served during that period.

During peak periods, firms increase staff and bring all equipment and physical facilities into the operation. When other opportunities to increase capacity are utilized, such as outsourcing, then quality control is the issue that has to be traded off with the cost and volume benefits. Firms may also investigate other customer value opportunities if it can put its value-creating assets to a different use. When the margins are attractive and the value-creating assets during low periods can be reconfigured to produce a different solution, firms might consider acquiring more capacity.

In general, capacity management is about expanding capacity during peak times and decreasing it during periods of low demand so that cost and volume efficiencies can be maximized. Demand management involves smoothing the peaks and valleys so that revenue and volume efficiencies are maximized; the most common techniques are pricing and promotions tactics.

An important question in this whole exercise is to determine whether the service lends itself to the various capacity management techniques. Ultimately, the customer-focused firm will maintain a caveat in adjusting capacity: how will it affect customer value?

Mixing Segments in the Customer Portfolio

When different segments must inevitably be handled at different times of the demand cycle, an important consideration to be made is availability of alternate segments. For example, Bermuda began targeting younger travellers, under the age of 49, to boost its offseason visitor revenues. With a resident population only one-tenth the size of the number of annual visitors, Bermuda's local economy depends on tourism.

About a third of Bermuda's visitors are passengers on cruise ships. These cruise ship arrivals being seasonal, Bermuda is looking to attract younger vacationers year round instead of just the spring and summer high season. Bermuda used a guarantee to support perceptions of off-season weather – at least 68 degrees or a 10 percent discount in any hotel, dining, shopping, or ground transportation service! Segments can be mixed by their time of use or time of purchase.

As a demand management tool, the timing of various consumption process activities such as purchase and use are levers that the firm can use to make its demand more predictable and to manage the utilization of its assets. For example, the time of purchase, use, and cancellation in travel, entertainment, hotels, and conferences, must all be considered in managing demand in service firms and in firms where assets are being used to produce services.

Group business is a savior for the hospitality business. It ensures a large volume of committed demand from one customer – but groups are usually booked far in advance and the price is discounted. The firm has to leave itself the appropriate amount of capacity for the anticipated "full-rated" customers for the same time period to be purchased closer to the time of use. When the anticipated demand is low, firms are forced to look for segments such as trade shows, business conferences, and executive seminars and the like.

The Royal Caribbean Cruises positioned one of its new ships as "the first million dollar conference centre at sea." Segments to be served at any given time can be selected based on their lifetime value and their responsiveness or sensitivity to customer value changes. Managing segments for maximum profitability by shifting demand involves understanding the sensitivity of the segments to the product bundle.

Adjustments to the product can change customer value and shift demand. The productive factors can be aligned by the sensitivity of the segments to changes in customer value in such a way as to shift segments to other points in the demand cycle.

But first, the firm must understand: What are the service preferences (value), sensitivity to price, and promotion specials? Will changing the customer value by changing either the benefits or costs of the value bundle change customer behaviour or shift demand to low-demand periods?

Modifying Customer Behaviour

Why do customers perform those interactions when they do? What will it take to change their behaviour to perform those interactions during other times? In other words, what is their behaviour sensitive to? Essentially, this analysis is reflected in a change in customer value. Segments differ in price sensitivity; different segments will switch their interaction times at different price levels.

Insofar as customer value is affected by price, pricing is a powerful tool to modify customer behaviour. Firms can do this with adjustments to the value bundle, by manipulating elements in the supplementary product. Adjustments to benefits and costs as reflected in customer value can be analyzed for its effect on customer behaviour. In how it affects customer value, the amount of customer participation sometimes allows flexible pricing.

Automation versus personalized service can be used to provide varying degrees of levels of service to the customer. Customers may choose the technology during peak periods such as in the case of the self-service checkout counters in many stores. Standardized versus tailored versions can be used to shift demand. Different versions of the product with different combinations of features using product bundling are effective demand shifting mechanisms. Firms in some industries do this instinctively without much sophistication while others such as airlines and hotels use very sophisticated methods.

Firms that have a good customer understanding are better equipped to adjust customer value without losing superiority among its competitors. Price promotions are powerful demand-shifting tactics. There are numerous examples of price promotions, from early bird specials to discounts during low periods. The problem with most price promotions is that they are not aligned with demand fluctuations, so that the effect on the customer is random — where the firm is simply hoping to build demand without a sense of timing and how it would affect demand fluctuation patterns.

Unless the firm's assets always operate at the same level of capacity, every firm should be offering price promotions to bring in customers during periods when the assets are idle. Anything from customer convenience in payment such as interest-free deferred payment schedules to outright price bargains are common uses of pricing for this purpose.

Customer behaviour can be modified to the benefit of both the customer and firm with customer education on how demand fluctuations can affect their own customer experience. Different industries have different norms in the attempt to inform the customer about peak times so that those customers who would not want to be subjected to long lines and wait times can choose to interact with the firm during low demand periods.

Most customer service phone lines will inform you of the expected wait times after you are greeted and logged in to their system. When there is an exaggerated peak and valley pattern, firms must find ways to educate customers to move their patronage to a different time or access point to help with the strain on capacity while reducing the risk of a poor customer experience that could be detrimental to customer loyalty and sustainable profits.

Customer lifetime value and customer preferences and priorities can and must be kept in mind when attempting to manage demand by changing customer value. Any type of membership benefits and loyalty programmes can be designed to essentially manage demand.

The terms of the membership programme need to ensure that the firm is managing the use of its productive resources according to the lifetime value of the mix of customers being served. Any change in customer value with demand and supply management technique should be monitored for its impact on brand loyalty and customers' lifetime value to the firm.

Chapter 7

Tourism Academics

RESEARCH

Although tourism as an activity has a long tradition, as an academic subject it is a development of the 1960s. Initial concentration of the subject development was in Europe but it is now seen as a worldwide phenomenon. In the 1960s there were few academic institutions which offered tourism courses (as differentiated from travel trade and hospitality specific programmes). Consequently, there were only a few academics who could term themselves as 'tourism lecturers'. However, as tourism expanded as both a domestic and international activity, it inevitably attracted the interests of academics from many disciplines with a consequent development of courses and degree programmes.

Tourism has developed at undergraduate level during a period of continual structural change within higher education institutions (HEI) and during changes in the purpose of the wider Higher Education (HE) system. There has been, without doubt, extraordinary growth of provision for Tourism in both further and higher education in the last ten years in the United Kingdom. Together with the arrival of other new subjects such as Media, Communication and Theatre Studies, Tourism represents an alternative to the traditional, yet popular, disciplines such as Geography, English and History. Over a four year period, the number of students accepting a place on an undergraduate Tourism programme in a UK HEI increased from 1666 to 2363, a rise of 42 per cent.

The study of Tourism as a subject has focused previously on the existence of, and need for, a minimum core curriculum. Research has also concentrated on the growth of provision and concerns of overprovision of tourism graduates due to the proliferation of tourism programmes in the last ten years or so, since the first two programmes at undergraduate level were introduced at Dorset Institute and Newcastle Polytechnic in 1986. However, no study to date has attempted to understand why Tourism has developed in the manner it has, and what factors have contributed towards that development.

This significant gap in research to date in the field of Tourism in HE offers the opportunity for this paper to evaluate Tourism lecturer perceptions of the key factors influencing the development of Tourism undergraduate programmes.

In the last few years, Leiper and Tribe have re-opened the debate surrounding Tourism's disciplinary status, following its initial airing in the early 1980s well before provision at an undergraduate level featured in HEIs in the UK. Tribe maintained that Tourism is not a discipline but two distinct fields, the business of tourism and the non-business aspect of Tourism. He defended the non-disciplinary nature of Tourism and proposed that 'tourism studies should recognise and celebrate its diversity' rather than 'hankering after an overly idealised concept'.

Leiper responded directly to Tribe's assertions of Tourism's non-disciplinary nature and favoured a recognition that a discipline can be seen to be emerging, and that 'the debate about whether or not a discipline of tourism studies exists is similar to debates about whether or not the industry exists'. These debates have played an important role in allowing the nature of Tourism as a subject and the extent of its academic maturity to be aired in the increasing number of academic Tourism journals.

In the 1990s there still appears to have been greater support for the view that tourism is still a subject rather than a discipline due to its relative youth as a subject area and because it lacks what Cooper and Westlake described as 'antecedents of a mature field'.

Tourism as a subject for study could strive to build a reputation not as a discipline, but based on its ability not only to draw on a wide range of established disciplines as above, but on its diversity and multidisciplinarity.

Tourism is still a relatively new phenomenon which has featured at postgraduate level for nearly 30 years and at undergraduate level for less than 20 years. While the existence or emergence of Tourism as a discipline and the need for a common curriculum has been disputed during this period these issues will not form the focus of this paper. Rather the aim of this paper is to analyse two key factors which have, according to Tourism lecturers, influenced the development of Tourism in HE against a backdrop of constraints at a national, institutional and departmental level.

METHODOLOGY

The research developed in two stages, firstly content analysis (of discussion documents, a new research tool, and programme validation documentation) and secondly, in-depth interviews with a variety of lecturers. The methodology is, in part, experimental in terms of the use of a previously untested research instrument, the 'discussion document', but also includes a more traditional method, i.e. in-depth interviews.

The process of content analysis involved the identification of 'bits of data which can be relied upon for the purpose of comparison'. Comparison in this case was between one lecturer's views and another's (in the same or different institution). As the research progressed, drawing on information from the two stages, certain influences on the development of Tourism programmes emerged as being more or less critical in terms of the actual nature of programmes.

The detailed 'discussion document' was designed to allow one representative from each of ten institutions delivering undergraduate Tourism to respond to a number of statements regarding programme structure and content. To date this type of research instrument has not been used to examine lecturers' views about aspects of programme development in HE and as such, the discussion document was an innovative test case which could be useful for future similar studies. A major problem which was recognised regarding the introduction of a new, untested research tool, is the fact that there could be no guarantee that it would result in collection of the necessary, or sufficient usable, comparable information.

For this reason piloting of the document was crucial in terms of highlighting potential problems which needed to be eradicated before completion by the actual selection of institutions. Piloting the discussion document with two institutions not involved in this stage of the research allowed the testing of wording (avoiding ambiguity), sequencing and layout of questions as proposed by Fink, Folz (1996) and Veal (1992) and very importantly in this case, finding out if the 12 page document was manageable in terms of the length of time it would take to complete.

A number of changes were made to the structure and design of the original piloted discussion document following telephone or personal interviews with the two respondents involved and analysis of the completed documents. The key change made involved a reduction in the number of open-ended questions and an increase in closed questions to make the instrument less demanding for the respondent and as a result, less time-consuming.

Criteria for selection of institutions to be analysed at the second stage were considered carefully and nine institutions, collectively covering the 'descriptors' of institutions delivering Tourism at undergraduate level, were approached and subsequently agreed to take part. The description included:

- Tourism programmes delivered in England, Scotland and Wales

- New Tourism programmes delivered at the former polytechnics
- Established Tourism programmes delivered at 'old' universities
- Tourism programmes delivered by colleges of higher education and university sector colleges, franchised and validated by a named university
- Tourism programmes of a 'general' or specialist nature (by programme title)

Respondents at this stage of the research held various positions within Tourism sections, schools and departments, i.e. lecturers, programme leaders, heads of departments and deans of faculties. The second stage of the research concerned the opinions of 27 lecturers responsible for teaching and researching Tourism in HE in the 1990s, as research to date in the field of Tourism education appears to have focused primarily on the quantitative aspect of programme delivery, rather than widespread interviewing of Tourism lecturers. According to McCracken 'the long interview is one of the most powerful methods in the qualitative armory...no instrument of inquiry is more revealing'.

Unlike the research carried out by Johnson where in-depth interviews were carried out with key Tourism educators who were known to be knowledgeable and to hold strong views regarding common core curriculum, this research aimed to interview not only the knowledgeable in terms of the subject, but also those lecturers who were relatively new to Tourism, and heads of department/school whose influence over programme structure and content was limited.

The aim was to gather views and opinions from individuals who had a wide range and level of interest and involvement in the development of Tourism programmes, from the highly informed, involved and influential individuals to those whose role in course delivery and programme structure was more limited.

This indicates the paper's emphasis on lecturers' views regarding Tourism's development, which needs to be viewed in the light of the recognition of three further possible levels of potential influence, at the national, institutional and departmental level. As it was not possible to undertake detailed interviews with staff across all the institutions which had completed the discussion document, it was decided to select a small sample of institutions which would represent these. Each of the five institutions selected met one or more of the criteria listed above.

The interviews were designed to focus on those substantial issues that emerged from the analysis of the discussion and validation documents and were semi-structured with specific objectives or outcomes. An informal approach was adopted with participating respondents being offered a list of topics or themes to be discussed prior to the interviews. Kahn and Cannell describe the in-depth interview as 'a conversation with a purpose' which is believed to be more fruitful than highly structured interviews. The aim of these interviews was to 'unfold' the respondents' perspectives on the 'phenomenon', in this case the nature of Tourism as an undergraduate degree subject.

Although there did need to be some form of systemisation in terms of the questioning (to aid the analysis and comparison of findings), it was vital to ensure that a flexible approach was maintained throughout in order to encourage openness and honesty on the part of the respondent.

Interview transcriptions and discussion documents were coded manually by the author according to four potential levels of influence on Tourism; national, institutional, departmental and individual. This allowed the critical issues to jump out due to their re-occurence at two or more of these levels. Analysis of the documents could have been carried out using one of the many software packages available, for example, QSR Nudist, which enables the analysis of qualitative data, possibly after the researcher's initial step of open coding of data. Nudist was, in fact, used to analyse and code the two pilot discussion documents.

However, it was not deemed successful due to the length of time it took to get the documents in a format which was acceptable to the Nudist package. It was felt that this time was better spent analysing and coding the discussion documents manually and subsequently the package was not used at the content analysis and coding stage of interview transcripts. As a research tool, Nudist was not designed to 'displace you as the researcher or your process as the central area of activity. Rather it supports the processes or activities that you engage in as you go about the business of doing qualitative research'.

As Nudist was not seen to support the research process - if anything it appeared to hinder progress - it was rejected accordingly. A limitation of the study with regard to methodology concerns the number of respondents interviewed. Although the interviews were comprehensive, allowing individuals to offer detailed explanations of their opinions and beliefs regarding Tourism in HE, the fact that they were relatively few in number means that it would be inappropriate to regard them as statistically representative of all Tourism lecturers.

From the outset the study was planned primarily as a qualitative, not quantitative study. The views of these lecturers should, therefore, be regarded as individual cases which illustrate the range of views and opinions at the five institutions. Additionally, the tendency for respondents on occasions to moan about certain issues regarded as important to their job satisfaction, rather than focusing on the concerns of the interview, resulted in a number of protracted interviews (nearly two hours) and a need to approach these grievances with a degree of caution.

As only five institutions (and 27 respondents) were included it would be inappropriate to regard these grievances as being reflective of all institutions and individuals involved in the design and delivery of undergraduate Tourism programmes.

Tourism as a subject is now found in many academic institutions throughout the world and many academics now designate themselves as 'tourism lecturers'. It is now possible for an academic to foresee a career in the academic study of tourism with a range of institutions in many countries offering a varied career path. The growth of tourism as a subject is reflected in the continuously expanding number of publications related to the subject in books, specialist journals, conferences and increasingly through postings on the Internet. As a group, academics have three main characteristics based on their traditional role of being thinkers, researchers, analysts and teachers:

- To advance both the knowledge and understanding of the subject;
- To disseminate information via teaching, publications and conferences;
- And, through teaching and publications, to educate and influence students, other academics and the industry.

Although there may be some debate about these characteristics they do seem to represent what most academics do. In the area of teaching the purpose is not only to inform students but also to influence their thinking by equipping them with concepts and techniques which are relevant to their future careers, an objective supported by the growing literature on tourism.

The need to publish in academic journals and through subject-specific books seeks to influence (if not always impress!) the peer group-fellow academics. The dissemination of information is essentially career-motivated and scholarly. Some of the central and continuing debates, for example defining the subject area, the nature and definition of 'sustainable' tourism, the role of tourism in society are all topics which advance our theoretical understanding of the subject but are unlikely to be of much interest to practitioners.

A further difficulty is that given the need for academic rigour in publications and the review system, many publications become dated and lose their usefulness before they are published. There may be a further problem where tourism practitioners do not read the academic press. It is suggested, from the basis of experience, that this is often the case. It follows therefore that academics write for and seek to inform fellow academics. Much of the innovative work being done by academics will tend to have a very limited influence on tourism development practice unless the academic is also a practitioner.

For example, the extensive and growing literature on ecotourism, on community participation in tourism development planning, and host-guest relationships are three areas of current interest to academics. Although these issues are also of concern to practitioners their concerns are essentially pragmatic, resource-constrained and implementation-oriented. Of necessity, practitioners must be focused within the parameters of the project and do not seek more general prescriptions.

Practitioners

In relation to development planning, tourism practitioners are either individual consultants or consulting companies. Consultants, unlike academics, operate in a business environment and may be identified as having three broad operational characteristics.

- Their work is contractual, project specific and profit driven.
- Knowledge dissemination is through project-specific reports, plans and studies which are commissioned by the client and have a limited circulation.
- They aim, by the development of expertise and reputation, to secure future contract work.

Consultants by the very competitive nature of their work do not readily make available to enquirers their past reports unless these are likely to be influential in securing future work. As most projects are in two stages, that is project preparation and subsequent implementation, consultants tend to protect their client base and are always, like any business, seeking to ensure their company sustainability through further contracts.

Much tourism development planning is funded by international agencies, for example World Bank, European Union, United Nations Development Programme, and, for regional development, by banks such as the Asian Development Bank. Many projects are large, long-term and require a variety of technical skills inputs. Few academic institutions would have either the resources or flexibility to compete for large contracts with the major consultancy companies in the area of tourism development.

For these reasons, where large contracts are available many consulting companies subcontract specialist requirements to individuals, often academics and sometimes academic institutions. In this way, there is a 'cross-over' between the academic and the practitioner.

Cross-over

Although it is postulated that academic institutions cannot realistically or effectively compete in the international tourism contract market, academics are employed as project specialists offering skills and experience usually on a short-term basis, for example tourism economists, forecasters and marketing specialists. However, these posts are filled after the contract has been signed and the project strategy and methodology agreed. A brief description of the project preparation stage will support this point.

Project Preparation

Although projects vary in scale and complexity there are basically five steps in the project cycle which are briefly discussed here:

1. *Project identification:* Depending on the nature and scale of the project there are usually three sub-components involved in this stage:

   a. *Technical specification:* At this stage of project identification the concept, for example to develop a tourism resort, or to specify a tourism planning exercise, is formalized into a project proposal. The project's objectives, activities and expected outputs (results) are identified. The aim is to establish wherever possible measurable indicators to eventually evaluate the project if it should go ahead.

b. *Feasibility studies:* For some projects a feasibility study will be done to assess the viability of the proposal. For international lending agencies a particular area of interest will be to determine how the proposed project fits into any indicative programme of general guidelines for co-operation between the beneficiary country and the lending institution. For example, what priority is given to the tourism sector in a particular country (perhaps indicated in a national development plan) and to what extent will the proposed project contribute to national and sectoral development aims? In some African countries, such as Zambia, tourism is not only recognized as a priority sector by the Government, but as Zambian tourism is almost exclusively based on wildlife viewing, which obviously takes place in rural areas, tourism development contributes to increasing rural development, incomes and employment-all national economic objectives.

c. *Financial proposal:* If the feasibility study confirms the viability of the proposed project and the overall objectives meet national development objectives, then a financial proposal will be drawn up for the project. At its simplest, the financial proposal sets out the budget for the project. At the project identification stage it is usual to employ a consultant(s) to prepare the various working documents. The technical specification and the financial proposal are used to prepare the Terms of Reference.

2. *Terms of Reference:* The Terms of Reference is the project 'bible'. It sets out in detail what the project aims to achieve, what activities are necessary, what outputs (results) are expected within a given budget. Usually incorporated into a comprehensive Project Document, the Terms of Reference not only guides the consultants undertaking the project but is also the main evaluating instrument to check performance against specification.
3. *The tender process:* Consultants may be invited to bid for a contract either on an open or restricted basis. The open system means that, with perhaps some qualification, any company can bid for the contract. A restricted tender operates where only selected companies are invited to bid. In the latter case this may be as a consequence of time pressures or more likely due to the specialist nature of the contract. The bids received will usually have three dimensions: a profile of the tendering company (including a record of previous experience); a technical proposal to indicate how the contract specifications are to be met (i.e. project methodology and the proposed team of consultants); and a financial proposal. It is not always the case that the lowest bid price wins the contract. Evaluations of tenders should involve careful scrutiny of past experience, an evaluation of the proposed methodology and of the team of consultants assembled to carry out the project, and of the financial proposal. The evaluation of tenders is a fairly mysterious process. The quality of the evaluation will depend very much on those doing it-their knowledge, experience and their understanding of the proposed project. Some project evaluations are guided by attempts to systematize the process often by using a points-scale reference to assess different project components. In some cases the process may proceed along more subjective lines. The outcome of the tender process is to award and sign a contract with a consultant(s).

4. Project implementation: The consultant implements the project by using the financial resources provided in the contract. Implementation will require the consultant to prepare a plan of operation and to present reports on the progress of the project as specified in the contract. It is also usual to appoint a project Steering Committee to oversee the operation of the contract and to monitor and discuss any issues arising. The Steering Committee is the main operational channel between the consultant/ contractor and the client.
5. Project evaluation: This involves the review and analysis of results and the impact of the project. Project evaluations can take place during or after a project has ended. In the case of a multi-stage project, the start of the next phase will usually depend on the conclusions of the previous stage.

   Although the outlined project schematic may vary between agencies depending on a variety of circumstances and practices, the main stages are common to development planning exercises. What is important to note is that the methodology for the project is devised by the bidding company/ consultant.

Procedure

Despite the increasing funds which are being channelled to tourism planning and development, very little is known about how project methodology is chosen, and on what basis. For example in the WTO report a brief synopsis of various country development plans is given for country projects, but there is no discussion of how a particular methodology was chosen, what alternatives might have been considered, and how this selection was made. Although much has been written on micro-methodologies, such as cost-benefit analysis, economic impact studies, social impact analysis, environmental assessment techniques, little has been written on macro-project methodology for tourism.

Methodological issues are usually conceptual, for example the debates on sustainability, on community participation and empowerment through decentralization. It is these conceptual but essentially pragmatic issues which are often project-relevant and are the main focus for academic writing and research. For many academics the issue is to ask 'why?' rather than 'how'; the latter question could be interpreted to be the main concern of the consultant.

It is suggested that in most projects, methodology is derived from past experience and it is the tried and tested methodology which prevails over anything innovative. In projects where profit margins are often tight, innovation might be costly. For example if, as is now generally agreed, community participation in tourism development is desirable, this might be written into the Terms of Reference.

How it is to be implemented is a challenge despite the extensive academic writing on this topic. In practice, participation may only involve consultation, and perhaps the consultant employed to undertake this task (academic or otherwise) may be methodologically constrained by the project manager, or the budget, or both.

In most large projects there are a series of methodological issues. At the project (or macro) level the main concern is to devise a methodological approach to cover the activities and to produce the outputs required within both the time-scale and budget. At the component (or micro) level, for example economic impact study, marketing survey, analysis of demand and forecasting, the same constraints apply but methodology and techniques are more firmly established. At all times, methodology is driven by pragmatism and is informed by experience rather than theory.

Although methodology is an area where one would expect academics to be most comfortable, it appears that few academics actually are involved in this at the project level. Some of the important contributions to tourism in the developing countries remain enshrined in the literature often unread by consultants. This statement is of course impressionistic and is based on the author's experience. It is a contention which might be tested via a survey of tourism practitioners or from responses to this chapter. A more important source of information could be derived from the financiers of tourism development and in particular, the institutional lenders.

Although organizations such as the European Union, the United Nations Development Programme, development banks and country-based donor organizations have and continue to fund tourism projects, very little information has been released about the relative success or failure of these projects. These lenders have the ability, and probably need, to create institutional memory, that is, to compare through project appraisal and evaluation a major databank of tourism-related information.

Such information is not only relevant to the prospects of future projects but, if disseminated, would become a stimulant to debate. Such an innovation would have to come from a project's lender; client confidentiality would preclude the consultant from revealing such information. Methodology has a particular significance in tourism because of its multidisciplinary nature. Various aspects of a single project can include economic, social, environmental and political inputs, each of which might require a specific methodological approach which will have to be harmonized within the operational framework of the project to meet the Terms of Reference.

Some of the major current debates in tourism development include: sustainability; the environment; social impacts; community participation; local empowerment; type, scale and location of development; globalization; indigenization; women in development and host-guest relationships. These are issues which have attracted major academic interest and publications-how can tourism practitioners and funding agencies be made more aware of this output? How can it be fed into project methodologies?

From the brief discussion of the project cycle it can be deduced that there are two points where the methodological approach can be influenced. First is at the stage of preparing the Terms of Reference for the project and second, at the implementation stage where the project's activities are undertaken. As noted previously, the Terms of Reference set out the activities, inputs and expected outputs from the project.

To a considerable extent the writer of the Terms of Reference can exert a direct influence on methodology by specifying certain activities which are integral to the project, for example that the planning process must incorporate some degree of community involvement; that the scale of the project take into account possible impact on the social and natural environment; that measures be devised to increase participation of women in the development process.

In each case the Terms of Reference will not normally specify how these activities will be done-but that they have to be incorporated into the implementation or operational phase. Well-written Terms of Reference can incorporate within a project most of the concerns that are of current academic debate-for example, how is the sustainability of the project to be achieved? The Terms of Reference are also informed by the client's perspective and any legal and planning framework perspective which might exist in the project's locale.

Where clients are international development agencies they will insist on certain development parameters which directly affect project methodology. For example, many development agencies, such as the World Bank, require that more development initiatives have to be channelled to and through the private sector. Long experience of state-dominated capitalism, for example in both Eastern European and African countries, has not generated the expected levels of development benefits.

In African countries, for instance Zambia, a 'privatization unit' is selling off the state's commercial assets such as copper mines to international and local private investors. Where part of a project's remit is to support more private sector involvement in the development effort specific measures have to be devised to do this. In both Zambia and Zimbabwe, although private sector companies were and are involved in the tourist sector, there was no representative body which had the recognized stature to provide an 'industry view'.

In both countries, aided by development assistance, industry representative associations were initiated in the Tourism Council of Zimbabwe and the Zambia Tourism Council which in the latter case is being formally incorporated within the proposed Tourism and Hospitality Bill. In terms of community participation in tourism development the Zimbabwean 'Campfire' project provided benefits for village communities in return for anti-poaching and wildlife conservation activities.

This type of initiative meets the requirements for more local participation in tourism development and also helps to increase rural development particularly related to employment and income. From these examples it can be seen how the Terms of Reference of a project can ensure that general development objectives are included within the parameters of a specific project. The Terms of Reference guide the formulation of project methodology-how the project is to be implemented. It is useful here to make a distinction between project methodology and project management.

The methodology determines 'how to' and project management monitors, changes and ensures that time-scales are adhered to. As noted above, very little is known about how project methodology in tourism is formulated. It is determined at the contract tender stage where the methodological proposal itself becomes an important aspect of the tender.

In fairly large projects, such as national development plans, experience suggests that methodology is derived from the 'tried and tested' approaches. These types of plans tend to break down into well-recognized components: marketing, transport, human resources development, environmental impact etc. To conform to the activities of the project and to meet the expected outcomes as specified in the Terms of Reference, little innovation is required.

The main opportunities for methodological innovation are related to the component activities. It is in these areas of activities where academics can become practitioners themselves through subcontracted inputs to the project or through academic writing which informs practitioners of developments in the field. This is the 'great divide' and where little is known about 'cross-over' activities.

To what extent are academics involved in tourism development projects as advisers or as temporary practitioners? How can they influence project methodology and/or implementation? Are tourism practitioners aware of the latest issues/developments/concepts in the field? It is these questions, largely unanswered, which should be incorporated into a new agenda.

If it is accepted that there is a gap between tourism academics and tourism practitioners then how might it be bridged to the mutual benefit of both parties? The following suggestions are not exhaustive but hopefully focus on some of the fundamental concerns raised by this chapter.

Research

At a country level it should not be difficult to identify those consulting companies with interests in and experience of tourism development projects. By means of a survey and probably personal interviews the issue of the formulation of methodology could be explored, as could the relevance and knowledge of academic publications on tourism. Information might also be gathered on the links with and use of academics in projects. A carefully structured research effort could yield information to lighten what is at present a black hole.

Publications

As noted above, the review system often has the effect of considerably delaying publications. In an era where the electronic media predominate, it should become increasingly possible to 'post' at least preliminary data and draft articles on specific networks accessible both to consultants and academics. There are the problems of copyright and plagiarism. However, it is one means of getting work more widely and quickly disseminated.

Another problem is that many academics would say this approach is essentially one-sided; what would the consulting companies offer in return? It may be that this type of information distribution would provide the consultancy companies with more information of what academic interests are, and who is working in what field-which may also lead to consulting opportunities for more academics.

This would facilitate 'cross-over' but some academics might argue that this would tend to compromise their objectivity as commentators on and analysts of the tourism sector. The required outputs of the project might limit if not preclude debate and experimentation on the more theoretical and conceptual issues which academics are mostly interested in.

Meetings

It is noticeable that in most academic conferences on tourism issues-of which there is a growing number-very few consultants or consulting companies attend. This may be due to pressure of work or perhaps because the practitioners do not have much interest in what academics are discussing? More effort should be given to inviting and involving practitioners in these fora, probably by asking for a written or/oral presentation. Creation of more common interest will again facilitate 'cross-over'. For many younger academics it may be an occasion to understand what the consultancy imperatives are.

Education

In an increasingly professional era, most consultants will have received a university-level education. The proliferation of tourism programmes and the growth of the industry worldwide, is creating more awareness of the career potential in tourism. Academics have an opportunity to influence students with a balanced view of tourism, how it has developed and what issues might have importance to its future. A well-rounded education in the subject area should become the basis for life-long learning.

The knowledge base must be continually refreshed. Academics can help to do this. The task would be facilitated if more of the practitioners' output could 'cross-over'. Unfortunately, as most of the practitioners' work is client-confidential, it will require dispositions from the clients to release non-sensitive project materials. For example, the large number of national tourism development plans which have been completed rarely find their way into the public domain. These project outputs could become very useful teaching aids and perhaps shed light on some of the methodological issues raised in this article.

Academic Participation

There are four areas where academics can influence tourism projects. First, is where they are invited to write the Terms of Reference for a project. Second is where they are employed by a consulting company to help devise the methodology for a project tender. Third is at the implementation stage usually involved as a specialist (e.g. economist, environmentalist). Fourth, where the academic is appointed to the project's Steering Committee which monitors the progress of the project. It is often possible through this involvement to input to the project methodology or to suggest changes as necessary and appropriate.

Participation will require that the academic has a reputation in the specialist field. Herein lies a problem. Although the academic may be perceived by his or her peers as a leader in the field, the practitioner may yet regard him as a citizen of an 'ivory tower'. Grossly unfair though this designation may be, tourism academics who do not engage in practical project work may find their influence marginalized or not even heeded at all. In part of course, this situation does derive from the nature of the academic's work which often involves theoretical and conceptual thinking which may not have an immediate application.

There does seem to be empirical evidence that there is a divide between tourism academics and tourism practitioners. There is a postulated need to facilitate more 'cross-over' and some measures have been suggested in this article. However what is important is to recognize that there is a synergy between the tourism academic and the tourism practitioner. There is a possibility of increasing mutual benefit, an objective which both groups should strive to achieve.

Essentially, tourism development is all about implementation. Sound or even innovative projects have no impact on development unless they are implemented. Perhaps too much of the concern of academics is about impact rather than the process of implementation. The two aspects are inextricably linked because the process of implementation is itself a methodological issue which can directly affect the impact of what is done.

To have a more central role in formulating methodology would allow the academic a real-world participatory function which should benefit the project, and the experience gained would also benefit teaching and future research. There are considerable 'cross-over' benefits to be gained by both parties if the great divide can be effectively bridged.

Integration has become a common and frequently used term in the tourism literature, particularly in the context of planning and development. Apart from Innskeep's volume relating specifically to the topic, the term finds considerable reference in writing by authors such as Gunn, Haywood, Murphy, Pearce, and Wall (1997) on general issues relating to tourism planning and development. In the more specific area of sustainable tourism, for example, we can find the term being supported in a considerable number of publications such as those by Bramwell et al. (1996), Priestley, Edwards and

Coccossis (1996), Nelson, Butler and Wall (1993), Stabler (1997) and Wahab and Pigram (1997).

This is not surprising, as the concept of sustainable development implies the linking or integration of elements of the environment in an appropriate manner, Wahab and Pigram (1997:4) commenting that 'sustainability is an integrative concept'. Although the term is widely used, like sustainable development, it is rarely adequately defined. A dictionary definition describes the verb to integrate as meaning 'to make or be made into a whole; incorporate or be incorporated', and goes on 'to amalgamate or mix... with an existing community'.

In the context of tourism, therefore, we can regard integrated planning and development as meaning the process of introducing tourism into an area in a manner in which it mixes with existing elements. It is implicit in such an understanding that this introduction and mixing is done in an appropriate and harmonious way, such that the end result is an acceptable and functionally successful community, in both ecological and human terms.

Successful integration in many cases is similar to the basic principles so eloquently presented by Ian McHarg (1967) in his book Design with Nature over three decades ago. As pressure from supporters of Agenda 21 to incorporate tourism development with the principles of sustainable development increase, the successful integration of tourism with other processes and activities in destination areas becomes more significant and important.

It is possible to note at least three principles which should make the concept of integration in the context of tourism appropriate and appealing to those involved in tourism development:

- Acceptability
- Efficiency and
- Harmony

The successful integration of tourism development into a community or destination should make the development more acceptable to local residents and existing resource users than when a tourism development is imposed in a segregated and unrelated manner. Successful integration can also be a much more efficient process. To most planners, developers and managers efficiency is a goal to be achieved, and steps and processes which speed the process of completion and acceptability of development are to be welcomed.

As important, perhaps, is the fact that successful integration can avoid problems that could otherwise materialize later in the operational phase of development through achieving synergy and even symbiosis with other existing activities and resource processes rather than competition or conflict. Finally, at a time when conflict resolution is an increasingly common process in development, the achievement of harmony and the avoidance of conflict through appropriate and acceptable development is another situation that is desired by planners and developers alike.

Despite this general support for the concept of integration in tourism development and planning, particularly in the last decade, in reality it is hard to find true examples on the ground. In many cases there are significant gaps between the concept as described in many plans and what actually appears and is operationalized in specific tourist destinations.

There are a number of reasons which can be put forward for this pattern of events which are discussed below. It can be argued that it is often not a lack of intent nor a lack of desire to achieve integration, but rather like the implementation of sustainable development, more a case of a lack of understanding and information about the nature of tourism which prevents the goal being achieved.

As with any process relating to development, the successful achievement of goals depends on a variety of factors. In the context of integration and its inclusion in planning there are a number of what may be termed policy issues which have to be taken into account. The integration of tourism development implies inevitably that tourism is being added to a set of one or more existing activities and processes in the particular destination.

Of key importance are the intra-relationships within this set of activities and processes and potential inter-relationships between them and tourism.

- *Priorities:* In the real world very few economic or social-cultural activities are equal in priority. There is normally a constant state of competition or at best uneasy alliance between activities in most communities, some being in the ascendance and others stagnating or being in decline. In many parts of the world in which tourism has been introduced, traditional primary activities have had a long established priority, both in terms of economic importance and because of their often intricate links with cultural patterns and behaviour. Tourism is often seen as being in direct competition with these traditional activities and in such situations integration rather than imposition is essential if development is to be successful.
- *Control:* In many areas in which tourism is being introduced or expanded control of resources and governance is often vested in those community members involved in other activities. In such situations tourism may be seen as a threat to the established power structure, as a force which seeks to obtain control of resources and space. Thus acceptance may be difficult if tourism is not carefully and appropriately fitted into the existing systems. This situation is often compounded by the fact that in the case of large-scale tourism developments, ownership and control of these developments commonly lies outside the local community, and the element of external control can make acceptance of such development much more problematic. Lack of appreciation of local preferences, patterns of activities and priorities can exacerbate such a situation.

- *Scale:* Clearly, small-scale developments can generally be integrated into communities and systems more easily than large complex developments which make major demands on local resources. Tourism development occurs in a wide range of scales from generally small local operations such as the provision of accommodation in private homes or itinerant selling of souvenirs to large, often foreign-owned inclusive resorts with major space and labour requirements.
- *Stage or timing of development:* Unless tourism is being introduced into an area devoid of settlement, the destination will contain a variety of activities at various stages of development and can itself be categorized as being developed, developing or undeveloped. Even where tourism development is taking place in an unsettled area, consideration has to be taken of natural processes. In a community the stage of development can be of crucial importance with respect to the probability of the successful integration of tourism. Mature, complex or sophisticated (in the economic sense) communities have a greater chance of successfully integrating tourism development into their pattern of activity and absorbing the economic impacts of tourism than more basic economies, where the effects may be much more severe and unanticipated.
- *Community harmony or conflict:* Communities rarely have uniform views, particularly on factors such as tourism that are seen as capable of causing considerable change to and within the community. Tourism, as other forms of development, is capable of generating the full range of emotions from enthusiastic support to outright antagonism, not only over time as in Doxey's over-simplistic unidirectional model, but also from the initial suggestion of tourism before development ever occurs. The issue may be not so much how feelings towards tourism develop over time, but whether there are opposing views at any

time. There need to be policies and practices in communities to determine views towards development and to enable the community to decide what type and scale of development can be accommodated in the community before development occurs, If such processes are in place and operational, then integration of the appropriate type of development should be much more easily achieved.

Other issues are also involved in determining whether tourism development will be successfully implemented in a particular community or not, and many are place and time specific, as well as relating to the nature of the specific development.

While the issues discussed above are perhaps more abstract and general in nature, there is also a range of practical issues which significantly affect the likely success or failure of the integration of tourism in specific locations.

- *Multiplicity of form*: As Simpson and Wall note, tourism comes in many forms and its effects are extremely varied. What may be appropriate procedures for the integration of tourism development of one form may not be suitable or successful for another form. Furthermore, it is rare for a destination to experience only one form of tourism or one form of tourism development during its life cycle. Thus the successful integration of one type of tourism does not guarantee that all development will be accepted and integrated in the same way, or that new forms of tourism will be able to be incorporated into the community as successfully. Different sectors, even within the same form of tourism, can place very different demands upon the destination resource base with varying levels of acceptability.
- *Dynamics:* In many respects the dynamic nature of tourism is the most difficult and greatest problem to be overcome in achieving the successful integration

of tourism. Rates of development and change are themselves inconsistent, and the faster the rate of development the more difficult the task of integration because the time available for consultation with the community and the study of ecological processes in the destination is reduced. As has been discussed elsewhere the agents of change themselves are subject to change, causing an infinite variety of inconsistency. Thus the integration process has to be dynamic and flexible itself, and capable of adapting to changing circumstances. The dynamism in the system extends to views about tourism, as well as change in economic activities and processes, in cultural behaviour, and in political viewpoints.

- *Benefits and costs*: It is not unreasonable to assume that if the attributes noted above accrue from the successful integration of tourism, then they can be regarded as benefits and will have a tangible economic form. An absence of conflict, increased speed and efficiency of planning and development and then of operation, coupled with an absence of post-development adjustment because of inappropriate scale of development, all have potential social and environmental benefits as well. However, the fact that benefits can accrue from integration does not necessarily by itself ensure the success or viability of the development. In many cases the benefits may be derived mostly or even exclusively by the developers and external agencies, allowing for dissatisfaction and opposition to continue or to develop at the local level. Benefits generally have a mirror effect, in that benefits in one area or at one level may be matched by costs in other areas and sectors. Successful integration needs to ensure that costs at the local level are at least matched by the benefits at the same level, and hopefully that they accrue to the same sectors which face costs because of the development. In many cases the benefits of tourism may accrue to new actors on the economic scene, while to other established operators there are only costs incurred by accommodating tourism development or expansion. If the principles of sustainable development are to be implemented in tourism development, then equity will become a major consideration, applying to the allocation of benefits and costs in the present as well as in the future.

In addition to the above factors, other elements such as politics and the origins of the actors involved can become significant influences on the success or failure of attempts to integrate tourism into a community. In reality the political structure and relationships within a community and with external agencies and levels of government can create strange associations and groupings of views. This can be complicated further by the origins of proponents and opponents of development and the ways in which tourism could be integrated into a community. The varying backgrounds, familiarity with the destination, and different levels of knowledge about tourism and the context for development can all affect the success or failure of attempts at integration.

The gap between the successful integration of tourism and partial or symbolic integration can be wide. A great deal depends on the attitudes of those with responsibility for tourism planning and development and the approaches which they take to co-ordinate and include the full range of viewpoints on proposed developments including those of local residents. It has been argued that if local participation is to be effective in overcoming the often inherent problems of entrenched decisionmaking and inequality in the allocation of benefits from development, then it must originate within the local communities themselves. The level of involvement and the ability to bring about changes in development proposals so that the final results are truly integrated into the local systems vary widely. One of the first researchers to describe the various stages of participation was Arnstein (1969), who proposed six 'steps' in her 'Ladder of Public Participation'. More recently, Pretty (1995) has described seven stages in a typology of participation. The five categories noted below reflect the same basic elements of level of participation and decision-making power vested in the communities involved, as do Arnstein's and Pretty's typologies. They range from 'imposition' through to 'equality', reflecting to a large degree the nature of decision making in the host country and community.

- *Imposition:* Clearly the least desirable, and probably the least effective, form of integration is where it is forced upon a community without input from that community. In such cases the development is normally controlled and financed from outside the community and has the support of external and higher levels of government. The Nusa Dua development on Bali serves as an example of such a type of development. A complex of international franchise hotels and associated facilities developed by external financing with strong support from the central Indonesian government was constructed over a period of years in southern Bali in the 1980s. The resort can be said to be integrated on the basis that it has strong economic links through transportation developments and employment with other parts of Bali, is promoted as a part of Bali, not as a separate destination, and to some extent has integrated water and other elements of environmental planning and operations. It is spatially segregated from the rest of Bali by virtue of its location and design, and by the market at which it aims, which is considerably higher than that attracted by most of the rest of Bali.
- *Petition:* Whereas the previous category implied a total absence of local involvement in the decisions on location, scale, design and other elements of

integration of development, this category suggests an opportunity for input. However, that input is made without obligation on the part of the decision-making agencies to accept such input or to modify their intentions. In these cases the proposal is presented to local communities for comment only after demands and petitioning for such an opportunity has been made and often at a point at which major decisions have been made. The opportunity for integration is mostly one-sided, that is, local operators and resource users may have an opportunity to adjust their patterns of operation to allow integration with the development before it is begun, or at least completed, thus allowing for an easier and possibly more successful insertion of the development. To some extent this situation reflects the process at Anuha Island discussed by Sofield, where the situation deteriorated rapidly following changes in ownership and operation and the perceptions of the level of involvement of local decision makers were abruptly changed with disastrous results.

- *Advice:* This category represents a situation in which local advice is sought as to the ways in which the development could be designed, located and operated in order to make it more integrated into the community, although the final decision-making authority still remains outside the community. There is the opportunity for local expertise and priorities to be reflected in the development, not only in its scale and operation, but also in its design and location. Integration that is effective is more likely to be achieved at this level and beyond in that there is for the first time the opportunity for adjustment to achieve integration on both the part of the developers and of the local communities. This process was followed by National Park authorities in Canada in the 1970s when public participation was introduced to park planning for the first time.

- *Representation:* At this stage the communities have formal rights to be involved in the process of integration through planning and operation of the development. This may take the form of representation on local boards or agencies to oversee the design, construction and even operation of the development. With involvement from an early stage local expertise can be incorporated more fully into design and operational procedures and the effects of development and use on the environment be minimized. The greater the sharing of knowledge about the local environment and the operation of the development the greater the opportunity for avoiding conflict and incompatibility as tourism develops. In Canada, tourism developments in those national parks which have permanent settlements are now designed and operated in such a way, and the residents are actively involved from the early stages (Parks Canada 1994). Final decisions are still taken outside the local area, and the process can still cause concern and generate opposition, because compromises still have to be made.
- *Equality*: True equality in the integration of tourism developments is rare. It can be taken to represent the situation in which the proponents and recipients of development are treated as equals and all elements of the integration process are agreed to by all parties. Adjustments in the design and operation of developments are as likely, or perhaps even more likely than adjustments in the operation of existing activities and lifestyles. Decision making rests in both locations, the communities and the source of the development. Clearly, where development is coming from within the community and the community operates on a democratic or equally acceptable format for its residents, then this situation should be automatic. Where development is proposed from outside, then procedures need to be in place to ensure

that proponents are required to treat the communities as equals. A workable veto is obviously one way of achieving this situation. It is likely that such a situation or something equivalent may materialize in Nunavut, the soon to be established Inuit controlled section of the Canadian North West Territories, where the local governing body will not only have control of development but also the funds to carry it out.

The categories which have been discussed above represent generalized levels of local involvement in decision making, and have been discussed in a variety of forms with respect to planning, but have not been applied specifically to the integration of tourism developments. As will be discussed below, one of the major problems is that it has taken a long time for the idea of local involvement in the tourism planning process to become a reality in many areas. In many parts of the world, unfortunately, a large proportion of which are the scenes of major tourism development and expansion, it still does not exist. However, the involvement of local actors in planning does not necessarily carry over into involvement in development and even less so in operations. Integration is much more than planning, however, and involves all elements from design, planning, construction and operation if it is to be truly successful. The presence of local involvement does not guarantee successful integration, but one may argue strongly that its absence is very likely to result in unsuccessful integration.

If it is accepted that current thinking and attitudes with respect to tourism development are strongly in favour of an integrative approach, and that such an approach is very much in line with the principles of sustainable development, which also appears to have widespread political and popular support, it is perhaps surprising that examples of the successful integration of tourism are hard to find. Pearce's example of such an approach in Sarawak is one case where external advisers have gone much further than most in clearly expressing the need for and utility of integration. The Integrated Rural Tourism Development Programmes for Andalusia, discussed by Cavaco represent another. In reality, while the intent may be present in other areas, although one may question whether there is little more than symbolic intent in some situations, there are a number of factors which make implementation difficult to achieve.

- *Lack of equality:* Despite long-standing calls for local and community involvement in tourism, echoed strongly in Our Common Future, local communities do not have the same power as higher levels of government or large-scale external development agencies. Local activities, especially where these are small-scale and highly fragmented, for example small family farms or individually owned fishing boats, can rarely be effectively and strongly represented when large-scale developments are being promoted and discussed. Different priorities are involved at different levels of government and local concerns may be subordinated to national or regional level policies. Such a situation can often mean that while tourism may be integrated in planning at national and regional levels, in reality it becomes imposed at the local level. Efforts may be made to integrate it at the community level, but in such situations existing activities are more likely to have to be adjusted to accommodate tourism than tourism significantly modified to fit in with established local activities. Such situations are common to development of all types. It is rare for local interests, generally represented by a small and limited power base, to be able to successfully achieve and retain equality with higher levels of government and large external private sector corporations. When they are able to do so, it is often because specific local conditions such as geographical attributes and timing, along with the contributions of key individuals, provide the means to achieve such equality of power.

- *Lack of desire*: To achieve successful integration can require considerable resources of time and money, as well as consistent commitment. In most countries elected representatives have relatively short-term viewpoints, often only as far as the next election. To ensure proper integration requires involvement from the first stage of the initial proposal for development through to monitoring the operational phase of developments. Even if the same decision-makers and officials were in power throughout that period, their priorities and commitments are likely to change and their concerns for specific developments in specific areas likely to wane after development has occurred. There are marked similarities with the issue-attention cycle of impact analysis. The environmental impact analysis process often attracts considerable attention in the early stages of a project, but decreasing attention is generally paid as the project continues, and in very few cases does monitoring continue and rarely are the original projections of impact reviewed and verified once the development is in place and operating. Resources are rarely allocated to ensure that integration of development continues into the operational phase, even if integration was achieved during the planning and development of a project. Development rarely stops when initial construction is completed and the dynamic element of tourism noted above almost always results in modifications to the physical and operational characteristics of most projects over time. Such modifications should also be reviewed and assessed as to their likelihood of being successfully integrated into the local environment.
- *Lack of appreciation*: Despite all of the research and attention given to tourism over the past two or three

decades, there is still considerable ignorance of its effects and the way in which it operates at all levels. The blindly optimistic view of tourism as an economic panacea promoted in the 1960s, when it was seen as the salvation of declining areas and thus pushed forward at almost any cost, has fortunately changed as the costs as well as the benefits of tourism are being more accurately assessed. However, to some extent the pendulum has swung too far the other way, and tourism is now often envisioned as a supplementary form of economic activity which can be easily accommodated in many peripheral or marginal areas with little adjustment. It is often assumed that tourism will automatically be compatible with existing activities, for example, that local farmers will supply hotels with food and local fisherman have ready markets for their catches, ignoring the fact that many hotel chains prefer to buy in bulk from offshore suppliers to ensure reliability and consistency in supply and quality, and that many tourists demand foodstuffs that cannot be produced locally. Tourism is a complex, resource-specific industry operating at a global scale, often with scant regard for local priorities. Failure to appreciate that it is an industry with global links, dependencies and relationships can result not only in an inability to achieve integration, but ultimately the replacement of a weak monoculture by one that is strong and dominant, at least in the short term.

- *Lack of mechanisms:* There is a general lack of appropriate mechanisms for ensuring the integration of tourism. There is widespread acknowledgment of the fragmentation and complexity of tourism, and the difficulty of exerting consistent control over the industry, along with its general failure to successfully regulate itself. For many other economic activities there are established agencies which are designed and empowered to control such elements as production, quality, price, marketing and participation, for example, agricultural marketing boards such as the Wheat Board in Canada, the White Fish Authority in Great Britain or Atomic Energy Authorities in many countries. No such bodies exist for tourism, and control and regulation is left with agencies not normally specifically equipped for the task. Planning authorities in most countries at the national level are either concerned with broad strategies or with promotion of development or both, and control and regulation including integration are found at regional and local levels if they exist at all. Whether tourism is sufficiently unique to require a specific mechanism to ensure its regulation and integration is uncertain. What is certain is that without appropriate mechanisms (along with the desire to enforce them, as noted above) tourism is not likely to be effectively integrated on principles of equity at even the planning stage, let alone the operational stages of development.

- *Lack of data and knowledge*: The lack of detailed knowledge of the way that tourism relates to and impacts on other activities has been noted above. One of the main reasons for this lack of knowledge relates to the lack of data on tourism and on the environment in which it operates. Traditionally data have been collected and analysed sectorally, which has mitigated against a holistic and integrated approach. In addition, data were often from one limited time period only, making it extremely difficult to identify and attribute changes over time to any particular causal agent. Monitoring change was not only expensive and time consuming, but often impossible on the scale necessary. Such change as was identified was often limited to small areas and was rarely placed in a regional, let alone a national context. Much data were collected for administrative units rather than for natural ecosystems, which made identification of causation and scale of effect much more difficult also.

Only in recent years has it become possible, through the use of remotely collected data, for example from satellite imaging systems, to collect data at a scale suitable to be able to understand and monitor change in natural systems. Even then, analysis of such data was difficult until suitable techniques such as Geographic Information Systems became available and were applied to tourism. The advent of a wide range of relatively user-friendly systems for the spatial analysis of data combined with increasing ease of access to large scale data means that one of the major blocks to effective integration planning may be removed.

The concept of integration is a popular one in the tourism literature and calls for its adoption have increased significantly with the popularization and support for the concept of sustainable development. Successful sustainable development inevitably neither requires the application of an integrative approach, since by definition it demands that the development process not eliminate future options nor prevents the continued operations, especially of indigenous peoples. In discussing planning the management of tourism for the future, Maitland comments:

There is increasing interaction between tourism and other industries and between visitors and host populations unconnected with tourism. The consequence is that we need tourism planning which integrates tourism development into broader strategies for the development of places, and of non-tourism businesses.

As tourism becomes tied ever more firmly to global processes and agents, so it will increasingly be involved with many activities and processes unrelated directly to leisure, and it will only be successful if its development is integrated with these other processes. While failure of a tourism enterprise at the global level through a lack of integration may be unfortunate, tourism development at a local level which is not suitably integrated with local activities and processes can be disastrous. The complete integration of tourism development is unlikely in many communities, just as the attainment of sustainability is more of a goal than a reality in most situations. However, sincere attempts at integration which include the involvement of local communities are more likely to be well received than development for which no effort is made to reach compatibility, if not symbiosis, with local ecological, economic and social systems. Even where sustainability is not an issue, development which is a part of a community is generally more successful than development which is apart from a community.

FACTORS INFLUENCING TOURISM

Before presenting the case findings, a number of broader comments need to be made regarding lecturers' perceptions of uncontrollable or system-wide factors which have been emerging as influential in the development of Tourism. Additionally influences are revealed which influence the way in which Tourism has developed at more than one 'level', for example, the issue of modularisation which, according to most lecturers, features at both the institutional and the department/school level, and the perceived importance of the subject's status or respectability which features at all four levels of influence. Despite the fact that there are system-wide factors or issues beyond Tourism lecturers' control which have had implications for the nature of the subject, Tourism is seen to have remained within the subject specialists' control during its developmental years.

Some of the general trends in HE, for example, the perception of a decline in students' academic ability and the increasing importance of quality assurance policies such as the Research Assessment Exercise (RAE) and Subject Review, have featured in the way in which Tourism has evolved, but are not perceived to have hindered its development.

At an institutional level lecturers felt that Tourism has represented for most, an opportunity for solid recruitment at minimal cost, rather than an opportunity to expand into previously uncharted academic waters. Competition between institutions is perceived to have heightened in the mid 1990s, resulting in the possible emergence of a virtual 'league table' of providers of Tourism at the turn of the century, and changing priorities with regard to research agenda at the institutional level compound similar frustration felt at department level.

Modularisation in HE receives mixed reactions from lecturers who perceive a reduced level of curriculum space and problems of contextualisation for Tourism as being unfortunate by-products of a system which is applauded within the wider HE system because of associated increased flexibility of provision and widening choice for students. Policies and activities at department or school level which influence Tourism subject development are numerous and in many cases filter down from the institution as a whole.

The issue of subject status is again prevalent at the department level and the extent of lecturers' concern about the appropriateness of individuals to teach Tourism is a reflection of their insistence that the subject still has to prove itself in academic terms. There is a clear message which emerges, that inappropriate individuals teaching Tourism have hindered the quality and integrity of the subject's development. In an environment where goal-posts regarding teaching and research are seen to change constantly, the importance of maintaining personal aims and agendas is regarded as critical in ensuring healthy development of the subject.

The remainder of the paper focuses on the two critical factors which have influenced Tourism's development, that of the individual lecturer's influence and the subject's perceived status in HE. The first of the two critical influences on Tourism's development focuses on individual Tourism lecturers. Members of the Tourism academic community interviewed have been seen to cope in the face of institutional change and constraints, resolute in their need, on occasion, to swim against the tide as a relatively content community.

At the same time they have accepted the continual, and what they regard as frustrating changes, whilst ensuring the community maintains a voice at department and institution level when human resources are being allocated and programme additions and deletions considered. In spite of the fact that lecturers interviewed regarded the Tourism academic community as playing a critical role in the way the subject has developed, this is not a community which can be characterised by togetherness, or involving a team approach to subject development. Becher has argued that 'being a member of a disciplinary community involves a sense of identity and personal commitment'.

Whilst the sense of identity for the Tourism academic community has not become as apparent (linked to a perceived lack of respectability) or consistent as one might have expected after 15 years of the subject's existence at an undergraduate level, the commitment of individuals to the teaching of courses cannot be doubted in the light of this study's findings.

The academic community which has emerged is one characterised by individuals' expectations, personal goals and values which have been critical in shaping Tourism and its developing curriculum. Trowler (1997) has emphasised the importance of individuals in HE and the potential impact that their aspirations and values can have on HE, and this study would lend support to this view. The fact that Tourism lecturers appear to cope in the face of considerable teaching pressures could also reflect, on the part of institutions' management, a soft approach to managing people where a committed group of individuals is developed by allowing Tourism lecturers a considerable amount of academic freedom regarding what they teach and how they teach it.

However, this soft approach, whilst encouraging committed individuals to pursue their own course development, does not appear to have been as successful in encouraging a truly committed Tourism academic community at institutional level when programme teams have been required to work together on programme validations or revalidations. Trowler noted that those lecturers who appear to be coping with their teaching workloads are likely to place activities like programme planning meetings very much at the bottom of their list of priorities.

The fact that a number of lecturers all but 'stick their heads in the sand' when such meetings are called, is reflective of a community which will busy themselves with what they perceive to be the more important issue of ensuring the delivery of their own courses. This is not to say that Tourism lecturers lack professionalism, which is evident in their commitment to research and teaching and interaction between these two key activities in HE.

This relatively young, still developing specialism remains at the evolutionary stage and realistically, is delivered by a diverging community, owing to the enthusiasm and determination of its members in delivering courses which meet their own personal aspirations and goals, rather than those of a collective, cohesive community. This does not, however, undervalue the achievement of those individuals in contributing towards a new subject which remains, for the time being, economically viable and diverse in its nature, reflecting the changing interests of the Tourism lecturing community.

What has emerged is a process of self-alienation from opportunities to contribute to subject development by the specialists who have, at the same time, made clear their discomfort with the lack of control they have over recruitment and promotion of the subject. This might be a reflection of the fact that some Tourism lecturers do not perceive the programme planning process to contribute towards the development of Tourism as a subject, perhaps favouring individual course development and research as the key factor in this process.

However, the trend which has emerged for lecturers to concentrate their efforts on course rather than programme development, could have implications for the subject's wider development as a cohesive curriculum, particularly if tensions emerge between those lecturers who do get involved in programme development and those who effectively choose to ignore it. A concern has been emerging for the appropriate matching of lecturer to course, extended in some cases to a concern that lecturers from other departments or schools have been drafted in to cover courses which require the knowledge and experience of other disciplinary areas.

Full-time Tourism lecturers interviewed expressed considerable concern over the fact that non-Tourism specialists were delivering generic Business courses to Tourism undergraduates, who were left to take responsibility themselves for providing the necessary contextualisation. The existence and quality of Tourism- specific knowledge amongst non-Tourism specialists appeared then to be of more concern to Tourism lecturers who have been defending 'their own patches of intellectual ground' in their attempts to ensure some level of influence over who is recruited from outside the specialism to deliver courses which contribute towards Tourism degree programmes.

Although there has been no evidence of a need to see Tourism recognised as a discipline per se, Tourism lecturers have been inclined to exert some level of ownership over their subject and to ensure the appropriate content of the curriculum, which has been after all, delivered by members of a wide variety of academic communities beyond the boundaries of the 'Tourism community'. This might account for the need amongst many lecturers to see Tourism's profile and respectability as an academic subject enhanced.

Little evidence has emerged to support a view that Tourism lecturers should take a step back from their teaching and consider the wider implications for the programme as a whole of removing entirely or amending the contents of a course. In the light of this evidence, not only has the Tourism curriculum been changing all the time, but it has been changing without any real attention paid to the implications of minor course amendments, exclusion and new additions to the overall thrust of programmes.

Individual desires and enthusiasms to alter the nature of a course or even to eradicate a course altogether could have been threatening the ability of students to meet programme aims and objectives. With regard to the subject's future in HE, the ad hoc addition and removal of courses from programmes could threaten the achievement of programme aims and learning outcomes. The nature of this divergent academic community is by no means unique to Tourism.

Previous studies have been able to clarify 'tribes' within disciplinary communities. For example, economists, sociologists and marketers are just some of the individual tribes within the Business Studies disciplinary community which has been described by Macfarlane (1998) as diverging in nature, made up of a number of 'refugees, nomads and tourists' due to its reliance on so many disciplines.

Tourism lecturers appear to belong to a community which is characterised by individuals from a wide variety of academic disciplines, although there does appear to be an increasing number who are gaining named Tourism academic qualifications at higher degree level. It might, however be inappropriate to talk about the Tourism community in terms of a tribe, as this might imply that there is, in fact, a sense of togetherness and working towards a common goal which has not yet, according to this study, come to light. In short, this paper has revealed the critical role played by the individual Tourism lecturer which is indicative of a still developing subject, reflected in the rapid movement of Tourism staff into and out of institutions, coupled with the frequency of inappropriate matching of staff to specialist courses and the incidence of curriculum change to suit particular circumstances rather than careful planning.

In essence, a situation has emerged where control of the logistics of offering Tourism as a subject in HE rests at the institutional level, as it is here that decisions are made about who studies Tourism at undergraduate level and what information is communicated to potential students regarding the structure and content of their Tourism programmes.

However, individual lecturers in their teaching have been given the freedom to deliver the subject according to their own personal desires and aspirations, but have not necessarily taken up opportunities to make changes to the curriculum through the programme planning and validation process. Having analysed the significant role played by individuals within the Tourism academic community on the subject's development, the discussion now turns to an evaluation of the continuing importance of the academic-vocational debate in the context of the developing curriculum, with particular reference to its contribution to the subject's status in HE.

TOURISM IN HIGHER EDUCATION

The academic-vocational debate and the perceived status of Tourism in HE clearly involves the individual lecturers described earlier playing a vital role in the subject's development. Interviews with Tourism lecturers reveal the continuing importance of the academic-vocational debate which surrounds the purpose and development of HE programmes and the perceived importance of academic respectability.

Whilst the two issues have not necessarily been explicitly linked in the context of Tourism's development in the first two decades in HE, this paper offers evidence which might support a view that the subject's status is inextricably linked to the Tourism academic community's relationships with the tourism industry. The extent to which Tourism programmes are delivered in accordance with the more vocational aims detailed in promotional literature and validation documents can certainly be challenged.

Undergraduate Tourism programmes have been promoted in recent years as preparation for work in the tourism, or other service industry, as evidenced in Airey and

Johnson's study of 1997. However, this study found that the majority of Tourism lecturers appear to have been taking on a form of liberal vocationalism in their approach to delivering their courses, which saw them combining academic and vocational aspects in what Raffe described as an aggregative approach to education, despite a tendency for stated aims to favour the employment preparation focus.

This flexible approach to focusing vocational programmes in HE on preparation for work in general rather than stating explicit Tourism careers has also been reflected in the emergence of undergraduate Tourism programmes which could be described as simultaneously offering both an education for, and an education about, Tourism, as in the case of Business Studies.

Tourism's development, according to Tourism lecturers, has been influenced by both a focus upon subject specific knowledge and skills development, and upon the development of transferable, academic skills. The critical factor here was the recognition that developing knowledge for Tourism was seen as just as important an aspect of preparation for work as the industry specific practical or skills-based aspects of Tourism education. Some lecturers were even beginning to argue that an education about Tourism could actually be a better preparation for employment in the tourism industry than an education for Tourism.

This supports an argument proposed by Ainley who felt that 'the independent ability of students to pursue knowledge, up to degree level and beyond' was even more useful to them in preparation for a given vocation than perhaps vocational information during their studies. It is now clear that lecturers are placing greater emphasis on traditional academic abilities than vocationally oriented skills at course delivery level, even when a Tourism programme's aim was essentially to provide graduates for the tourism or other service industry. There is however, a further possible explanation for lecturers' tendency to avoid the overtly vocational courses, and to focus instead on the more academic aspects of the subject.

However clearly an institution promotes the vocational aims of its Tourism provision, the individual lecturers' need to focus on the academic, more respected aspects of the subject, might have overshadowed the vocational intent of that provision. Whereas respectability for Tourism as an academic subject has been viewed by lecturers interviewed as an issue over which they feel they have little influence or control, their decision to focus on the academic aspects of Tourism, and to distance themselves from courses which have clear vocational links, is to an extent, evidence of the considerable impact they have exerted over the subject's perceived respectability. There are in fact a number of further reasons why lecturers focus upon the provision of academic courses, other than reasons of respectability.

Firstly, lecturers might be intrinsically interested in the academic aspects and, as long as they have the apparent freedom to teach what they are interested in, they will continue to do so. Secondly, as mentioned earlier, institutions might not be capable of delivering vocational courses due to the nature of the lecturing staff they recruit; this might be the reason why institutions do not lean heavily on staff who are not delivering what the documentation states should be happening.

Thirdly, there might be a total misunderstanding on the part of programme planners about the needs of the industry. Given that lecturers probably know more about these needs (which may involve general as opposed to specific skills) than senior programme planners, they may believe they are, in fact, delivering what the industry wants. With this evidence in mind, therefore, a contradiction has been unearthed regarding the provision of Tourism as an undergraduate subject in HE.

Whilst the stated focus remains that of preparing graduates for the world of work in the Tourism and other industries, lecturers admit to being reticent in involving tourism industry professionals in the planning, design and delivery of Tourism courses. This is despite the fact that much of the validation documentation and institutions' mission statements highlight the importance of industry involvement.

Whilst institutions say they are offering an education for Tourism in programme validation material which reflects the mission of the institution as a whole, the industry which could benefit the most from graduates with that education is rarely offered more than a token role in its delivery.

The vast majority of Tourism industry involvement in an education for itself, and other service industries, involves a seat on the validation or revalidation board and the occasional guest lecture arranged by individual Tourism lecturers on an ad hoc basis, which are regarded as one-off insights into industry practice rather than a valuable contribution to the overall Tourism education package.

This might not, however, be indicative of approaches to industry involvement at all institutions which offer Tourism undergraduate programmes but is, nevertheless, an emerging trend which featured in this study. This apparent trend for some individuals to distance themselves from opportunities to work with the tourism industry in preparing programmes and coursescould be further evidence of an attempt, on the part of Tourism lecturers, to rid the subject of vocational links which they perceive to be detrimental to its respectability in the wider academic community.

Another reason for avoiding links with the tourism industry could be that many Tourism lecturers come from other disciplines or subjects and do not necessarily want to sever these links. Reluctance amongst Tourism academics to foster links with the industry might also account for the difficulties experienced by the National Liaison Group for Higher Education in Tourism (NLG), now the Association of Tourism in Higher Education (ATHE), to gain widespread support over the last seven years.

Despite its aim to 'promote the development and recognition of tourism as a subject for study in the UK' and 'to identify and communicate good practice, statistics and other information about first degrees and postgraduate qualifications in tourism', it has been perceived by Tourism lecturers interviewed to be a body made up of committed individuals but was regarded as having been 'an outside body looking in' to Tourism in HE.

In this sense, lecturers interviewed did not feel that they had any control over the activities taken on by the Group. In view of the efforts of the NLG to bring as many representatives from HE and the industry together in the last seven years or so to discuss the nature and direction of the subject, it is difficult to understand why this perception has emerged. What is more, of the 50 institutions which offered Tourism at undergraduate level in the academic year 1998/99, only 30 were paid up members of the NLG therefore it could easily be argued that membership of the Group would itself lead to opportunities to influence its key activities.

The NLG has reported continual problems in encouraging a greater proportion of institutions to become active members of the Group, and this could be put down to its professed industry links which have been regarded as countering Tourism academics' desire to see vocational links severed in order to enhance the subject's academic respectability. If you do not agree with the fundamental aims of the organisation, you are simply not going to join. It is important to note that four of the five institutions which took part in the interview stage of this study were members of the NLG during the academic year 1998/99.

Therefore, it would appear that comments reflecting a lack of awareness of the Group's activities and its key purpose might reflect gaps in communication between NLG representatives and Tourism lecturers within institutions/ schools or an unwillingness or inability for tourism lecturers to take on board the potential importance of a group whose remit has focused on facilitating and advising on the nature and delivery of Tourism in HE.

Whilst the activities of the NLG have been perceived by some lecturers as being beyond their control, the Group has in fact been committed to increasing its membership, widening participation in its conferences and encouraging those involved in the design and delivery of Tourism, (in education and industry) to produce practical written guides which reflect the developing Tourism curriculum and areas of good practice in its design and delivery in higher education.

The debate surrounding the role and effectiveness of the NLG continues into 2001. In adopting its new name, ATHE has in fact opted to drop its industry-link role and to take on the role of subject association for Tourism in HE. If this is an indication of a more direct approach to gaining academic respectability for the subject, then ATHE might well see its membership increase and a true community approach to curriculum development emerge. In spite of this apparent trend for Tourism academics to distance themselves from the tourism industry, one of the key concerns of lecturers regarding the RAE was the fact that the exercise was not supportive of practical or industry based research.

A key characteristic of Tourism research carried out by Tourism lecturers in the last few years has been the fact that it was in most cases 'RAE-led'. In short, lecturers felt that departments and institutions as a whole were seen to be very supportive of individuals who would and could write for the RAE and were seen, in fact, to create research appointments and sabbaticals for that very purpose, irrespective of the increased teaching workloads for non-research active lecturers.

This has led to criticism from some who felt that industry relevant research output which would not be suitable for contribution to the RAE was not supported or encouraged. Completion of academic or pure research which was sure to get published in one of the handful of highly acclaimed, refereed Tourism journals was the only way in which Tourism lecturers could be sure of gaining valuable remission from teaching to carry out research.

This approach to research, whilst recognised as a fact of life in HE in the late 1990s, was regarded as unfortunate in the context of Tourism as an emerging subject, as it has important vocational content which, it could be argued, had just as much right to contribute to research evaluations. These complaints from a few lecturers, however, need to be considered in the context of an academic community which, for the most part, is not all that supportive of links with the tourism industry and are contradictory to the more general view that academic aspects of the subject need to be pursued if respectability is to be gained.

Chapter 8

Indigenous Tourism and Service

INDIGENOUS TOURISM

Aboriginal tourism gives Indigenous people the chance to tell their story in their way, to share cultural insights, traditional practices and contemporary concerns with non-Indigenous Australians and international visitors. Indigenous communities view tourism as a means of both educating others about Indigenous culture, and creating employment and training opportunities at a local level. Aboriginal tourism experiences are varied, but a common thread is the inclusion of insights about the cultural knowledge, lifestyle and beliefs of Australia's Indigenous people.

Aboriginal tourism goes beyond the lifestyles and traditions of Indigenous people who live on homelands, out-stations and remote communities to include the urban experience of Australia's Indigenous persons. Rock art tours, politically themed art exhibitions, live theatre and stories from the Dreamtime told around a campfire are all expressions of Indigenous culture. The National Aboriginal and Torres Strait Islander Tourism Industry Strategy defines Indigenous tourism as including all forms of participation by Indigenous persons in tourism:

- As employers
- As employees
- As investors

- As joint venture partners
- Providing Indigenous cultural tourism products
- Providing mainstream tourism products.

In Aboriginal culture the significance of land is intimately bound in the spirituality surrounding the origins of landscapes, animals, plants and people. Traditional owners, or custodians, have a responsibility to look after the environmental, cultural and spiritual wellbeing of the land. This unique relationship and respect for the land is increasingly attracting visitors seeking to 'touch the earth'.

Another key element of Aboriginal tourism is cultural control, considered crucial to maintaining authenticity and preventing cultural exploitation and cultural appropriation. Intellectual and cultural property rights, along with copyright issues, are of particular concern to Indigenous. Authenticity is important to international visitors.

The Wet Tropics World Heritage Area (WHA) was declared in 1988. It covers an area of 894 420 hectares and mainly includes tropical rainforest extending from Townsville to Cooktown in northeastern Queensland. It is managed by the Wet Tropics Management Authority (WTMA) based in Cairns, and the Queensland Parks and Wildlife Service (QPWS) is responsible for field management and permits for activities in the WHA.

There are twenty Indigenous language groups in or near the Wet Tropics WHA, which also includes Indigenous communities such as Yarrabah, south of Cairns, Mona Mona, near Kuranda, and Wujal Wujal, in the Daintree region. The involvement of Rainforest Indigenous communities is set out in Wet Tropics WHA legislation, the Wet Tropics Management Plan 1998, and in the key policy document Protection through Partnerships. WTMA negotiates with Rainforest Indigenous groups on cultural protocols, planning, site management, infrastructure, walking-tracks, and joint management agreements. Three Indigenous community liaison officers are employed on contract by WTMA, to consult Indigenous groups on management issues.

Rainforest-based nature tourism and ecotourism is a major activity in the Wet Tropics WHA. In 1998, more than 210 commercial tour operators had permits to operate in the Wet Tropics region. Half of all Queensland nature-based tour operators are located in Far North Queensland, with the majority visiting sites in the Wet Tropics. The region has an estimated 2.8 million visitors per year. High-use areas include Mossman Gorge with 500 000 visitors and the Daintree with over 300 000 visitors per year. Indigenous tourism ventures include Kuku Yalanji Dreamtime Walks in Mossman Gorge; Native Guide Safari Tours conducted by Hazel Douglas in the Daintree; Tjapukai Aboriginal Cultural Park in Cairns; Menmuny Museum in Yarrabah; Nganyaji Cultural Centre in Ravenshoe; and guided rainforest walks at Malanda Falls with Ngadjonjii elder, Ernie Raymont. Kuku Yalanji art and craft workshops, storytelling and Indigenous-guided rainforest walks are included at the Daintree Ecolodge.

New Indigenous tourism ventures in 2002 include Kuku Yalanji Coastal Habitat Tours marketed by Daintree Ecolodge; Bunda Dibandji Art Site Tour near Kuranda, a joint venture between Djabugay Tribal Aboriginal Corporation and Cedar Park Resort; and Gugubarabi Echo Creek Walk in the Tully Valley, a partnership between El Rancho del Rey and local Jirrbal guides, Robert and Ernie Grant. Other Rainforest Indigenous participation in Wet Tropics tourism includes employment as QPWS rangers, the construction of boardwalks, and cultural heritage signs in national parks.

Tourism in the Wet Tropics WHA directly generates $179 million, while flow-on tourism expenditure in the local region is around $753 million. At present, Rainforest Indigenous groups do not receive any licensing income from tourism operations in the Wet Tropics and visitors do not pay park entry fees at popular rainforest sites such as waterfalls, lakes and rainforest boardwalks in National Parks.

Tourism use should contribute to the conservation and understanding of Aboriginal cultural heritage and help Aboriginal people as tourism industry participants to achieve economic and social benefits.

Apart from consulting with traditional owners about site management, there is limited Indigenous participation in the development and management of tourism in the Wet Tropics WHA. Indigenous cultural and land issues are addressed by the North Queensland Land Council representing Wet Tropics native title claimants, Indigenous land management agencies and by Indigenous community liaison officers. New cultural protocols will guide consultations with Indigenous peoples about permit applications in the Wet Tropics. Wet Tropics nature-based tourism strategy Indigenous involvement in rainforest-based tourism is a central part of the Wet Tropics Nature Based Tourism Strategy.

This tourism strategy for the Wet Tropics World Heritage Area of North Queensland aims to 'facilitate Aboriginal involvement in (nature) tourism and tourism management'. It also acknowledges that 'Rainforest Aboriginal people have native title rights and are partners in management of and participation in nature-based tourism in the Wet Tropics'.

The Strategy has policy statements on 'Rainforest Aboriginal People's Rights and Interests', including the cultural responsibilities of native title landholders, visitor site management involving traditional owners, and Indigenous involvement in nature-based tourism. This included participation, employment and training in tourism, interpretation of natural and cultural values and partnerships in tourism, such as cultural tours at Mossman Gorge.

The Bama Wabu Rainforest Aboriginal Association was listed as a key partner in Wet Tropics marketing guidelines, monitoring visitor sites, and setting accreditation levels for tour operators. Indigenous groups, though, were not involved in permit approvals for commercial tour operators in the Wet Tropics. This Strategy endorsed nature-based tourism in the

Wet Tropics WHA that promotes Indigenous cultural heritage values and empowers Indigenous peoples as participants in the tourism industry. ATSIC, Bama Wabu and local Indigenous groups contributed to the policies and principles for the Wet Tropics Nature Based Tourism Strategy.

Consultation with traditional owners about site planning and management was required for most of the popular visitor areas in the Wet Tropics WHA. Rainforest Indigenous interests in tourism or cultural interpretation were also mentioned for eighteen visitor sites, including Mossman Gorge, Cathedral Fig Tree, Lake Barrine, Lake Eacham, Tully Gorge, and five scenic waterfalls: Murray, Josephine, Millstream, Blencoe and Wallaman Falls.

Other sites are under review with traditional owners about tourism concerns. The Strategy also states the need for assessment of the impacts of tourism on Indigenous cultural landscapes in the Wet Tropics. It does not address the specific programmes or training required for developing Indigenous tourism ventures at key visitor sites.

Wet Tropics Walking Strategy

The Wet Tropics Walking Strategy identified 145 managed walks in the Wet Tropics WHA region. Rainforest peoples were identified as key stakeholders with opportunities for walk management and cultural tourism. This Strategy acknowledged the cultural significance of walking tracks with many based on traditional trading routes through rainforest areas. Indigenous participation in this Strategy included employment through tourism operations, guided walks, track construction and maintenance.

Negotiation on walking-track routes, protection of cultural sites, permits for commercial operations, and resources to fund Rainforest groups in track construction were highlighted. The Indigenous cultural setting was one of four key criteria used to assess walk experiences, focusing on Indigenous history, use, perceptions, names, cultural associations and stories about walkways. Walkingtrack management by community rangers and Indigenous cultural walks were also identified for key rainforest areas such as Malanda Falls, Bare Hill, Wabunga Wayemba, Echo Creek Falls, Barron Gorge, and Murray Falls/ Kirrama Range. Some eighty percent of the Wet Tropics WHA is claimable under native title legislation and sixteen claims covering 282 966ha have been lodged to date.

Land-use agreements have been negotiated recently by WTMA with the Mona Mona and Wujal Wujal Aboriginal communities. Indigenous Land Use (ILU) agreements have also been reached with major tourism developments in the Cairns region. These agreements cover Skyrail Rainforest Cableway and Tjapukai Aboriginal Cultural Park, located on adjacent sites under a native title claim, with guarantees of employment for the local Djabugay people, protection of cultural heritage, and Indigenous approval of cultural presentations.

In 2002, the Mamu Aboriginal Corporation and Johnstone Shire Council, based in Innisfail, signed an ILU Heads of Agreement for a proposed new rainforest canopy walkway in the Wooroonooran National Park. This Agreement also provides for Indigenous employment, protection of cultural heritage, and cultural tourism input at the Mamu canopy walk, during and after construction. The Queensland Ecotourism Plan 2003-2008 (Tourism Queensland 2002) also recognises the importance of negotiating native title claims in managing protected areas for ecotourism.

Indigenous Tourism in the Wet Tropics WHA

Kuku Yalanji Dreamtime Walks in Mossman Gorge won the 2002 Tourism Queensland Award for Aboriginal and Torres Strait Islander Tourism, previously won by Tjapukai Aboriginal Cultural Park. However, this tourism venture operated by the Mossman Gorge Aboriginal Community depends on CDEP wages for guides and is not open on weekends. Indigenous tour operators also require QPWS permits in national parks and approval from WTMA to build new infrastructure such as visitor centres and walking tracks in the WHA. Indigenous tours also compete with other rainforest day tours offered from Cairns, Port Douglas and Mission Beach, and mainly attract self-drive independent travellers rather than regular tour groups. Thus new Indigenous guided tours in 2002 are partnerships with established rainforest lodges in the Wet Tropics.

There are other key issues for developing Rainforest Indigenous tourism in the Wet Tropics WHA. Tasting rainforest fruits (bush tucker) are part of an Indigenous cultural experience that may be constrained by seasonal availability, or environmental laws that prohibit taking or using natural resources in protected areas. One Indigenous tour operator in the Wet Tropics used to let visitors taste rainforest fruits, but a sign in the operator's vehicle now asks guests not to touch or eat anything in the rainforest. Telling tourists how (Rainforest) Indigenous peoples ate bushfoods and utilised the natural environment, as a past practice, seems to contradict the image of Indigenous culture as 'alive and authentic'.

Since 1990, Rainforest Indigenous peoples have sought to have the Wet Tropics officially re-listed by the World Heritage Convention for its Indigenous cultural values, along with current natural heritage values, in order to manage jointly the WHA. With this official cultural recognition, 'they would become equal partners rather than seen as "stakeholders"' in Wet Tropics' management, including tourism. Rainforest Indigenous groups did not consent to WHA listing of the Wet Tropics region, neither have they benefited economically from rainforest tourism in the area.

Funding for new tourism infrastructure such as rainforest walking tracks and cultural centres has been provided through the Queensland Heritage Trails Network. Ongoing funding for Indigenous groups to maintain and preserve Wet Tropics WHA values is required, drawn from an environmental levy on visitors. ILU agreements for major tourism projects such as Tjapukai, Skyrail and the Mamu Canopy Walk have generated Indigenous employment and protection of cultural heritage.

Allocation of commercial tourism permits to Rainforest Indigenous groups for key sites, with leaseback or licensing arrangements for tour operators, would also increase the economic benefits of tourism for Indigenous communities.

Putting the 'ECO' in Tourism

Bicycling on back roads. Trekking a 2,000-year-old trail. Crouching in the sand to measure a giant sea turtle. Sipping chai and savoring chapati prepared at a local Indian restaurant. However diverse the modern vacation, there's a common thread that ties each together: the traveller's thirst for discovery, passion for authenticity and interest in helping preserve and protect the planet.

"We're longing for gung-ho, do-something, learn-something, give-back-something vacations that will exhilarate us and leave us feeling good," write Daniel and Sally Wiener Grotta in The Green Travel Sourcebook, eloquently capturing the sentiment of the globe-trotting environmentalist. "We want vacations that will allow us to experience intimately the people and places we visit, while not inadvertently polluting the environment or contributing to an oppressive political regime, and perhaps make the world a better place."

Defining Green Travel

Ecotourism, or ecotravel, strives to do just that. "Ecotravel helps conserve fragile ecosystems, support endangered species and habitats, preserve indigenous cultures and develop sustainable local economies," sums up Megan Epler Wood, president of The International Ecotourism Society. "By looking at travel alternatives and making informed choices, you can minimize your impact and positively contribute to the conservation of natural environments, local economies and cultures."

That's something the mainstream travel industry has yet to accomplish. In popular resort areas like Cancun and Hawaii, overbuilt waterfront hotels have contributed to beach erosion, flooding and the disappearance of natural wetlands, while generating mountains of garbage without adequate means of disposal. The rapid growth of the trekking industry in Nepal has increased pollution in Kathmandu and caused dangerous crowding and destruction of trails; logging for hotel building materials and cooking fires has led to deforestation, flooding and landslides as far away as Bangladesh.

More than 500 million people travel for leisure each year, making tourism the world's largest industry at $425 billion and climbing, according to the World Tourism Organization. Tourism provides 10 percent of the world's income and employs almost one-tenth of its workforce. Ecotourism, although growing by 20 to 30 percent a year, still represents less than one-tenth of the total tourism industry.

Although "ecotourism" attempts to recognize the incredibly complex interactions among the environment, culture, economy and travel, it often eludes a clear definition. Guidelines are offered by such diverse groups as the United Nations Environmental Programme, Conservation International, the American Society of Travel Agents, Sierra Club and Mountain Travel Sobek. "Certified ecotourism" has recently been introduced in Australia, offering consumers a "Good Housekeeping"-type seal like those used for certified organic produce and sustainably harvested wood.

Touring with a Purpose

Ultimately, however, the responsibility for the impact of your travel rests not with a label, but with you. Be an activist – traveling the world as a dedicated ecotourist is not a spectator sport. "Ecotravellers ask lots of questions," says M.J. Kietzke, team coordinator of Co-op America Travel Links, which matches members requesting ecotravel with the operators or destinations that meet their needs. "Because ecotourism is consumer driven," she says, "these questions help create a green demand for responsible travel options."

If you choose all organized ecotour, ask about the trip fee. Besides responsibly sourced food and lodging, it can also help defray the cost of fieldwork, support local education or health programmes and leave economic dividends with the host community. (Often, if paid to a nonprofit organization, the fees for service trips are also partially tax-deductible.) Ask whether you'll be visiting a place during the most heavily traversed time of year, contributing to overcrowding, and whether you'll be using mass transportation, to reduce pollution, and eating regional cuisine, to support local markets.

The answer to the most vital question, however, still hangs in the air: Can ecotourism help connect us with the rest of the world, and by doing so, actively make it a better place? There are many who believe it can. The following examples are but a sampling of the vast array of ecotravel options and operators, for all budgets and for all age groups.

Whether you have a few days or a few months, these ideas offer a glimpse into an amazing world, one we must either learn to protect or lose forever. Participants on Oceanic Society Expeditions need no prior scientific training, but their enthusiastic contributions will support the research that leads to environmental protection of marine life in Belize. This small, diverse Central American country nestled along the Caribbean Sea is still captivatingly wild. As of 1992, 90 percent of Belize's forests were very much intact, and much of the reef system – the second longest in the world – was considered so valuable that it received World Heritage protected status.

Oceanic Society groups in Belize, under the guidance of top specialists in the field, alternate between conducting scientific research on dolphins – including observing their behaviour and recording their vocalizations – and taking naturalist-guided excursions, snorkeling in the pristine waters around Sergeants Caye, or birdwatching in the mangrove lagoons. To avoid tourist-saturated San Pedro on Ambergris Caye, the Expeditions are now based on Spanish Lookout Caye at the Belizean-owned Spanish Bay Resort.

The solar-powered resort offers its guests sun-washed cabanas over the water and native family-style cuisine in the main lodge. Evening slide shows and discussions about the dolphins, reef and mangrove ecology supplement the daily experiences. "These trips help us learn, grow and give back," says Elly Schaefer, a recent volunteer. Beginning in 2001, the dolphin project will move to the Blackbird-Oceanic Society Field Station at Blackbird Caye, and Spanish Bay will host a project on coral reefs.

For over 30 years, Mountain Travel Sobek has helped thousands of cubicled office workers transform themselves into modern-day replicas of Indiana Jones. Although this ecotravel doesn't scrimp on comfort and cuisine, environmentally sensitive practices like solar showers and leave-no-trace camping are part of the painstakingly planned cultural and wilderness experience.

Breathtaking describes both the spectacular landscape and high-altitude effects that come from trekking with Mountain Travel Sobek's ecotrip in the Annapurna Himal region of Nepal. The magical panorama includes some of the highest mountains on the planet, 20,000-plus-footers like Annapurna South, Annapurna I and III and Machapuchare, the so-called "Matterhorn of Nepal." A tattered topographic map will lead you along ancient, stone-stepped passageways and narrowly carved trails, through terraced rice paddies, rhododendron, oak and bamboo forests. The journey brings you, too, in close contact with the Gurung and Tamang clans, who have practiced sustenance agriculture in the region for centuries.

An active supporter of global nonprofits, Mountain Travel Sobek and the grassroots conservation work of white-water rafters led in 1993 to the preservation of the Tatshenshini River in Canada and Alaska as an international park, saving it from development as a giant, open-pit copper mine.

In the rainforests of Guatemala, slash-and-burn agriculture and other deforestation pressures continue to close in on the four-million-acre Maya Biosphere Reserve, which contains the popular Mayan temple complex of Tikal and the El Peru and Tikal National Parks. Conservation International (CI), along with USAID/Guatemala, the Guatemalan government, the National Council for Protected Areas and local conservation organizations, has set out to redirect development there in a more life-preserving direction.

The Mayan Trails, or Caminos Mayas, provides ecotravellers with the opportunity to explore both the cultural and natural heritage found beneath the forest canopy of Guatemala's Peten region. Three distinct trail systems await the ecotraveller: The Scarlet Macaw, El Mirador, and Zotz-Tikal. Hosted by communities along the path and guided by local experts, each offers a spectacular glimpse of flora and fauna – tropical birds such as Mot Mots, Macaws, Toucans and Trogons, and spider and howler monkeys – and the ancient Mayan ruins. Accommodations are at rustic campsites where guests rest in hammocks with protective mosquito nets, falling asleep to the late-night symphony of nocturnal rainforest life.

"The services, including meals, lodging, guides and horses or boats, are offered by the communities themselves," says Juan Carlos Bonilla, former coordinator for CI's Ecotourism Enterprise Development and Marketing Programme. "Conservation International is trying to build community-based, conservation-savvy entrepreneurship, not that big of a stretch."

Scotland is a hill walker's paradise. A journey there features rugged mountains, heather-covered moors, sparkling lochs, swift-flowing streams and cragged coastlines. The country's wilderness – from alpine flowers to colonies of Max shearwaters, guillemots, razor bills and Arctic terns – complements its ages-old castles and ancient Standing Stones.

Ecotravellers on the Wilderness Travel trip make their way through the highlands to the poignant Isle of Sky, rich in tradition and a spectacular landscape created by ancient volcanic activity. At a local pub, the Gaelic language still hangs heavy during discussion of the latest rugby match. After a spirited day of hiking, you'll find yourself warmly invited into this proud culture – perhaps for a "wee dram." A quaint country inn will welcome you to stop and rest for the night.

"Many of [our clients] see tourism as contributing to a more sustainable economy," says Barbara Banks, director of marketing and new trip development for Wilderness Travel.

Rather than engage in destructive activities that may "benefit a region in the short term," she says, "the host communities can safeguard their land and bring money into the economy for years to come."

The sun-bleached and wind-swept slope on which Concordia Eco-Tents rests contrasts with the lush green landscape of the surrounding Virgin Islands National Park on the island of St. John. It's difficult to imagine that Maho Bay Eco-Tents, Concordia's sister resort, nestles among the forested terrain just a short drive away.

Concordia Eco-Tents is an ongoing experiment in the practical use of sustainable design. On St. John, where water is a precious commodity, owner and developer Stanley Selengut was inspired to create truly low-impact accommodations – a resort that brings people literally closer to nature. Guests collect their own solar-heated water in a cistern. Solar panels and wind generate much of the electricity that powers energy-efficient lighting and a small refrigerator. Floors and boardwalks are made with a recycled composite wood and each eco-tent includes a composting toilet with low-water flush.

"Living within the Earth's resources is something that we have to do to survive as a race," says Selengut. "There are a growing number of people interested in these problems, and we're probably one of the most popular resorts in the Caribbean because of it." Vistas of undeveloped coastline and sparkling turquoise water, accompanied by a constant breeze, certainly don't hurt either.

Great, fluttering butterflies, dragonflies the size of softballs, and huge spiders resting on shimmering strands of web, melt into the lush forest understory of the Gunung Leuser National Park in Sumatra, Indonesia. This steamy, tropical rainforest is also home to endangered orangutans, known locally as the "humans of the forest," and the subject of the Earthwatch expedition called Orangutan Health.

Joining an Earthwatch expedition is an opportunity to both explore the world and assist the scientific community.

Volunteers for the Sumatran project follow orangutans, making behavioural observations from close distances, in the hopes of learning how these lumbering primates use specific plants to heal themselves. Situated at the edge of the park along the Bohorok River, the base camp is what you might expect from such a jungle adventure: a simple, clean bungalow with a bed and mosquito net, cold-water showers, Asian toilets and freshly made Indonesian dishes of rice, fish, chicken, vegetables and amazing tropical fruit.

The diverse projects and global presence of Earthwatch attracts volunteers from all over the world. The trips, which usually last several weeks, are organized by research focus, and the fee, which covers the meals and accommodations of volunteers, also directly supports the research of leading scientists in the field. On the Sumatra expedition, besides tough hiking terrain, high humidity and manic mosquitoes, the nearly two-million-acre park also harbors 130 mammal species (including gibbons, leopards and Sumatran rhinos) and 325 species of birds. So there's plenty to do when not observing orangutans.

When travellers to any of the U.S. national parks venture forth from their cars for more than just a quick bathroom break, their experiences can be transforming. Numerous wildlife interpretive programmes, which offer travellers valuable insights to area flora and fauna as well as the unique histories of the parks themselves, help put the all-important aspect of education in ecotravel. Grand Teton National Park in the U.S.

Rocky Mountains is one of the most majestic – high enough to support a dozen mountain glaciers, with 12 Teton peaks that reach above 12,000 feet. Grand Teton itself rises 13,770 feet above the bucolic valley of Jackson Hole, the Snake River threading the terrain below. Plant communities thrive there, from ribbons of riparian plants to sagebrush fiats, lodgepole pine forests, subalpine meadows and alpine stone fields.

The nonprofit Teton Science School offers Wildlife Expeditions, a programme in which locally trained wildlife biologists teach people not only about the wildlife, but also wildlife viewing ethics and habitat preservation. These specialized safari-style tours help visitors turn a casual trip to the park into a more intimate, ecologically friendly experience. "Often times, people approach wildlife, endangering themselves and disturbing an animal's natural behaviours," says Christy Bradburn, administrative coordinator for Wildlife Expeditions. "We teach people how to enjoy wildlife and understand their natural history."

Immeasurably rich in geography, ecology, culture and history, Bolivia is home to expansive cloud forests, unique salt flats, savannas and the snow-capped Andes, making it one of the most biodiverse portions of the Amazon region. Tread Lightly trips to Bolivia, completely set up through in-country operating partners, offer backstage views of the prehistoric ruins and indigenous villages of the mystical islands of the Sun and Moon in the expansive Lake Titicaca, at 3,810 feet the highest navigable lake in the world.

Tread Lightly provides intimate cultural and natural experiences for ecotravellers to Latin America. It favours lodges that respect natural surroundings, carefully use water and other valuable resources, and employ alternative energy and waste-disposal techniques. Tread Lightly partners sponsor guide-training courses that provide rich careers for locals, helping preserve community integrity while increasing awareness for the environmental diversity and fragility of their surroundings.

Visits to Potosi and the magnificent capital city of Sucre offer ecotravellers an opportunity to enjoy Bolivia's unique cultural, as well as natural, attractions. Located at an altitude of nearly 13,100 feet, Potosi is one of the highest cities in the world and best known for the extraordinary quantities of silver extracted from Cerro Rico, "Rich Mountain."

Amidst a sea of cruise ships competing for the honour of biggest and most grandiose, the 100-passenger Galapagos Explorer II is putting luxury in a more intimate, and environmentally sustainable, context. "We want to be the most environmentally friendly ship in the Galapagos," says Freddy Espinel, hotel manager of the Explorer II. He proudly points to practices like on-board desalinization of water; its purification with ozone, rather than chlorine; composted biodegradable waste and recyclables flown to the mainland; and the use of only biodegradable soaps and detergents.

While the service is impeccable and on-board atmosphere inviting, the islands themselves are the real showstoppers. On excursions escorted by the ship's naturalists (trained by Galapagos National Park) visitors see firsthand the unique adaptations of island fauna, such as flightless cormorants, marine iguanas, giant tortoises and Darwin's finches. Opportunities for photography are rife, as is snorkeling with schools of brightly-coloured fish or hiking in search of the more perfect vista.

Small group size and tight Park Service control help protect the fragile ecosystem and ensure that even on this limited terrain more wildlife than tourists are encountered. The new interpretation centre on San Cristobal Island is well worth exploring, and after you return to the ship for some native Ecuadorian cuisine and to sail to your next destination, you can watch a slide show about the natural history of the archipelago, discuss with fellow shipmates environmental challenges faced by the islands, or browse through the science library on board.

Winding along the sweeping valleys and rolling hills of unglaciated southwestern and central-western Wisconsin, the Elroy-Sparta State Trail tempts both bicyclists and walkers alike. Interrupted occasionally by cavernous rock tunnels through which bikers pass, the trail showcases local history and wildlife as it crosses trout streams and weaves through farmlands and hardwood forests. By staying in quaint bed and breakfasts, eating at family-owned restaurants and shopping for unique gifts or handmade Amish furniture along the 32-mile trail, visitors help preserve the area, support struggling agricultural communities and revive interest in natural corridors for wildlife and recreation.

The Elroy-to-Sparta trail is among the first of the U.S. rail-trails, recreational trails created from abandoned railroads, advocated by the nonprofit Rails-to-Trails Conservancy. Such trails provide a link among historic, cultural and natural sites, boost sagging local economies and, in some cases, completely revive economically depressed towns. Playing hopscotch across the landscape, the number of trails has grown from 75 in 1986 to more than 1,000 today; they cover 11,000 miles.

Ecotourism operators and "free independent travellers" each share a commitment to tread lightly on the land and culture, and support the local economy at their destination. Ecotourism is not defined by the distance traveled, but rather how it's accomplished and what is experienced, so don't overlook natural attractions like rail-trails right in your own backyard. After all, for most travellers, a fully satisfying journey can be one of less than 100 miles.

Eco-Cultural Tourism in India

There is an urgent and growing need for local/regional/national/international peace and security. This may be broadly ascribed to the increasing conflicts arising out of social, economic, religious and political factors. Peace and sustainability, considered as the indicators of development are threatened due to a myriad of conflicts and they are more visible than ever before in India.

Tourism considered as a Global Peace Industry has greater potentials to reduce these conflicts. This paper analyzes the threats to peace and sustainability and indicates that the newly emerging Heritage Eco-cultural Tourism holds the key for the promotion of peace and sustainability.

> "Tourism is like a fire; you can cook your soup in it;
> but you can also burn down your house with it."
>
> — *Asian proverb*

As we enter into the next millennium and the birth of a new global era, we are confronting the urgent need for local/regional/national/international peace and security more than in the past. This may be broadly ascribed to the increasing conflicts arising out of social, economic, religious and political factors. The widening gap between the haves and have-nots, have further accelerated these conflicts.

Hence, we are seeking universal human rights and universal human progress and prosperity. One powerful indicator of such a development is the fact that more people are traveling from more countries than ever before, making travel and tourism the worlds largest industry. Its growth is expected to continue with globalization and as people everywhere seem determined to exercise their right to travel and to make their world a more familiar place in the spirit of peace and friendship.

Tourism itself has always been a peace-based industry and may be considered as a Global Peace Industry. In the face of current human population increases and worldwide ecological degradation, intact and healthy ecosystems are becoming the world's most sought-after tourism destinations. Culture and Heritage besides peace and harmony in such areas attract special groups of tourists, who demand quality products.

Peace and sustainability, considered as the indicators of development are threatened due to a myriad of conflicts – Social, Economic, political, cultural and Environmental. These conflicts usually confront multiple and diverse stakeholders such as state institutions, religious organizations, communities, indigenous ethnic groups, local institutions, private development and non-government organizations, international organizations, and many other players.

Wide differences in culture, knowledge, power, influence, and resources characterize these groups. Even though most conflicts essentially develop in a local framework, they are also frequently connected at regional, national and even international levels, transcending political and geographical boundaries including non-represented interests (e.g. future generations). Such complexity explains, in part, the lack of sustained attention that conflicts receive. In addition, many conflicts in India are often dealt with unprofessionally and result in frustrations, violence, greater inequities, and negative impacts on quality of life, economic and social processes and in the natural resources themselves.

The most common methods of intervention in conflicts tend to be centralized, hierarchical, and sectorial, with a predominantly technical and adversarial (judicial) and at times political. Seldom do they achieve a reasonable level of satisfaction for all interested parties. Hence, we are urgently in need of alternative paradigms for development – we are moving from the narrower 'reductionist', 'reactive' and 'bureaucratic' approaches to 'wholistic/Integrated or Systems' view of looking at issues, 'pro-active' policies and 'participatory' strategies. How quick and how effective we are in reorienting ourselves according to these shifting paradigms will determine our sustainable futures.

The word 'conflict' carries negative connotations. It is often thought of as the opposite of cooperation and peace, and is most commonly associated with violence or the threat of violence. This view of conflict is not always helpful. In many settings it should be seen as a potential force for positive social change – its presence a visible demonstration of society adapting to a new political, economic or physical environment. A potential non-violent approach to solve these conflicts at the least social/economic/Environmental costs may be through evolving alternative tourism strategies.

In the midst of growing tensions and worries everywhere "Getting away from it all," is understandably popular. With so many wonderful places in the world, prices of international travel falling, and the stresses and strains of everyday life increasing, more people are traveling. And as the population grows and incomes rise in many societies, the trend is steeply up. In 2000, international tourist arrivals reached an all time high of 698 million, an increase of 7.4 % that was double the growth rate of 1999, according to the World Tourism Organization. Tourism sector employs 11 per cent of the global workforce – over 200 million people – either directly or indirectly.

The Tourism Sector in India

India's tourism potentials are immense – with a large variety ranging from rich cultural diversity, world-renowned historical, religious, heritage and architectural monuments, unique fairs, festivals, folklore and folk dances besides the costumes and customs to wildlife sanctuaries with exquisite flora and fauna. Besides, there are cool hill stations and long stretches of sunny beaches all round the peninsula.

The diversity is not only in climate but is all pervasive and as J. Nehru put it, "India is a land of contrasts – with the rural tranquility of simplicity and urban bustle, pomp and show". Added to this, there are plenty of traditional arts and crafts to carry back as souvenirs; Indian hospitality and variety induce tourists to make repeated visits. India's wide choice of adventure sports ranges from the daring to the exotic – trekking, camping, rock climbing, white water rafting, skating, air/water gliding, etc. In spite of such attractions, tourist arrivals in India are less than 1% of the world arrivals.

Tourism in India is different from other sectors by some special characteristics that include:

A wider variety of stake-holders but with lack of communication and coordination.

Uniformity of artificial structures in Tourism areas does not blend with the natural diversity of undisturbed areas.

Inter-sectoral linkages and complexity with several intangible costs and benefits; conflicts leading to problems in analysis, monitoring and coordination; mixed priorities and conflicts, make cooperation & participation difficult.

Research on tourism especially on policy and planning has been given low priority – as a result, it is poorly studied & understood as a sector in general and its Environmental & Social/Cultural impacts in particular; hence, we are confronted with fragmented & poorly coordinated policies, riddled with ad-hoc decisions for short term gains at the cost of long term sustainability.

Multiplier effect is prominent – can enhance poverty alleviation and alternative livelihoods; but is rarely understood by the planners and the implementing agencies.

Seasonality in Tourist influx has implications for carrying capacity analysis and Tourism policy/planning/implementation, but rarely taken into account by the planners/policy makers

Spatial and temporal dimensions – implications for Physical planning:

Positive & negative feed backs – implications for absorbing capacity, carrying capacity, Sustainability, and resilience; a typical tourism cycle would involve – Exploration/developmen/tconsolidation/stagnation/decline/rejuvenation; however, negative impacts, on a cumulative basis destroy the resource base, affecting the natural, cultural, and Heritage attractions, culminating in declining tourism trends.

Life supporting systems are impacted, culminating in debates on Ecological integrity Vs Economic security.

'Profit maximization' is the prime motto of Tourism enterprises (irrespective of whether they are private or Govt. sector undertakings) and hence, tourism is largely out of control for planners; some impacts are irreversible and hence tourism itself is affected due to degradation in Environmental health/quality.

The Ecological impacts of tourism are more on Common Property Resources – air, soil and ground water, leading to tragedy of the commons as they are treated as 'open access commons'.

Lack of know how and trained man power in Govt. agencies on Eco-cultural tourism lead to lack of appreciation and Govt. support for community based initiatives.

Tourism industry is fundamentally dependent on the diversity and quality of the natural and cultural resources. Hence, it has grater reasons to conserve/protect the same. But are we giving adequate attention/priorities for natural and cultural resources while planning and implementing tourism projects in India?

Though tourism is India's one of the largest foreign exchange earners and one among the fastest growing industries, the natural resource base that supports tourism is "heavily stressed" in and around the main tourist destination areas. In spite of the overwhelming technological and information revolution, we have trapped ourselves in a vicious circle of self-destruction by adopting the typical "boom and bust" tourism paths paved by the ill-conceived and unplanned/uncontrolled mass tourism, promoted for short-term profit maximization at the cost of degradation in Environmental quality. Ironically, this in turn, ultimately detracts the tourists and destroys the Tourism industry itself.

The question is whether we, in the blind pursuit of rapid Economic growth and earning more foreign exchange Q an afford to sacrifice the higher Environmental quality and our rich cultural Heritage upon which tourism so strongly depends. Though we have already learnt many bitter lessons, we tend to overlook them. Changes in the physical, spatial, and socio-economic structure of a tourist area as well as the existence of several, sometimes burdensome, environmental/ social problems testify to the presence of these conflicts and the crying need for evolving appropriate strategies to sustainably manage the Environmental quality, and to improve the local livelihood opportunities.

However, the researchers as well as policy makers in India largely ignore the inseparable links between the Environmental quality (EQ), sustainability, peace and tourism and pay little attention to participation of local communities, by focusing only on setting up infrastructures, promoting marketing strategies and make only adhoc/piece meal efforts to improve the EQ, sustainability and peace in the destination areas. This is self-evident from the "tell-tale symptoms" or "indicators" such as garbage dumps, foul smell, very high rates of pollution, overexploitation of natural resources, alienation of local communities, increasing conflicts and violence in several destination areas.

The industry has learned these bitter lessons only after the irreversible damages have already set in. Examples can be seen every where the mass tourism went out of control – starting from Ooty and Kodai lakes in the South to Dal lake in the North; from Kovalam in the South to Goa in the North; even our nation's pride Taj Mahal is not spared! As a result, tourism has become a dirty word amongst many communities, environmental groups and human rights campaigners. This is really unfortunate as the tourism sector has greater potential to enhance local livelihoods, if it is properly planned.

The Ills of the Tourism Industry

Though tourism could lead to a variety of potential benefits, uncontrolled mass tourism, the most predominant form of tourism today, inevitably increases the already existing conflicts, besides creating new ones. Tourism's voracious appetite for basic resources – land, water and energy – has meant that the tourism industry and Government Agencies are increasingly finding themselves opposed over land rights and water rights by local people. Lack of access by locals to public beaches, violation by hotels of environmental regulations, and heavy-handed tactics by local authorities to free-up beach areas for hotels' use, have all been cited in legal disputes throughout the world.

For instance, three quarters of the sand dunes on the Mediterranean coast between Spain and Sicily have now disappeared, largely because of the construction of hotels and holiday flats. One of the most famous long-term tourism protests has been in Goa, India. With one five-star hotel consuming as much water as five local villages and one five-star tourist consuming 28 times more electricity per day than a local Goan, local discontent over resource-use is understandable.

Thus, the modern world is characterized by mass concentrations of people, mass production, and mass activities.

Diversity and beauty of land and life are more and more replaced by uniformity and ugliness. Human settlements in their mad rush for development have turned beautiful tree-clad landscapes into desolate concrete jungles, and fertile lands with diverse native vegetation are increasingly destroyed by monocultures. Tourism is no exception to this general rule.

The Green Signals

Over the last decade, understanding of these complex and interconnected issues by the world tourism industry, tourists, governments and communities has increased as indicated by the evolution of numerous alternative forms of tourism such as 'green' tourism, 'alternative' tourism, 'responsible' tourism, 'sustainable' tourism, 'eco' tourism, 'eco-cultural' tourism (ECT), 'eco-development' tourism, 'Heritage eco-cultural' tourism (HECT), 'community' tourism, "ethical' tourism, 'fair-trade' tourism and even, most recently, the particularly un-catchy, 'pro-poor' tourism(PPT).

Unfortunately, we, in India have not sufficiently re-oriented ourselves, to meet the future international market demand for these specialized forms of tourism. The concept of sustainable tourism should not be confused with ECT. According to WTO, all tourism activities, be they geared to holidays, business, conferences, congresses or fairs, health, adventure or ECT itself, must be sustainable.

This means that the planning and development of tourism infrastructure, its subsequent operation and also its marketing should focus on environmental, social, cultural and economic sustainability criteria, so as to ensure that neither the natural environment nor the socio-cultural fabric of the host communities will be impaired by the arrival/activities of tourists; on the contrary, enterprises, as well as the communities in which they operate, should benefit from tourism, both economically and culturally.

Eco-tourism, a growing trend, is the most commonly understood term as tourism that focuses on an appreciation of the environment. In 1993 the World Tourism Organisation

(WTO) estimated nature tourism generates 7 per cent of all international travel expenditure. More recent research reveals this is now much higher, accounting for 20 per cent of international travel in the Asia-Pacific region and some areas, such as South Africa, experiencing a massive growth in visitors to game and nature reserves, of over 100 per cent annually.

Research by The International Ecotourism Society (TIES) reveals that coo-tourists are likely to be higher spenders on their holidays than 'ordinary' mass tourists. And high spending, nature-loving, responsible tourists are undoubtedly an attractive option for governments looking for ways of earning foreign exchange.

The recent Amman Declaration on Peace Through Tourism reflects many of the strategies discussed above and has recognised that peace is an essential precondition for travel and tourism and all aspects of human growth and development. Hence, it has recommended the development of tourism as a global vehicle for promoting understanding, trust and goodwill among peoples of the world through an appropriate political and economic framework.

The New Threats

The alternative tourism strategies, evolved in response to the concern for the Ecology, culture, Heritage and local livelihoods, have created both new opportunities as well as new threats. One of eco-tourism's first problems is one of definition. Although, there are several definitions, there is no certification system to abide by or international monitoring body. The term can be used by anyone at anytime for anything from a small-scale locally run rainforest lodge where the money goes to support a local community, to a large, luxury, foreign-owned resort which has little community involvement and uses masses of natural resources. Eco-tourists may even visit areas of national beauty and wildlife significance without realizing that local people have been evicted from the area in order for eco-tourism to be developed, as has happened in East Africa, India, Southern Africa and many other destinations.

Ill-conceived and/or ill-planned Eco-tourism, as practiced now by a majority of the business communities has caused serious, irreversible negative impacts in environmentally and culturally sensitive areas, even in countries that are well known as eco-tourism destinations like Belize or Costa Rica. The Malaysian-based Third World Network working with the Thailand-based Tourism Information Monitoring team (TIM-team) cite examples throughout Asia, including the eco-tourism policy promoted by the tourism working group under the Greater Mekong Sub-region (GMS) development scheme, led by the Asian Development Bank, which covers a vast area across Burma, Cambodia, Laos, Thailand, Vietnam and Yunnan/China. They are riddled with several problems relating to accusations of 'human zoos' being created and financial exploitation of hill tribe villages by outside tour operators.

Besides, the increasing link of eco-tourism to the multi-million dollar biotechnology industry through bio-piracy in key eco-tourist sites like rainforests, and the use of eco-tourism by the World Bank's Social Investment Project to support massive development projects, some involving logging operations are becoming common in many developing countries. The revolution in information and communication technologies would enable both the promoters and the tourists to exploit the hidden potentials ECT in a region, more efficiently than ever.

However, the lack of discipline of government and the escalating demand for growth will undermine efforts to create sustainable eco-tourism economies that are small but beautiful. Under extreme conditions of land grabbing and unplanned structures, it may create concrete jungles, surrounded by degraded vegetation, thus destroying the once tranquil zones. Hence, we have to be extremely careful while promoting ECT.

Despite these problems, an International Year of Ecotourism (IYE) was declared by the United Nations for 2002. This will be co-ordinated by the WTO and UNEP and a range of activities held, including a World Ecotourism Summit from

19-22 May 2002 in Quebec, Canada plus various regional conferences. Oliver Hillel, the UNEP tourism programme co-ordinator sees the IYE as a chance to "assess what eco-tourism is, or can be, rather than only a promotional event for UN member governments, for the private sector and for recipients of development aid."

It is clear to many that nature-based tourism is presently seen as one of the most lucrative niche markets, and powerful transnational corporations are likely to exploit the IYE to dictate their own definitions and rules of eco-tourism on society, while people-centred initiatives will be squeezed out and marginalised.

While the commitment of the tourism industry in India to tackle these complex issues seems limited, a few smaller operators are keen to work closely with local people in order for the communities to support their business and out of an honest desire to protect environments and optimise benefits to local people. However, such small operators lack the know-how to tackle the issues involved. As a result, alternative tourism strategies for which India has a greater potential, make up a very small proportion of overall tourism facilities.

The Potential Alternatives

In any outdoor tourism activity, human experience, knowledge, expectation, and socio-cultural contexts interact with environmental elements and environments as entities to produce an outcome that affects both the humans and the environment. Thus, sustainable tourism development depends in many important ways on the proper handling of the relationships between Tourism and the Environment. Sustainability, Peace and Environmental quality occupy the central table in the wake of global terrorism.

Greater sustainability of the tourism would mean more regional products, less noise and emissions, lesser solid wastes and appropriate sewage treatment measures, creation of jobs, lesser social conflicts/violence by learning to live in harmony and higher quality of life for the local populations well as improved quality of holidays for the guest. The conventional mass tourism, by its very nature cannot cater to these demands. Hence, alternative tourism strategies are emerging.

Sustainable tourism is defined as "Tourism that meets the needs of the present tourists and host regions while protecting and enhancing opportunity for the future. It is envisaged as leading to management of all resources in such a way that economic, social and aesthetic needs can be fulfilled while maintaining cultural integrity, essential ecological processes, bio-Diversity and life supporting systems (soil, air and water)". Thus, it has the inbuilt mechanism for promoting peace and harmony among the tourism stakeholders.

A related alternative is Eco-cultural Tourism (ECT). ECT activities are offered by a large and wide variety of operators, and practiced by an even larger array of tourists. While there is no single universal definition for ECT, its general characteristics can be summarized as follows:

All nature-based forms of tourism in which the main motivation of the tourists is the observation and appreciation for admiring, enjoying and/or studying nature as well as the traditional cultures and Heritage (both past and present) prevailing in relatively undisturbed or uncontaminated natural areas

It contains participatory, interactive, educational and interpretation features. It is generally, but not exclusively organized for environmentally, socially conscious small groups by specialized and small, locally owned businesses. Foreign operators of varying sizes also organize, operate and/or market ECT tours, generally for small groups.

It minimizes negative impacts upon the natural and socio-cultural environment. Heritage Eco-cultural Tourism (HECT) is a newly emerging type of alternative tourism. When Heritage of the destination areas can be exploited along with the local Ecological and cultural attractions, we have a case for Heritage Eco-cultural Tourism.

Heritage embraces magnificent natural, indigenous and historic landscapes (natural or man-made), wildlife and healthy, intact ecosystems, historical elements (that has helped to shape the regional/national identity), cultural elements and human values, shaping regional, national, global identity; it also incorporates a strong connection to 'place'; that is, people come to the place by choice, they are somehow transformed by it, and they choose to identify themselves with it even if they don't live there. This may be because of the outstanding universal value of the areas visited from the point of view of science, conservation or natural beauty.

Historical places, objects and manifestations of cultural, scientific, symbolic, spiritual and religious values are important expressions of the culture, identity and religious beliefs of societies. Their role and importance, particularly in the light of the need for cultural identity and continuity in a rapidly changing world, need to be promoted.

Tourists are actively seeking such lost values. They come hoping for a profound psychic or spiritual experience in some quiet corners of the destination areas. Hence, we have greater responsibility to conserve the cultural Heritage areas.

The following are the key potential benefits of HECT:

- Protection and active conservation of natural and built heritage resources, justified by their own intrinsic value for posterity and the revenue which visitors contribute.
- Enhancement of the natural and built environment to meet rising quality standards necessary to sustain modern travel and tourism.
- Reconstruction for visitor usage of urban environments and environments degraded by the industrial practices of former extractive and manufacturing industries.
- Establishment of attractive environments for tourism destinations, for residents as much as visitors, which may support other compatible new economic

activities, from agriculture and fishing to service and manufacturing industries.

- Creation of economic value and protection for resources which otherwise have no perceived value to residents, or represent a cost rather than a benefit-livelihood opportunities – micro-enterprises?
- Opportunity to communicate and interpret the values of natural and built heritage and of cultural inheritance of residents of visited areas.
- Effective management of visitors within an environment so that it can support long-term economic development and repeat visits.
- Research and development of good environmental practices and management systems to influence the operation of travel and tourism businesses as well as visitor behaviour at destinations.

Opportunities, through the direct customer contacts that all travel and tourism businesses have, for operators to communicate and interpret the values of natural and built heritage and culture to visitors, thus helping to create a new generation of responsible consumers

The available knowledge indicate that the following may be considered as the major criteria for selecting HECT sites:

- *Geography* – proximity to mass-tourism sites; sufficiently closer for easy accessibility but adequately away from motorable roads and other human disturbances.
- *Climate & Ecology* – microclimates/habitats conducive enough for the tourists without any need for artificial comforts
- *Rarity & Uniqueness* – Ecosystems like mountains, rivers, mangroves, coral reefs and islands endowed with unspoiled beauty, unique culture and Heritage.
- *Infrastructure* – only reasonable – to the barest minimum but with desirable conditions – hygienic

ethnic food (locally produced/prepared), protected water supply, natural ventilation and local architecture.

- *Diversity* – higher habitat/community/Ecosystem/cultural (food, cloth, architecture, crafts, festivals etc.) – diversity and purity – potentials/opportunities for viewing/appreciating more attractive species/cultures as well as Heritage elements; Potentials for a variety of nature/adventure tourism activities such as camping for wildlife observation, traditional healing camps, caving, bird-watching, trekking, rock-climbing, mountain biking, skating, para-gliding, wind-surfing, funky jumping, canopy walkways, white water rafting, snorkeling, scuba diving, recreational fishing
- *Unpolluted/relatively undisturbed areas with higher Environmental quality* – in contrast to polluted/degraded landscapes/seascapes
- *Minimum health/safety risks* – to avoid costly demands from the tourists
- *Opportunities for Environmental Education & interpretation* – for all the stake-holders
- *Opportunities for generating and sustaining new livelihoods* – to cater to the demands of the tourists – e.g. Apiculture (the science and art of raising honey bees), agriculture, horticulture, floriculture, community dairy/piggery/poultry, preparation of Ethnic foods, rich diversity of arts and crafts.
- *Community cooperation* – to make and enforce their own decisions on eco-tourism development.
- *Presence of dedicated NGOs* – for catalyzing cooperation.
- *Cooperation of other stake-holders* – Govt. and other institutions – their policies, programmes and goals.
- *Marketing opportunities* – potentials for targeting different types of eco-tourists (hardcore, dedicated, mainstream and casual); marketing linkages and potentials.

"The future belongs to those who give the next generation reasons to hope."

— *Pierre Teilhard DeChardin*

The HECT will enable the tourists as well as the local communities to find ways to live sustainably, and in peace with nature, Cultural Heritage and intact, functioning ecosystems. More importantly, we will be reconnecting ourselves with our forgotten treasure of the diverse culture and Heritage of the bygone era. In this process, tourism will promote peace and sustainability by closer mutualistic interactions between tourists and the local communities.

Among the several organizations that could be involved in the promotion of HECT, mention must be made of UNESCO (World Heritage sites programme) and the International Institute for Peace through Tourism at international levels and the Indian National Trust for the promotion of Arts and Cultural Heritage (INTACH) at the national level. The Indian Tourism Development Corporation and the State Tourism Development Corporations have to recognise the potentials of HECT and reorient themselves to the tasks ahead.

Broad guidelines for promoting HECT strategies may be modified and adopted from UNEP that has prescribed Environmental codes of conduct for tourism and Gonsalves' (1991) paper on guidelines for alternative tourism for the third world. The adoption of the Global Code of Ethics for Tourism, the Green Globe programme, the ECOTEL Certification awarded by HVS Eco Services, Certification Programmes for Sustainable Tourism and Eco-tourism, Exemplary Practices by Canadian Tourism Commission, The National Eco-tourism Accreditation Programme of the Eco-tourism Association of Australia and the Australian Tourism Operators Association and equitable community participation in tourism are a few other such initiatives to name, globally. Recently, Mastny (2002) from World Watch Institute has provided policy guidelines with examples for sustainable tourism. The recently emerging pro-poor tourism approaches, have to be ideally integrated into HECT.

Index

F

G

H

I

J

K

L

M

N

O

P

Q

R

S